M 58

# PAPERS OF ISAAC HULL

### Commodore Hull

# PAPERS OF ISAAC HULL
## COMMODORE UNITED STATES NAVY

EDITED BY
GARDNER WELD ALLEN

Printed from the Income of the
Robert Charles Billings Fund

THE BOSTON ATHENÆUM
1929

ROBERT CHARLES BILLINGS FUND
PUBLICATIONS   NUMBER EIGHT

# Preface

IN 1924 the Boston Athenæum received a large collection of the papers of Commodore Isaac Hull. It was labelled: "The Property of the late Mrs. Sara Jarvis Pattison presented to the Boston Athenæum by her daughter, Mrs. Frederick Nichols." The Trustees of the Athenæum voted to have a number of the more interesting papers printed. In carrying out this purpose, biographical matter has been incorporated in order to make a connected story. No Life of Isaac Hull has ever been published — only a few magazine sketches.

The collection is a noteworthy one. To describe it in detail would exceed reasonable limits of space. In addition to letter-books, log-books, and other bound manuscript material, there are letters and documents, filed and tied together in bundles, more than two thousand in number, including enclosures. The one letter-book of importance covers the year from August, 1840, to August, 1841. The log-book of the frigate *United States* — January 5, 1824, to April 24, 1827 — is in three volumes which, having been water-soaked, are in large part illegible, but the remaining parts are of decided value and interest. There are three log-books of the *Ohio,* ship of the line, for the period extending from October 11, 1838, to July 28, 1841, with an interval uncovered between December, 1839, and October, 1840. There are only two letters of any importance during the War of 1812, and a few before that; a good many papers for the following years up to 1838; and a much larger number, in fact the bulk of the collection, covering the cruise of the *Ohio,* Commodore Hull's flagship while in command of the Mediterranean Station in the years 1838 to 1841.

The papers for the most part consist of official correspondence and reports relating to the routine business of the navy, many of which, nevertheless, have interest for the general reader. Very much the greater number are addressed to Hull. Such of his own letters as the collection contains are nearly all official; a few relate to private business, but there are none of an intimate sort. In the text of this volume, however, will be found extracts from a few of his letters in the Library of Congress and the Yale University Library, and elsewhere, which help to fill gaps and give a little more personal touch.

In selecting from the collection papers to be printed, the attempt has been made to choose those which throw light on the character and personality of Isaac Hull, those which illustrate life in the old navy or have historic value, and those which possess a human interest. One hundred and eighty-three papers have been selected for the purpose. They include all of Hull's letters which seemed sufficiently important. All the papers are printed with headings, signatures, etc., in full. Supplementary extracts, whether taken from log-books or other papers in the collection or from outside sources, are quoted in the text.

Acknowledgment is due, for assistance and suggestions, to Mr. Charles K. Bolton, Librarian, and to Miss

Wildman, Miss Whitcher, Miss Gregory, Miss Coker, and Mrs. Hodgdon of the Athenæum, and to many others. The library of the Massachusetts Historical Society has been much used in the search for material, and Mr. Worthington C. Ford and Mr. Julius H. Tuttle have given valuable advice.

GARDNER W. ALLEN

Boston, February, 1929.

# Contents

| Chapter | | |
|---|---|---|
| I. | Early Years in the Navy | 1 |
| II. | In Command of the *Constitution* | 11 |
| III. | The War of 1812 | 24 |
| IV. | The Boston Navy Yard | 37 |
| V. | The Pacific Station | 42 |
| VI. | The Commodore Has Enemies | 62 |
| VII. | The Washington Navy Yard | 68 |
| VIII. | Private Affairs | 78 |
| IX. | The *Ohio* | 84 |
| X. | The Mediterranean Squadron | 98 |
| XI. | The Officers of the Squadron | 151 |
| XII. | Midshipmen | 166 |
| XIII. | The Man Before the Mast | 184 |
| XIV. | Health and Sanitation | 199 |
| XV. | Port Mahon | 207 |
| XVI. | A Riot in the Theatre | 221 |
| XVII. | Discipline | 253 |
| XVIII. | Impressment | 267 |
| XIX. | A Slave Ship | 277 |
| XX. | War Clouds | 296 |
| XXI. | A Statue of Washington | 320 |
| XXII. | Home Again | 329 |
| | Index | 333 |

# Illustrations

ISAAC HULL . . . . . . . . *Frontispiece*
   From the original portrait by Gilbert Stuart in The Metropolitan Museum of Art, New York. Courtesy of the Museum.

*Facing Page*

BIRTHPLACE . . . . . . . . . 2
   From a photograph in possession of The Society for the Preservation of New England Antiquities. Courtesy of the Society.

THE FRIGATE *CONSTITUTION* . . . . . 26
   Engraved by J. Thackara and Son, Philadelphia. Inscribed: "The United States Frigate *Constitution* getting under way with reefed topsails." Courtesy of the Massachusetts Historical Society.

THE FRIGATE *UNITED STATES* . . . . . 44
   Painted by T. Birch; engraved by S. Seymour. Part of a battle scene, inscribed: "This representation of the U. S. Frigate *United States,* Stephen Decatur, Esq., Commander, capturing his Britannic Majesty's Frigate *Macedonian,* John S. Carden, Esq., Commander, is respectfully inscribed to Captain Stephen Decatur, his officers and gallant crew, by their devoted humble servant, James Webster." Courtesy of the Massachusetts Institute of Technology.

THE SHIP OF THE LINE *OHIO* . . . . . 84
   Drawn by J. A. Knight. Inscribed: "U. S. Ship of the Line *Ohio,* 108 Guns, struck by a White Squall in the South Pacific Ocean, Nov. 1849. — Capt. C. K. Stribling, Commander." Courtesy of Charles H. Taylor, Esq.

MAP OF THE MEDITERRANEAN . . . . . 98
   Drawn for this work.

xii  ILLUSTRATIONS

*Facing Page*

ISAAC HULL . . . . . . . . . . 222

    From *The Polyanthos,* January, 1814. Engraved by I. R. Smith from a portrait by H. Williams. *The Polyanthos* says: "Before the engraving could be finished, another appeared in the *Analectic Magazine* [the Stuart portrait], and the dissimilarity in the two pictures induced us to postpone the publication of ours, till it should have been submitted to the inspection of his friends. Having done this, we are authorized to say that it has been honored with their entire approbation."

BOWL . . . . . . . . . . . 296

    From a photograph of a carved wooden bowl presented to Isaac Hull by his officers.

TOMB . . . . . . . . . . . 330

    From a woodcut in Lossing's *Pictorial Field-Book of the War of 1812,* pages 441, 442.

# PAPERS OF ISAAC HULL

## Chapter I
## EARLY YEARS IN THE NAVY

THE name Hull was common in eastern Massachusetts in early Colonial days. In 1639 Richard Hull, who had been living in Dorchester, migrated to Connecticut and settled in New Haven. His son, Dr. John Hull, moved to Derby and there the family continued to live. Derby is nine miles west of New Haven, on the Housatonic River. Joseph Hull, of the sixth generation from Richard, was born at Derby October 27, 1750. He married Sarah Bennett and built a house just across the river in Huntington, now Shelton. Here was born the future commodore. Early in the Revolution Joseph Hull was a lieutenant of artillery and later he is said to have commanded a flotilla of whaleboats on Long Island Sound. He was captured, and for a time was confined on the prison-ship *Jersey*.[1]

Isaac Hull was born March 9, 1773.[2] When quite young he was adopted by his uncle, William Hull, who later, as General Hull, figured in the War of 1812.

[1] Mason, *A Record of the Descendants of Richard Hull*, 22; Weygant, *The Hull Family in America*, 490, 507. See Middlebrook, *Maritime Connecticut During the Revolution*, II, 212.

[2] *New Haven Genealogical Magazine*, IV (December, 1926), 886. Various dates are given for the birth of Isaac Hull, but this is without doubt authentic.

While living with his uncle, Isaac spent part of his boyhood in Newton, Massachusetts.[1] He went to sea at fourteen as a cabin-boy. At sixteen he was shipwrecked and he saved the life of his captain. Before he was twenty-one he commanded a ship and made voyages to England and the West Indies.

On his twenty-fifth birthday, March 9, 1798, Isaac was appointed a lieutenant in the navy. At this time difficulties with France had reached an acute stage and, although war was not declared, hostilities continued nearly three years, the navy was greatly increased, and several important battles were fought on the sea.

Hull was ordered to the frigate *Constitution,* then a new ship, commanded by Captain Samuel Nicholson. The *Constitution* sailed from Boston on her first cruise July 22, 1798. Her first service was patrolling the coast for the protection of commerce, until November. Later she cruised in the West Indies. She returned to Boston and Captain Silas Talbot replaced Nicholson in command. Hull then became her first lieutenant. Talbot was ordered to the West Indies, where, in October, 1799, he took command of the San Domingo station and a squadron of half a dozen vessels.

While on this station the captain of a British frigate offered to race the *Constitution* for a wager of a cask of Madeira. Commodore Talbot accepted, and the ships sailed from sunrise to sunset, beating to windward all day. The American frigate was sailed by Isaac Hull.

---

[1] Clarke, *Records of Some of the Descendants of Richard Hull,* 10. The very meagre known facts of Hull's pre-naval career are taken from various sources and are believed to be approximately correct.

BIRTHPLACE OF ISAAC HULL

At sunset, says James Fenimore Cooper, the British frigate "was precisely hull down, dead to leeward. . . . The manner in which the *Constitution* eat her competitor out of the wind was not the least striking feature of this trial, and it must in great degree be ascribed to Hull, whose dexterity in handling a craft under her canvas was ever remarkable. In this particular he was perhaps one of the most skilful seamen of his time."[1]

In the spring of 1800 Lieutenant Hull commanded a cutting-out expedition into the Spanish harbor of Porto Plata, on the north coast of San Domingo. The objective of the attack was a French armed ship lying in the harbor under the protection of a fort. As the *Constitution* drew too much water, a sloop called the *Sally* was impressed and was taken into the harbor in open day by Hull, with a force of ninety seamen and marines, most of whom were concealed while going in. "They ran alongside of the ship and boarded her, sword in hand, without the loss of a man." The marines landed and spiked the guns in the fort. "Perhaps no enterprise of the same moment was ever better executed," said Commodore Talbot, who commended Lieutenant Hull and his party "for their avidity in undertaking the scheme I had planned and for the handsome manner and great address with which they performed this daring adventure."[2] It was about noon when Hull took possession of the ship, and he found her completely stripped of sails and rigging, which were stored

---

[1] *Putnam's Magazine,* I (May, 1853), 476.

[2] Goldsborough, *United States Naval Chronicle,* 171, 172, report of Commodore Talbot, also printed in the form of a broadside.

below; only the lower masts were standing. By sunset she was fully rigged and only waiting for a breeze to take her out of the harbor.

In the summer the *Constitution* sailed north with a convoy, returning to her station in December. In the spring of 1801 this little war with France came to an end. The navy was reorganized and much reduced. Many vessels were sold and many officers were discharged from the service. On the new list of lieutenants Charles Stewart stood first and Isaac Hull second.

The war with Tripoli soon followed, and in 1801 a squadron was sent to the Mediterranean, in which Lieutenant Hull did not serve. In 1802 another squadron under Commodore Richard V. Morris was sent, and Hull went as first lieutenant of the frigate *Adams*, Captain Hugh G. Campbell. The *Adams* arrived at Gibraltar July 22, but saw practically no service during the remainder of the year. In the spring of 1803 Hull was given command of the schooner *Enterprise*. Off Tripoli, on the evening of June 21, with the frigates *John Adams* and *Adams*, the *Enterprise* intercepted a large vessel attempting to run into the port. The next morning the three American vessels attacked this ship, which was supported by nine gunboats and a large armed force on shore. After about two hours the ship blew up.

Commodore Morris, having accomplished little, was recalled, and Commodore Edward Preble was given the command. His flagship, the *Constitution*, arrived at Gibraltar September 12, 1803. The *Argus*, Lieutenant Stephen Decatur, a new brig built at Boston especially for this service, arrived November 1. Hull, being senior

## EARLY YEARS IN THE NAVY

in rank, took command of the *Argus,* turning the *Enterprise* over to Decatur. May 18, 1804, Hull was promoted to the grade of master commandant, now known as commander. Meanwhile the frigate *Philadelphia,* Captain William Bainbridge, having grounded on a reef, was captured by the Tripolitans and all her crew made prisoners. She was taken into the harbor of Tripoli and was there destroyed by an expedition under Lieutenant Decatur — a brilliant exploit, for which he was promoted to captain.

The *Argus* arrived off Tripoli in April, 1804, and took part in the blockade. From August 3 to September 3 Commodore Preble made five attacks on Tripoli. Besides the *Constitution,* he had three brigs, three schooners, and six gunboats. The squadron carried one thousand and sixty officers and men and forty-two heavy guns, besides many light ones of little use in bombarding fortifications. The battery of the *Argus,* sixteen twenty-four pound carronades, was of this class. Most of the fighting was done by the gunboats, which ran into the harbor and engaged the enemy gunboats. Some of the hand-to-hand contests in these boats were of the most thrilling character. The *Argus,* with the other larger vessels, supported the gunboats. Great loss and damage were inflicted on the enemy by these attacks, but Tripoli was not captured. August 9 the *Argus* reconnoitred the harbor and was struck by a large shot.

On September 4, in the evening, Commodore Preble sent into the harbor the ketch *Intrepid* as a fireship, with one hundred barrels of powder on board, in the hope that many of the enemy's gunboats might be destroyed and other injury inflicted. Commander Richard Somers took the *Intrepid* in, escorted by the *Argus* and other vessels. By some tragic mishap, never understood, the explosion was premature and all hands were lost.

Meanwhile another and larger squadron was sent out from the United States. Unfortunately, it was deemed necessary to supersede Preble, as there were no captains junior to him to take the ships out. Preble was doubtless better qualified than any one else to carry the enterprise through and his loss was irreparable. His successor, Commodore Samuel Barron, arrived off Tripoli September 10. The *Argus* took Commodore Preble to Syracuse not long afterwards.

The next important service rendered by the *Argus* was in support of the operations which culminated in the capture of Derne by General William Eaton. Commander Hull's orders were "to proceed with Mr. Eaton to Alexandria in search of Hamet Pasha, the rival brother and legitimate sovereign of the reigning Pasha of Tripoli, and to convey him and his suite to Derne," for the purpose of coöperating with the American squadron against the common enemy. General Eaton was landed at Alexandria November 27, 1804, and two months later Hamet was found. Eaton's plan had been to embark with Hamet on the *Argus* and proceed to a point near Derne where he would meet his troops, but for various reasons it was decided to go by land. Arrangements were made with Commander Hull to meet the expedition at the Bay of Bomba, with supplies and reinforcements. Early in March, 1805, Eaton began his arduous and perilous march across the Libyan Desert at the head of his heterogeneous army of about four hundred Arabs, with a handful of Americans and a few Greeks. He arrived at Bomba April 15 and the next day the *Argus* appeared. The sloop *Hornet* and schooner *Nautilus* also took part in the enterprise. The attack on Derne was made April 27. An attempt was made to land two fieldpieces from the ships. One of these, with great difficulty, was hauled up the steep and rocky precipice that bordered the bay, while the other, to avoid delay, was left behind. "The *Hornet*, Lieutenant Evans, anchored with springs on his cables within one hundred yards of the battery of eight guns and commenced a heavy fire upon it, the *Nautilus* took her Station to the eastward of the *Hornet* and half a mile's distance from shore and opened upon the town and batteries, the *Argus* anchored without and a little to the Eastward of the *Nautilus* and began firing on the town and battery, the fort kept up a heavy fire for about an hour, after which the shot flying so thick about them they abandoned it and run into the town."[1] The vessels' guns then cleared the beach of the enemy. All this time General Eaton had been attacking the town vigorously by land, and after a hard fight the place was captured. On June 11, Eaton was under the painful necessity, in obedience to orders, of evacuating the town and yielding all the advantage gained by the expedition. The *Argus* returned to Syracuse June 22.

After this tour of duty the *Argus* remained in the

[1] Library of Congress, John Rodgers Papers (Hull to Barron, April 28, 29, 1805). The correspondence of Hull and Eaton while in Egypt, including nine letters of the former, is printed in *Proceedings of the American Antiquarian Society*, XXI (April, 1911), 107–116.

Mediterranean about a year, for several months at Syracuse, later at Naples. She sailed for home early in June, 1806. Meanwhile Commander Hull had been promoted to captain April 23, 1806. "The U. S. Brig *Argus*, Captain Hull, arrived on Sunday [July 13] in 39 days from Gibraltar. She brings no news of importance. Yesterday the President of the U. S., attended by the heads of departments, visited the *Argus*, which was dressed for the occasion. A salute was fired on their going on board and another on their departure. The state of this vessel indicated the utmost order and cleanliness, which is further evinced by her not having a sick man on board, although directly from the Mediterranean."[1]

Captain Hull's next service was at Middletown, Connecticut. August 24, 1806, he wrote to Commodore Preble, then at Portland, Maine: "You will doubtless be informed of my being ordered to this place for the purpose of building Gunboats. I am now about compleating the contract and hope to have them in the water this fall. As you have built several (I believe after the same Moddle) if you have any improvements that you could recommend I should be pleased to be made acquainted with them." In this and later letters he asks for suggestions as to the rigging of gunboats, dimensions, masting, etc., and thanks him for information received. October 16 he wrote to Preble: "I wish you all the pleasure you anticipate on your eastern Journey and should be happy in being one of the party, but I have been so much absent from this place that I dare

[1] Washington *National Intelligencer*, July 16, 1806.

not venture on so long a Journey at present, but have hopes of paying you a visit this Winter." November 27: "I have once received orders to go to Newport but they were countermanded. Whether I shall again receive them I cannot tell."[1]

In 1807 occurred the famous *Chesapeake* affair. On June 22 the frigate *Chesapeake,* bearing the pennant of Commodore James Barron, was fired on by the British fifty-gun ship *Leopard.* Three of her crew were killed, many wounded, and four supposed deserters from the British service were carried off. A Court of Inquiry was appointed, consisting of Commodore Edward Preble and Captains Isaac Hull and Isaac Chauncey. There was delay in assembling the court on account of Commodore Preble's illness, and he died August 25. Captain Alexander Murray was appointed in his place and the court convened on board the *Chesapeake* October 5. Barron was charged with being unprepared, prematurely surrendering his ship, and many other things. In January, 1808, he was tried by a Court Martial and sentenced to be suspended from duty for five years without pay or emoluments.[2]

Isaac Hull's movements during the year 1808 are not revealed by any source of information at hand. April 24, 1809, he wrote a letter from Boston to Commodore Rodgers, which indicates that he was probably on recruiting duty at that place. He says: "I have received

---

[1] Library of Congress, Preble Papers (Hull to Preble, August 24, October 16, November 27, 1806).

[2] *Columbian Centinel,* July 8, 22, September 23, November 28, 1807, May 21, 1808.

a letter from Mr. Hunt covering one to Mr. Goldsborough relative to the accounts of the men sent by the *Argus*. I shall see that they are sent on immediately; it would have been done before but the officers on the recruiting Service were not here to give the purser the time of entry, etc. Mr. Eakin leaves this tomorrow with thirty men, fifteen of them Seamen, the remainder good ordinary Seamen. A Vessel will also leave in a few days with from thirty to forty Marines and perhaps some Seamen."[1]

A few months later the captain was able to relieve the monotony of a long term of shore duty by a short cruise, as a few newspaper items will show. July 1: "The U. S. frigate *Chesapeake,* Capt. Hull, will leave our outer harbor this day, weather permitting, for the purpose of taking a summer cruize off the coast." The *Chesapeake,* since her mishap two years earlier, had been commanded by Captain Decatur. August 2: "Several of the United States frigates, etc., are now making short summer cruizes on the coast, to exercise their crews." August 9: "When the *Chesapeake* came to anchor in our harbor on Saturday [August 5], her sails were unbent and on deck in ten minutes after the yards were manned. We mention this in honor of the discipline and dexterity of her crew."[2]

---

[1] Library of Congress, John Rodgers Papers.
[2] *Columbian Centinel,* July 1, 22, August 2, 9, 1809.

## Chapter II

## IN COMMAND OF THE *CONSTITUTION*

FOR many years, especially since the *Chesapeake* affair, strained relations had existed between the United States and Great Britain, and the feeling towards France was hardly more friendly. Naval officers were on the alert and did what they could to keep their ships in order. The Government, however, did practically nothing in the way of military and naval preparation and drifted with blind fatuity into collision with the greatest naval power on earth.

With the opening of 1810 Captain Hull, still in Boston, doubtless began to feel a desire for active duty afloat and evidently made application to the Navy Department for a command. In reply he received the following:

Navy Department[1]<br>20 Feby, 1810

Sir

I have received your letter of the 13th inst.

Remain at Boston for the present. Your services may be highly useful at that place in superintending the repairs of the *Chesapeak*. When the other frigates shall be put in commission you shall be gratified, if possible, in your wishes.

I am respectfully<br>Your obt. servt.<br>Paul Hamilton<br>[Secretary of the Navy]

Capt. Isaac Hull
Boston.

---

[1] This is the first letter in the Boston Athenæum collection of Hull Papers.

In the spring Hull was given the frigate *President*. A squadron was organized under the command of Commodore John Rodgers for the protection of American commerce against English and French cruisers. Rodgers had the *Constitution,* but he preferred the *President,* so an exchange was effected June 17, 1810, each captain taking with him his officers and crew. Charles Morris was Hull's first lieutenant. The squadron was to patrol the coast of the United States; and the other vessels were the brig *Argus,* Lieutenant James Lawrence, and the schooner *Revenge,* Lieutenant Oliver H. Perry. During the late summer and fall the *Constitution* cruised between Cape May and Cape Henry and went into winter quarters at New London.[1]

For a short time the *Constitution* continued her cruising in the spring of 1811. In the summer Captain Hull was ordered to Europe with a large amount of specie for payment of the interest on the Dutch debt. Annapolis, Maryland, was the point of departure and the ship was at that place about the end of June. Thursday, August first, "At 2 A.M. the Boat went on shore for the purpose of bringing Mr. [Joel] Barlow, and Suit on board. At ½ past 7 A.M. it returned with Mr. Barlow, Minister to the Court of France, Mr. Warden, Consul General at Paris, Mr. Lee, Consul at Bordeaux, and Mrs. Barlow and sister; hoisted in the Boats. At ¾ past 7 got under way and stood down the Bay."[2] The ship anchored in Hampton Roads and got to sea August 5.

[1] Paullin, *Commodore John Rodgers,* 210, 211, 215.
[2] Journal kept on board the U. S. Frigate *Constitution,* Isaac Hull, Esq., Comdg. By Frederick Baury, Midshipman. This journal (July 5, 1811, to June 21, 1812), apparently a copy of the official log, is in the library of the Massachusetts Historical Society.

The Consul General, David Bailie Warden, kept a journal, and August 9 he notes: "I dined today with the officers of the Ward Room, with whom I am much pleased. The dinner was good. . . . It is not permitted to smoke a Segar except in the forecastle, or on deck near the prow."[1] The English Channel was reached about September first. On the fifth Midshipman Baury enters in his log: "At ¼ before 5 took in Top Gal[lan]t Sails, the 2d Reef in the Top Sails and bore away for the [British] Blockading Squadron off Cherbourgh. At 5 P.M. Beat to Quarters and cleared Ship for Action. At ½ past 5 P.M. hauled up the Courses and was spoken by the frigate of the Squadron. Set the foresail and stood for the Commanding officer of the Squadron. At 6 P.M. hauled up the fore Sail and backed the Main Top Sail, a boat came alongside from the Comodore Ship, the boat returned again. Made a Signal, filled away, made Sail and stood off the Land. . . . At ½ past 6 P.M. secured the Guns."[2] The next morning the *Constitution* anchored in the harbor of Cherbourg. "Saluted the commandg officer of the Harbour with 15 Guns, it was returned with the same number." In the afternoon Mr. Barlow and the other passengers went on shore. "Maned the Yards and saluted him with 17 Guns." The French admiral, with his staff, visited the *Constitution* and on leaving was saluted with nine guns, which was returned by the French flagship.

In about ten days the *Constitution* made sail for the

[1] *Maryland Historical Magazine*, XI (June, 1916), 206.
[2] Baury's Journal. All quotations in this chapter, unless otherwise noted, are from this log. When necessary the date is corrected from nautical to civil time.

Texel. An English squadron of thirteen sail of the line was seen at anchor off Flushing. On arriving off the Texel, early in the morning of September 20, several Dutch men of war under French colors were seen in shore and a British squadron was cruising off the harbor. "Filled away and ran down to the Admiral who sent a boat on board of us. At 10 A.M. . . . Hove too and took a Pilot on board. Mr. Garrison [Garretson, the purser] left the Ship for Amsterdam."

September 21: "Laying too. At 1 P.M. an English Officer came on board with a letter to the Capt. from the Admiral of the English Squadron. . . . The English Blockading Squadron consisting of 7 Sail of the Line and a number of smaller sail came to an anchor in the Offing." The next morning a pilot boat came off from the Texel with a letter for Captain Hull. "At ½ past 12 [September 22] sent the 4th Cutter to the Pilot boat for Mr. Garrison." On the following day the frigate got under way and cruised off shore several days. Meanwhile the difficulties encountered by Captain Hull in carrying out the purpose of his visit to the Texel are set forth in his correspondence.

Amsterdam 18 September 1811

Isaac Hull, Esqr.
Commander of U. S. Frigate *Constitution*
Texel.
Sir

We have received from Mr. D. B. Warden the letters intrusted to his care by the Honorable A. Gallatin

Esqr, Secretary of the Treasury, announcing to us that on board the United States Frigate *Constitution* were shipped two hundred twenty thousand spanish dollars, which on your arrival are to be delivered to us. Mr. Warden at the same time desired us to promise a pilot to watch the arrival of the Frigate under your command, which we have done accordingly, Mr. Hooglant at the Helder having our orders to that effect.

Mr. Gallatin desired us to adopt such measures for landing the money as may be required; and in order to procure you every possible dispatch we have been immediately with the Intendant General and with the Director of the Douanes, who both regretted that their orders are so strict as not to admit of their giving any directions whatever without previously having received orders from Paris; they have in consequence written immediately to the Comte de Sussey and we have informed Mr. Warden of this circumstance requesting him to consult with Mr. Barlow, the American Minister, and to take such steps as they may think proper. We hope that we may soon have a decision, and assuring you of our zeal to promote the intention of Mr. Gallatin, we shall be happy to be of service to you and have meanwhile the honor to be very respectfully
      Sir
       Yr Most Obedt. Servt.
        Wilhem and Jan Willink
     For selves and Messrs. Van Staphorst

U. S. Frigate *Constitution*
Off the Texel 19 Sept. 1811

Sir

Having arrived off this Port with the U. S. Frigate *Constitution* under my command, I have dispatched an officer for a Pilot, which I will thank you to procure if possible. The ship draws twenty three feet six inches water and I am told there is not that depth on the Bar; will you make enquiry on that subject and inform me, also whether in case I come in I can get out again before the next spring tide. I have business of great importance to transact at Amsterdam, of which Mr. Garretson the bearer of this will inform you.

Any assistance you can give him in the execution of it will be duly acknowledged by

Your obt. servt.

To the American Vice Consul     [Isaac Hull][1]
    or
Commercial Agent
    at the Texel


U. S. Frigate *Constitution*
Off the Texel 21st Sept. 1811.

Sir

I have this moment received your letter of the 20th and have to thank you for your polite attention to Mr. Garretson in forwarding the wishes of Government. I have by the same conveyance received a letter from the agents of the Government at Amsterdam, saying

---

[1] This and the following four letters of Captain Hull are unsigned copies.

that permission cannot be had to land the specie without writing to Paris; that being the case, I am at a loss how to proceed. At least ten or fifteen days will be taken up in hearing from Paris. The season of the year very bad and the ship not able to enter the port, has determined me to leave the Coast and take the chance of an arrangement being made to land the specie at Cherbourg.

I will thank you to give me your opinion and advice on the subject. I am sorry to hear of your indisposition and hope you will soon recover. Would it not be possible for the ship to stop at Flushing until I hear from Paris.

Respectfully<br>I am etc.

William Warsdale, Esqr.          [Isaac Hull]
Consul for the United States,
at the Helder

U. S. Frigate Constitution<br>Off the Texel 21st Sept. 1811

Gentlemen

I have had the honor to receive your letters of the 16th and 18th inst, and regret extremely that an arrangement cannot be made for landing the specie immediately. I find that the ship cannot enter the Texel and the season so far advanced that I consider it very unsafe to remain at sea the length of time it will take to get an answer from Paris, and the risque of landing the specie from the ship at sea in bad weather would be great, particularly so as we shall be obliged to send it on shore in our own boats, otherwise it would be subject to detention by the British Cruisers. Cannot an arrangement be made to receive it at Cherbourg, if so, I shall sail immediately for that place. I shall remain here until I get an answer to this letter unless the bad weather drives me away. Should the weather set in bad and the ship does not appear off on the first good day, you may take it for granted that I have left the Coast for Cherbourg and I shall hope to find that you have been able to make arrangements for receiving it there.

  I am with great respect
    Gentlemen
      Your obt. svt.
        [Isaac Hull]

Messrs. Wilhem and Jan Willink
N. & J. & R. Van Staphorst
  Merchants
    Amsterdam.

    U. S. Frigate *Constitution*
      off the Texel 21st Sept. 1811

Sir

I have received your letter of the 20th and regret extremely that some arrangement cannot be made to get the money on shore but I find it is impossible. I have this moment received a letter from the Agents at Amsterdam saying that they have written to Paris for permission to land it and must wait an answer, this being the case and it being impossible to get the ship in I have pretty much determined to return and take the chance of getting it on shore some where else; you will take advice for me of the Consul and other men of intelligence and find out what difference it will make to the Government. The risque of lying off here ten or fifteen days and then be obliged to get the money out at sea, would be great, besides we should not be able to land it in a Dutch vessel, provided the Squadron[1] off here chose to be saucy. Weigh all these things and see what can be done.

Be pleased to call and make my acknowledgements to Admiral DeWinter, and thank him for his polite offer of assistance. I am sorry that my not being able to leave my ship prevents my paying my respects to him in person. After you have advised with these people, come off to night if possible with such letters as may come to hand for me; if you cannot get off to night be underway by daylight in the morning if the ship is in sight, if not the moment we appear stand off to us, I shall be anxious to get you off.

Respectfully etc.

Isaac Garretson Esqr.             [Isaac Hull]
Purser U. S. Navy at the Texel.

U. S. Frigate Constitution<br>off the Texel 22 Sept. 1811

Sir

I have this moment received your very polite letter in answer to mine of the 19th.

I find so much difficulty in getting the specie out of the ship and myself made accountable for it, when in

---

[1] The British blockading squadron.

fact I can have no control over it whilst lying in lighters on shore, that I have determined to leave the Coast immediately.

It would have given me great pleasure to have taken charge of any communications that you might have for the Treasury department, but I fear my stay will not be long enough to allow them to reach here. I have written to the Agents of the Government to know if some other arrangements cannot be made for the safe keeping of the specie other than lying on board of the lighter that receives it. Their answer will determine my stay. I have given Mr. Garretson permission to visit Amsterdam on his way to Paris. Any aid you can give him will be acknowledged by

Your ob. svt.

Sylvanus Bourne, Esq.                [Isaac Hull]
Consul for the U. S.
Amsterdam.

Captain Hull evidently changed his mind and determined to make another effort, for after cruising off shore about a week, he brought his ship in to the anchorage again. Meanwhile the Director of the Douanes authorized the landing of the specie in lighters, and permission was also received from Paris. September 29, "At Meridian two pilot boats came alongside for the purpose of taking the Money from the Ship. . . . At ¼ past 1 P.M. the Dutch Pilot boat left the Ship with the Money under charge of Lieut. Swift, — filled away and made sail."

## IN COMMAND OF THE *CONSTITUTION*

The *Constitution* anchored in the Downs October 3. Early on October 8 she made sail out of the Downs and the next morning "At 1 A.M. saw a Sail on the Weather Bow. At ½ past 2 A.M. she fired two Shott at us, one struck under the Quarter and the other on the Weather Beam. Cleared Ship for Action and beat to Quarters. At 3 A.M. hauled up the Courses and bore up, at ½ past 3 A.M. spoke his B. M. Brig *Redpole,* who sent an Officer on board to Apologise for firing at us. Made Sail, secured the Guns." A few days later, October 12, off Cherbourg, the *Constitution* was the victim of another mistake. "At ½ past 3 [P.M.] four Shotts was fired from the French Battery at us, two struck us, one passed through the Hammock cloths, struck the Stern of the 2d cutter, carried it away and passed through the Mainsail, and the other struck the water about 5 yds from the Starboard Gangway and went into the side just abaft the fore Chain." The frigate then came to anchor.

After remaining at Cherbourg nearly a month Jonathan Russell and several other passengers came on board. Mr. Russell, who had been looking out for American interests in Paris before Mr. Barlow's arrival, was now to take charge of the American legation at London. The ship got under way November 9 and the next day anchored in St. Helen's Roads, Portsmouth. Captain Hull and Mr. Russell left the ship and proceeded to London. The incidents relating to certain deserters, told by various writers, then took place. Everything on the subject found in the log-book is here quoted.[1]

---
[1] See *Autobiography of Commodore Charles Morris,* 44, 45.

November 12: "At ½ past 8 P.M. an Officer came on board from the Admiral to inform us of their having taken up a Man who had swam from us, it proved to be Thomas Holland (sea[man])." Captain Hull being away Lieutenant Morris sent for the man, but he claimed British protection and the admiral refused to give him up. November 17: "At Midnight William Wallace (sea) swam from on board his B. M. Ship *Havanna* (44) on board of us, claims our protection as an American." November 18: "At ½ past 11 [A.M.] Capt. Hull returned from London." November 19: "At Meridian hove up the Starboard Anchor and stood down St. Helens Roads under the Top Sails. . . . At ½ past 1 P.M. took in the Top Sails and came too in St. Hellens Roads . . . with the Larboard Anchor." November 20: "At ½ past 3 P.M. hove short on the Larboard Cable, beat to Quarters and cleared away the Guns, expecting a disturbance on account of William Wallace who Capt. Hull refused to give up, he claiming our protection. At ¼ before 4 P.M. hove up the Anchor and stood out for the Channel. . . . From 4 to 6 P.M. employed stowing the Anchors and preparing for Action." November 21: "At ½ past 5 A.M. filled away." The British made no trouble, the ship was soon under full sail, and the next morning anchored again in the harbor of Cherbourg.

December 1: "The French Ships were Dressed and fired a Salute of 21 Guns in honor to the Emperor's Coronation." December 30: "At ½ past 9 [A.M.] Dis[covere]d an Amer'n Ship in the Offing, made the private Signal of the Day which was answer'd. At 10

A.M. She hoisted her Number. She proved to be the Am. Ship *Hornet* [sloop of war], Capt. Lawrence. Sent a pilot to her. . . . At ¼ past 12 the U. S. Ship *Hornet* came too astern of us." The *Hornet* sailed January 2, 1812, and the *Constitution* a week later, with several passengers.

January 9: "At ½ past 8 A.M. got under way and stood out the western passage. Disc'd a Ship of War in the Offing. . . . At 10 A.M. . . . Disc'd another Ship of War to windward, both standing for us. All hands emp[loye]d getting the Ship ready for Action. . . . At ½ past 12 beat to Quarters and cleared Ship for Action. At ½ past 1 P.M. shortened Sail, hove too and spoke his B. M. Frigate *Hotspur,* the Hon. J. Percey comdg. Requested permission to send a boat on board, which was granted by Capt. Hull. At ½ past 2 P.M. the Boat left us, filled away, bore up and made sail." January 15: "At 2 A.M. spoke his B. M. Ship *Mars* (line of Battle Ship)."

The *Constitution* was now homeward bound and came to anchor in Hampton Roads February 19. In the spring she made her way slowly up the Potomac River to the Washington Navy Yard, arriving April 5. On the 15th, "At 4 P.M. removed the Ship's Company on board the *Gen. Green,* Rec[eivin]g Ship."

CHAPTER III

THE WAR OF 1812

THE *Constitution* received a thorough overhauling at the Washington Navy Yard. She was hove down and her bottom found in better condition than was expected. The copper sheathing was repaired. The foremast and bowsprit were found badly decayed and were replaced by new. Her trim was altered by restowing her ballast and, Cooper says, "the effect was magical." Within a few weeks her increased speed was her salvation. June 9, "At 4 P.M. the Crew removed on board the *Constitution*," and during the next two days, by towing and sailing, she was brought down the river and anchored off Alexandria, where her stores were put on board. On the 18th she made sail and stood down the river. War was declared against England that same day and when the news came, "The Crew manifested their Joy and Zeal by giving three Cheers."[1]

The *Constitution* was then brought out of the Potomac and up the bay to Annapolis. Here she filled up her crew and made every other necessary preparation for a cruise in search of prizes and glory. All these things took time, and it was July 5 before the frigate began to work her way down the Chesapeake. Just a week later she passed out between the capes into the

[1] Baury's Journal, which ends here; *Putnam's Magazine*, I, 487. See *Autobiography of Commodore Charles Morris*, 51.

open sea. She was under orders to join the squadron of Commodore Rodgers at New York.

The next adventure was the remarkable chase of the *Constitution* by a British squadron. During the War of 1812 the frigate had three narrow escapes from capture by British squadrons and this was the first and most notable. July 16 the *Constitution* fell in with a squadron consisting of a ship of the line and four frigates. The chase which ensued lasted nearly three days. For much of the time a dead calm prevailed, kedges were made use of for warping the ships, and boats employed in towing. The British had the advantage in towing, as all the boats of the squadron were employed in towing the nearest frigate. By consummate seamanship Hull escaped, and reached Boston in safety, July 26.[1]

The captain was more magnanimous than is sometimes the case with military and naval commanders, and soon after his arrival issued this statement: "Capt. Hull, finding his friends in Boston are correctly informed of his situation when chased by the British squadron off New York and that they are good enough to give him more credit by escaping them than he ought to claim, takes this opportunity of requesting them to make a transfer of a great part of their good wishes to Lt. Morris and the other brave officers and the crew under his command for their very great exertions and prompt attention to orders while the enemy were in chase. Capt. Hull has great pleasure in saying that, notwithstanding the length of the chase and the officers and crew being deprived of sleep and allowed but little re-

---

[1] *Naval Monument*, 1–5; *Autobiography of Commodore Charles Morris*, 51–55.

freshment during the time, not a murmur was heard to escape them."[1]

On August 1 the *Constitution* again set sail, on a cruise to the eastward, and on the 19th, off the Banks of Newfoundland, fell in with the British frigate *Guerrière,* one of the squadron which had chased her in July. After a period of manœuvring, during which the English ship kept up an active though ineffective fire, the *Constitution* delivered her first broadside at about six o'clock in the afternoon, within pistol-shot. Fifteen minutes later the *Guerrière's* mizzen-mast went over the side, in another quarter of an hour the main-mast went by the board, and about the same time the fore-mast also fell. The British frigate then surrendered, a complete wreck. Although the *Constitution* was superior in number of guns and men, the injury inflicted on her adversary was out of all proportion to the difference in force. The British loss was fifteen killed and sixty-four wounded, eight of them mortally; the American, seven killed and seven wounded. The *Constitution* suffered some damage to her spars and rigging, while the *Guerrière,* a helpless hulk, could not be brought into port and was set on fire and blown up. This and nearly all the later naval battles in the war proved the superior seamanship and gunnery of the Americans.

In his report of August 30 to the Secretary of the Navy Captain Hull says: "After informing you that so fine a Ship as the *Guerrière,* commanded by an able and experienced Officer, had been totally dismasted and otherwise cut to pieces, so as to make her not worth towing

[1] *Naval Monument,* 5.

THE CONSTITUTION

into port, in the short space of thirty minutes, you can have no doubt of the Gallantry and good Conduct of the Officers and Ship's company I have the honor to command. It only remains therefore for me to assure you that they all fought with great bravery and it gives me great pleasure to say that from the smallest boy in the Ship to the oldest Seaman, not a look of fear was seen. They all went into Action giving three cheers and requested to be laid close alongside the enemy. . . ."[1]

Captain Hull, in another letter to the Secretary, says: "I cannot but make you acquainted with the very great assistance I received from that valuable officer Lieut. Morris, in bringing the ship into action and in working her whilst alongside the enemy; and I am extremely sorry to state that he is badly wounded, being shot through the body. We have yet hopes of his recovery, when I am sure he will receive the gratitude of his country for this and the many gallant acts he has done in the service."[2]

The *Constitution* returned to Boston with the news of her victory and with the crew of the *Guerrière* on board. The house of Josiah Quincy stood close by the shore of Boston Harbor in the town of Quincy and every ship passed in full view of the windows. Edmund Quincy, in his Life of his father, quotes an account of this time written by his sister. "Toward evening on the 29th of August, 1812, a frigate (recognized as the *Constitution*, commanded by Captain Hull) came in under full sail

---

[1] Extract from a copy of Hull's official report, in the Yale University Library. See *Autobiography of Commodore Charles Morris*, 55–59.

[2] *Naval Monument*, 14.

and dropped her anchor beside Rainsford Island, — then the Quarantine Ground. The next morning a fleet of armed ships appeared off Point Alderton. As they rapidly approached, the *Constitution* was observed to raise her anchor and sails and go boldly forth to meet the apparent enemy; but, as the frigate passed the leader of the fleet, a friendly recognition was exchanged, instead of the expected broadside. They joined company and the *Constitution* led the way to Boston. It was the squadron of United States ships, then commanded by Commodore Rodgers, unexpectedly returning from a long cruise.

"A few days afterwards, Hull, who had just taken the *Guerrière,* came with Decatur to breakfast at Quincy. When this incident was mentioned, he said: 'I must acknowledge I participated in the apprehensions of my friends on shore. Thinking myself safe in port, I told my officers to let the men wash their clothes and get the ship in order to go up to Boston; and, being excessively fatigued, went to my stateroom. I was sound asleep when a lieutenant rushed down exclaiming, "Captain, the British are upon us! an armed fleet is entering the harbor!" No agreeable intelligence, certainly; for I was wholly unprepared to engage with a superior force. But, determined to sell our lives as dear as I could, I gave orders to clear the decks, weigh anchor, and get ready for immediate action. I confess I was greatly relieved when I saw the American flag and recognized Rodgers.' In speaking of the conflict with the *Guerrière,* he said: 'I do not mind the day of battle; the excitement carries one through, but the day after is fearful; it is so dreadful to see my men wounded and suffering.' These naval officers formed a striking contrast. Hull was easy and prepossessing in his manners, but looked accustomed to face 'the battle and the breeze.' Decatur was uncommonly handsome, and remarkable for the delicacy and refinement of his appearance."[1]

Midshipman Matthew C. Perry, on board the flagship *President,* wrote in his journal under date of August 31, 1812: "At daylight [August 30] discovered a frigate lying in Nantasket Roads, cleared ship for action and stood for her. At 7 she proved the frigate *Constitution* from a cruise, having captured the British frigate *Guerrière.* This day moored ship in Boston harbor."[2]

Great was the rejoicing in Boston when the victorious frigate sailed up the harbor. "On Monday morning [August 31] the *Constitution* came up to town and was welcomed and honored by a federal salute from the Washington Artillery under Capt. Harris and by the hearty, unanimous, and repeated cheers of the citizens on the wharves, the shipping, and housetops."[3] A few days later a dinner was given in Hull's honor at Faneuil Hall. The streets and shipping were decorated with bunting and the captain was escorted to the hall by a procession of five hundred citizens. He received the thanks of the Legislature; and, as the news spread over the country, honors and gifts were bestowed in various cities. Congress gave him a gold medal and awarded fifty thousand dollars in lieu of prize money to the officers and crew of the *Constitution.*

[1] Quincy, *Life of Josiah Quincy,* 262.
[2] Paullin, *Commodore John Rodgers,* 257.
[3] *Columbian Centinel,* September 2, 1812.

If Captain Hull had delayed his cruise of August 1, he would have missed the greatest opportunity for glory that ever came to him, for the Secretary of the Navy had already written him to remain at Boston until further orders; and the letter was on the way. Now, however, he was ready to give way to another, and having urgent private business to attend to, he asked to be relieved. Commodore Bainbridge, therefore, who had had command of the Boston Navy Yard, was ordered to the *Constitution,* and during his absence on a five months' cruise, Hull took charge of the Boston Yard. Bainbridge returned about the first of March, 1813, having captured the British frigate *Java,* and resumed command of the Navy Yard. Meanwhile Hull's command seems also to have included the Portsmouth Navy Yard, and during the remainder of the war he was occupied at that place.[1]

Late in December, 1812, Hull was in New York, where he received further honors in recognition of his naval victory. During this visit to New York the captain was married, January 2, 1813, to Anna McCurdy Hart,[2] daughter of Captain Elisha Hart, of Saybrook, Connecticut, a privateer officer of the Revolution.[3] This was a happy though childless union, and the couple were less frequently separated than is usually the case with

[1] Preble, *The Navy and the Charlestown Navy Yard,* in Winsor's *Memorial History of Boston,* III, 341, 343; Fentress, *Centennial History of U. S. Navy Yard at Portsmouth, N. H.*

[2] Miss Hart was the second of seven sisters and had no brother; Isaac Hull was the second of seven brothers and had no sister.

[3] Middebrook, *Maritime Connecticut During the Revolution,* II, 204, 205.

seafaring people, for Mrs. Hull accompanied her husband on most of his voyages. In after years "Admiral Porter . . . told a cousin of Mrs. Hull . . . that of all the beautiful and brilliant women he had ever met in any country, Mrs. Hull surpassed them all."[1]

During Hull's command of the Portsmouth Navy Yard — about two and a half years — he was perhaps unduly apprehensive of enemy attacks, particularly in 1814, when the British blockading squadron lay outside and one of the new seventy-fours authorized by Congress was under construction in the Yard. It was natural to suppose that an enterprising admiral might send in a boat expedition to destroy this vessel and other property. Hull kept strict watch with the small force at his disposal, and as early as the summer of 1813 the local paper recorded that "the Volunteer Company for the defence of the Navy Yard met at that place on Saturday last and went through their evolutions at one of the batteries and on board one of the gunboats with unexpected celerity and precision."[2] At times the watchers were aroused in the night by false alarms.

In September, 1813, Captain Hull was greatly interested in the brilliant exploit of the U. S. brig *Enterprise,* which, a few days after sailing from the Portsmouth Navy Yard, encountered off Portland, fought, and captured the British brig *Boxer,* both captains being killed. Hull went to Portland a few days after the battle and on the 14th wrote to the Secretary of the Navy: "I have the honor to forward you by the mail the Flags

[1] Salisbury, *Family Histories and Genealogies,* I, 88, 89.
[2] *Portsmouth Oracle,* July 24, 1813.

of the late British brig *Boxer,* which were nailed to her mast heads at the time she engaged and was captured by the United States brig *Enterprise.* Great as the pleasure is that I derive from performing this part of my duty, I need not tell you how different my feelings would have been could the gallant Burrows have had this honor. He went into action most gallantly and the difference of injury done the two vessels proves how nobly he fought." A few months later Hull served as president of a court-martial on board the frigate *Congress* in Portsmouth Harbor for the trial of the sailing master of the *Enterprise* for cowardice during the action with the *Boxer.*[1]

The keel of the new seventy-four-gun ship of the line *Washington* was laid in March, 1814, at the Portsmouth Navy Yard; and she was launched the following January. The oak knees for this ship were at Gloucester and the difficulties of land transport were so great that Captain Hull resolved to attempt running them through the blockade. This was accomplished in several trips by Captain Henry Trefethen in his smack, the *Yankee.*[2]

On May 11, 1814, Captain Hull wrote to Hon. William Jones, Secretary of the Navy: "I have the honor to enclose you a Copy of a letter I have this day received from a respectable gentleman in New Haven. The information contained in this letter agrees precisely with information received from other sources and forwarded you, which leaves but little doubt on my mind

---

[1] *Portsmouth Oracle,* September 18, October 2, 1813, January 1, 1814.

[2] Fentress, *Centennial History of U. S. Navy Yard at Portsmouth, N. H.,* 38, 39, 40.

but an attack will be made on this place before the Summer is out. I have written to the Governour of the State on the subject, giving him such information from time to time as I have received, and have given him very freely my opinion of the defenceless state of the Harbor, but no measures have as yet been taken by the State Government, except furnishing from fifty to seventy-five men to man three Guns I had mounted on Pierce's Island; nor do I believe that the least calculation ought to be made on the Militia of this part of the Country to act against the kind of force that will be sent against it. If the enemy should land for 24 or 48 hours, the Militia would no doubt in that time get ready to act. But that will not be the mode of warfare. If the enemy come, it will be with a considerable force, and what they do will be done in a short time.

"A force ought therefore to be ready to receive them. The Forts are not manned, nor do I know of regular troops enough in this neighbourhood to man them. About one hundred men have within two or three weeks been ordered here, but I understand by Colonel Upham (whose command they are under) that they are to leave this on Monday next, when Fort Sullivan with three heavy Guns on a very commanding height will be left without men. I shall write to Governour Gilman again tomorrow and urge him to send some force to the defence of this place.

"By returns I had the honor to enclose you some days since, you will observe that there is only Two hundred men attached to the Gun Boats and Navy Yard, and when the boats are manned we have not enough

34    PAPERS OF ISAAC HULL

men in the Yard to work more than two or three Guns, and I can make but little calculation on the Carpenters in case of an attack, particularly if it should take place in the night, for they will have their own affairs to attend to before they come to assist us on the Island, if they come at all, so that in the event of a force coming against us of from one to two thousand men, you can easily suppose what the result will be, situated as we now are."[1]

Navy Department
May 26th, 1814

Sir

Your letter of the 11th current with enclosed copy from your friend at New Haven, have been submitted to the Secretary of War, who says, "its substance shall be communicated to General Cushing, with orders to reinforce Portsmouth as far as may be practicable. I shall send Col. Walback to command the troops at Portsmouth."

I am respectfully
Your obedt. Servt.
W. Jones
[Secretary of the Navy]

Isaac Hull Esqr.
Commanding Naval Officer
Portsmouth, N. H.

[1] Library of Congress, James Madison Papers.

Navy Department,
June 17, 1814

Sir,

I have received your letter, of the 9th instant. You are misinformed as to the defence of the ships at New London; they have not one third of the number of men on board that you mention, nor do I believe the military force is one half that you suppose, though in the actual presence of a very strong blockading squadron, and the means of defence vastly inferior to those at Portsmouth.

The Secretary of War has been regularly informed of all you have said on the subject, and has taken such measures as he presumed the occasion calls for.

As to the crew of the *Congress,* they formed no part of the defence of Portsmouth, for, could she have recruited 50 additional men, she would have been at sea long since. I am sure you do not expect that other places much less tenable than Portsmouth are to be abandoned in order to defend Portsmouth.

Your own observation and experience must prove to you the difficulty of recruiting men, and if you cannot get them in the very quarter of the union where they most abound, where are they to come from? The want of seamen has, as you have seen, compelled the Department to strip from ships that were ready for sea, to man those on the Lakes. Are we to strip the remainder in order to defend those that are building in the Atlantic ports? If so, policy and economy would dictate the burning of the latter, in order to remove the temptation, rather than to defend them at an expense far transcending their value.

You must see, Sir, that this Department can give you no other additional means of defence than such as you may derive from recruiting. The War Department will, I presume, send such as can be spared from other branches of the service, but if the people of a populous place, with such powerful means of defence natural and artificial, will not defend themselves, I see nothing to prevent the force you have mentioned from burning the town and everything in its vicinity.

I am, very respectfully,
Your obt. Servt.<br>W. Jones.

Capt. Isaac Hull
U. S. N. Portsmouth, N. H.

CHAPTER IV

THE BOSTON NAVY YARD

THE Board of Navy Commissioners was established by law February 7, 1815. It had long been felt that a board of experts on whom the Secretary of the Navy could rely for advice and assistance in technical matters was greatly needed. While still at Portsmouth, Captain Hull had written three letters to Hon. David Daggett, United States Senator from Connecticut, freely expressing his opinion of conditions in the navy and making suggestions. November 18, 1814, he wrote: "It has long since been my opinion that at least three Admirals ought to be made. . . . If the Government wish a grade between a Captain and an Admiral, let them . . . give out commissions for Commodores and attach to that grade of Officer pay and emoluments accordingly. . . . If we are to have a Navy (which I almost despair of) we ought and must have Admirals.[1] A Navy Board must be established and be composed of men capable of bringing everything that relates to a Navy into some sort of system, and make regulations for its government that will be sure to fit out our ships at the least possible expence. . . . As for myself, I feel that I am so far

---

[1] The grades of admiral and commodore were not established until the Civil War. Before that time captains in command of squadrons were given the title, but not the rank, of commodore; and by courtesy they usually bore the title through life.

out of the reach of Admirals . . . that I have but little to hope for. Indeed our memorial presented to Congress a few years since was treated with so much indelicacy (I may say indecency) that every officer had determined never to ask again for anything. If you will look over that Memorial you will find nothing asked but what ought to have been granted, and if you will look at the debates on that subject I am sure you will blush for some that spoke against it." The captain goes on to complain of the treatment that he personally had received. He was strongly opposed to brevet rank in the navy, which had been proposed.

On November 28 he wrote: "It has ever been my opinion that a Naval Board was absolutely necessary, and *that* Board composed of Officers that are capable of fixing on what is necessary to fit out every class of Ships, and after having given what they absolutely require, they should have nothing further, nor should any alteration be made in the equipment or stores furnished. It has also long been my opinion that whatever class of Ships we build, they ought to be of the largest size of that class; say if 74's, build them of the largest size, and the same with Frigates and Sloops."[1]

The Secretary of the Navy having asked Commodore Rodgers his opinion of the qualifications of certain officers for appointment to the new Navy Board, Rodgers spoke of Hull as "a man of most amiable disposition; and, although he does not pretend to much science, he is an excellent seaman and at the same time he unites all the most essential qualifications necessary for such a

[1] Original letters in the Yale University Library.

situation."[1]  The Board consisted of three Commissioners, and those first appointed, February 27, 1815, were John Rodgers, Isaac Hull, and David Porter. The Board met and organized April 25.

Although, as appears from Captain Hull's letters to Senator Daggett, the work of the Navy Board was something that interested him greatly, he retained his membership a very short time. July 1, 1815, he was appointed Commandant of the Boston Navy Yard at Charlestown, and took up this new work a few weeks later. His service on this station was long — more than eight years — yet there is practically nothing to say of it. It was the routine work of a navy yard during the dull period which usually follows a war. The only vessel built at the Yard while Hull was there was a schooner in 1821. Nothing more important than repair work was done. One unpleasant episode of this service will be related in another chapter.[2]

In January or February, 1819, Mrs. Hull was in Washington with the captain and attracted the attention of Elijah H. Mills, Member of Congress, who wrote to a correspondent: "Mrs. Hull, the wife of the Commodore, who is now in the city, is said to be the reigning beauty here. If you have seen her, therefore, you may be able to form some idea of the others. She is not a beauty; to my taste too insipid and too much like wax-work. But I did not intend to fill this whole letter with nonsense and will stop."[3]

---

[1] *Massachusetts Historical Society Proceedings*, Second Series, IV (1888), 208; Paullin, *Commodore John Rodgers*, 303.

[2] See Chapter VI.

[3] *Mass. Hist. Soc. Proc.*, XIX (1881), 31.

The subject of rank and command was still a matter of concern to Captain Hull and he believed that if prevailing conditions continued they would "go far to ruin the Navy," as he expressed it in a letter of November 29, 1820, to Nathaniel Silsbee, Member of Congress. He adds: "If we cannot get a permanent Grade, the nominal one of Commodore must be done away; . . . it cannot be supposed that the President intended, in giving the command of one or more ships to some of the youngest Captains with the nominal rank of Commodore, that he intended to give them permanent rank and honor. If so there is an end to the Service, and I hope if the question is brought forward an inquiry will be made, whether the President did intend permanent honors, etc., when giving those Commands. Believe me it is a subject that ought to attract the attention of both Houses.

"The Navy Department must have considered that there were permanent honors attached to the rank of Commodore, or why should they, after that command ceased, address letters to 'Captain' Isaac Hull, to 'Commodore' Isaac Chauncey . . . and forty other Commodores that were Midshipmen when I was a post Captain? I am now informed that those Commodores have commenced a correspondence with each other to endeavor to make interest with their friends to get their rank confirmed. You must readily conceive what my feelings are to see their letters come addressed to them as Commodores, and by the same mail mine are directed to 'Captain Hull.'

"In short, my dear sir, it will be impossible to prevent duelling and all sorts of quarrels unless Rank and Command is better defined, understood, and practised than it now is."[1]

Up to this time Hull had never commanded a squadron, but a few years later he did so, and thereafter was addressed as Commodore. August 23, 1823, he was relieved of his command of the Boston Navy Yard and it was once more taken over by Commodore Bainbridge.[2]

---

[1] *Mass. Hist. Soc. Proc.,* XLV (1911), 29, 30.
[2] *Memorial History of Boston,* III, 351.

## Chapter V
## THE PACIFIC STATION

ABOUT the beginning of the year 1824 Isaac Hull was ordered to the west coast of South America to take command of the Pacific Station, relieving Commodore Stewart, whose instructions were sent to Hull for his guidance. These orders, dated September 8, 1821,[1] took cognizance of the disturbed political conditions in South America, the independence of the revolutionary governments not yet having been fully achieved.

The instructions required that in case it should be found that American commerce had been molested by either party at war, the causes of this and the best means of protection should be inquired into and respect for the United States secured. Blockade of the coast without sufficient force to maintain it and the right to exclude American merchant vessels from the coast or to seize them for violation of the blockade must not be recognized. Yet, being a struggle for liberty, the United States should avoid any collision with the revolutionary governments or any appearance of favoring Spain. In case of violation of our neutrality, a spirited appeal must be made through the United States Agent to the Chilean Government. The commodore must decline to take on board for either party, men, money or supplies,

[1] Hull's copy in the Athenæum collection.

## THE PACIFIC STATION 43

to be carried to any port whatever, except specie to be brought to the United States on his return. He must observe strict discipline, requiring exemplary conduct on the part of officers and men visiting shore.

Commodore Hull set sail from Hampton Roads in the frigate *United States* January 5, 1824.[1] He was accompanied by Mrs. Hull and her sister, Miss Jeannette Hart. Three weeks later the ship crossed the equator and February 11 anchored in the Bay of Rio de Janeiro, where she remained one week. On March 9, says the log, "At 4 [A.M.] discovered the land (Cape Horn) on the weather quarter, bearing per Compass W. ½ S., about 20 miles distance." The frigate arrived at Valparaiso March 27, sailed April 4, and just a week later anchored in Callao Bay. "In port U. S. Ship *Franklin* and Schr *Dolphin*. . . . Saluted the *Franklin* with 11 Guns and hoisted the Red broad Pendant, which was returned. At 11 saluted the Castle with 21 Guns, which was returned by 18. Sent an Officer on Shore to demand the reason why an equal number was not returned and immediately 21 Guns were fired. Commodore Stewart visited the Ship." Callao Castle was held by the Spaniards at this time.

During the next few weeks several American vessels came into Callao, among them a brig from New York which had been captured by a Spanish privateer. Some Americans who had been confined in Callao Castle were received on board the *United States*. The Spanish governor of the Castle was General Rodil. There were

---

[1] Log-book of the *United States*, in the Athenæum collection of Hull Papers.

also in port a squadron of the Peruvian navy, under the command of Admiral Guise, and a few vessels of the British navy, including the line-of-battle ship *Cambridge*. A number of British officers serving in the Peruvian army and navy visited the *United States*.

The United States consul at Lima at this time was William Tudor, a Boston man, who graduated at Harvard College in 1796 and founded the *North American Review* in 1815. He was afterwards *Chargé d'Affaires* in Brazil. He carried on a voluminous correspondence with Commodore Hull, and Lima being only about six miles distant from Callao, they could often meet.

Brig Rimac<br>[Bay of Callao, May 24, 1824]

Dear Sir,

. . . . . . . . . .

With regard to this blockade, I have the same opinion I have always had, to me it seems illegal, unauthorized, injurious to us particularly and impolitic on their parts and I apprehend will be disavowed by Gen'l. Bolivar.

I will put on paper a sketch of such thoughts as occur to me, in the shape of a letter addressed to him, which you can make use of partially or entirely as you may deem expedient as I have little doubt but a representation from you of all the circumstances will cause a countermand of Guise's proceedings.

. . . . . . . . . .

I am always yours,<br>W. Tudor.

Comm. Hull

THE *UNITED STATES*

Lima   May 27th, 1824

Dear Com[modor]e

You must protect your countrymen and I am one of them. I have been three days to Callao at your request. I consider these three days equal to 12 working days of your caulkers; do pray let them go to work on the Brig *Frederic* which will keep her from sinking and balance all demands. I will besides acknowledge myself to be in your debt for this favor.

I wish you would be kind enough to send me that national calendar I saw yesterday by the first opportunity and I will return it in a few days. We had an earthquake this morning.

My respects to the ladies

Yours truly<br>W. Tudor

Com. Hull.

U. S. Frigate United States<br>Callao, July 15th, 1824

Sir,

In compliance with your order I disembarked at Huacho from the U. S. Schooner *Dolphin* with the despatches entrusted to my care for Genl. Simeon Bolivar, Protector of Columbia and Liberator of Peru. From thence I took my departure for the Head Quarters of his Excellency who I fortunately met at Huaras, a city about sixty leagues in the interior and seventy from Huacho.

I was received in the most polite and friendly manner and treated with marked attention during my stay. His

Excellency expressed himself in the warmest terms of gratitude for the friendly attention you had given to the misunderstandings with the Peruvian Admiral saying that it was consistent with the principles of our government and the lively interest our country has ever shewn in the welfare and happiness of South America. He repeated these sentiments several times and assured me that the patriots of South America felt with peculiar satisfaction the disinterested sympathies of our countrymen.

He moreover assured me that every thing in his power should be done to remove all unpleasant subjects of communication, to which end he would send by me new instructions to the Peruvian Admiral requiring him in future to make the laws of nations his rule of conduct, that blockades should be confined to Callao and Pisco and that no place should be considered in a state of blockade where there was not an efficient force. He remarked that you had just cause of complaint, that the Peruvian Government would hold itself responsible for all just claims, but that for any *private offence* which the Admiral might commit he must be held personally responsible. Accompanying is the reply of his Excellency to your despatches together with a package from the Liberator to Admiral Guise.

The situation of the country through which I passed having rendered travelling extremely difficult from the scarcity of horses and mules together with the absolute necessity of employing a guide throughout my journey will account for my having expended more money than would be necessary to perform the same in our own country, and knowing it was important that I should perform it in as short a time as possible, I did not hesitate to incur extra expense whenever it facilitated my progress.

I have the honor to be, Sir, with the highest respect,

Your m . obdt. and hbl. Servt.

H Paulding, [lieutenant, U. S. N.]

Commodore Isaac Hull
Commanding the U. S. Naval Forces
in the Pacific Ocean.

The *United States* weighed anchor July 22 and stood out on a short cruise along shore to the northward. The next day a Spanish privateer was boarded but no proofs were found of depredations on American commerce. It does not appear that at this or any other time during her stay in the Pacific the frigate extended her cruising any considerable distance to the northward. She returned to Callao about the middle of August. Political conditions in Lima were precarious. The Peruvians having just won a great victory at Junin, there was apprehension of disturbance and mob violence in the city, and General Rodil proposed the landing of marines from the British and American ships for the protection of lives and property. The battle of Ayacucho in December was a still more decisive victory for the Peruvians, but the Spaniards continued in possession of Callao Castle for more than a year longer.

Lima    August 19th 1824

Dear Sir,

As soon as I heard of the proposition of General Rodil to yourself and Captain Maling respecting the sending of a detachment of marines to this City, for the purpose of protecting the property and lives of your countrymen, and that the English merchants had joined their solicitations to the commanding officer of their nation, I supposed a similar application would be desirable to you, and I drew up a request which was signed by such of our countrymen as I could find at a short notice. All I have seen since have expressed their desire to join in the request, which was, that you would concur in the measure proposed by General Rodil. The paper was forwarded to Mr. Nixon[1] but I understand has not yet reached your hands.

I drew up and signed this request not to influence your opinion but to support it in case, as I was informed, that you and Captain Maling were acting in concert. The English detachment arrived last night, have good quarters assigned them in the Consulate and ample rations furnished by the government. The ground they have taken is a very noble one, which is to serve as a main guard and point of support for the whole city, instead of being distributed about in the houses of their countrymen, which would have had injurious effects on the discipline of the men, besides greatly circumscribing their utility and rendering it invidious. I may say

---

[1] Lieutenant Z. W. Nixon, who had resigned from the navy and was in business in South America.

## THE PACIFIC STATION

that their presence has poured consolation into every dwelling in this unfortunate city.

Former experience has shewed the horrours this city is exposed to on such a change of power as is now impending and I beg leave to explain the circumstances as they have been stated to me in justification of the request that has been addressed to you. When the rear guard of the evacuating party leave the city, all government and controul cease as the civil and military power expire together. During this period which may last one day or two or three, the lives and property of the citizens who are all unarmed, are at the mercy of the abandoned part of its populace, and the most dreadful disorders have been the consequence. A small force like the one proposed to be sent from the American and English ships is however sufficient to avert all this danger, because the Alcaldes and watchmen having their support do not abandon their posts, and the populace who are timid and easily overawed are afraid to commit outrages. The moment any regular officer appears from the entering army, the care of the city is given up to him, and the labours of this neutral force cease.

It seems to your countrymen here that the English by their humane interference, will most deservedly gain credit, which on national grounds we should have been glad to have shared with them if circumstances would permit. As the Spanish government spontaneously made the proposition, both sides must be gratified by such a step because the patriot government cannot but be grateful to those who volunteer to protect their friends and families all alike exposed, until they can arrive to do it themselves.

I have stated these facts that you may know the circumstances of this case, in regard to the course which is best to be pursued. I leave that to your own better judgement and better knowledge of what is proper under your responsibility. I do not pretend to advise, or even to give an opinion and have only written this letter to explain the situation of things here that you may be apprised of all the facts to form your own decision.

I remain with respect

Yours truly

W. Tudor

Commodore Hull
Comg. the U. S. Squadron
in the Pacific.

P.S. I go on board the *Cambridge* tomorrow to serve a friend, but not being very well, the distance to your ship will prevent my having the pleasure of calling upon you, but if you wish to write me, a letter will reach me on board before 2 o'clock.

Lima, August 20th, 1824.

Dear Sir

I understand from Mr. Nixon this morning that you propose sending a few trusty seamen to guard the houses of your countrymen. Will you permit me to state what was the first impression on my mind and that of others on hearing this, that it would be inexpedient. The main object of preserving the City from tumult during the period of evacuation will be obtained by the presence of the English forces. If then you send us men for our individual protection which I think now is unnecessary, it may hereafter be tauntingly said, that we protected ourselves and the English protected the City, and it would operate very disadvantageously to us.

Not having seen you since the proposal of General Rodil I do not know what steps you may have taken. Everyone whom I have heard speak of it thinks it does him great honor. I feel perfectly that it is much more easy for Captain Maling to take the step he has done than for yourself, he has 160 marines and three officers on board one ship. Your situation is very different and the risk and inconvenience greater to you. Would it not be well to write General Rodil on this subject to prevent any unfavorable impression being entertained by any party at our not being able to join in the proposed arrangement for protecting the City.

I need not hint to you the difficulty we should have in controlling the sailors scattered about in 5 or 6 houses, without officers to command them, and the impossibility of preventing their getting drunk and in fact instead of being a guard to us, obliging us to be a guard to them. I write in haste but am

Truly yours<br>W. Tudor.

To Commodore Isaac Hull

In January, 1825,[1] the *United States* was in Callao Bay, and on the 16th saluted the Chilean frigate *O'Higgins*, flagship of Admiral Blanco. Ten days later Com-

---

[1] From August, 1824, to the end of the year the log-book of the *United States* is almost entirely illegible. She seems to have passed most of this time at Callao.

modore Hull made another short cruise to the northward and on his return anchored in the harbor of Chorillos, just south of Callao. At this time he had with him the sloop of war *Peacock*. February 22 the log records: "At Sunrise fired a salute of 17 guns accompanied by the *Peacock*. At 10.30 A.M. the Ship was visited by Genl Bolivar and suit, fired a Salute of 21 Guns and manned the Yards, beat to quarters and exercised the Crew." On March 3 the *United States* went to sea bound for Valparaiso, where she arrived on the 22nd. Ten days later she went as far south as Concepcion, thence back to Valparaiso, and later returned to Chorillos, arriving June 7, having spent three weeks at Coquimbo, Chile, on the way. During this three months' cruise she spent four weeks in the harbor of Valparaiso. American commercial and whaling interests occupied the attention of Commodore Hull at these various ports.

The next six months were passed by the *United States* almost wholly in port, either at Chorillos or Callao. Commodore Hull received instructions from the Secretary of the Navy directing him to visit the Hawaiian Islands at the first opportunity, in order to give his attention to American interests there, which seemed to require the presence of a naval force. The commodore, feeling that conditions in Peru and Chile were too insecure to admit of his absence, sent the U. S. schooner *Dolphin*, Lieutenant John Percival, to Hawaii.[1] The commodore was also requested by Edwin Bartlett,[2] an American in business at Guayaquil, to visit that place.

[1] Paullin, *Diplomatic Negotiations of American Naval Officers*, 335, 337.
[2] Ruschenberger, *Edwin Bartlett*, 39.

Mutinies in the merchant service were not uncommon and constituted one of the problems of a naval commander on a foreign station.

Navy Department
29th April 1825

Sir,

I transmitted to you under date of the 18th January last, a copy of a Memorial signed by sundry Merchants residing in Nantucket, in relation to some of the Mutineers of the American Ship *Globe*.

I now enclose to you herewith a copy of another Memorial to the President of the United States from the same quarter, on the subject of protection to our commerce in the neighborhood of, and at, the Sandwich Islands.

As soon as the situation of the service will permit, you will proceed with the Frigate *United States* to those Islands for the purposes mentioned in the Memorial, and after having made an examination you will then be better able to judge of the necessity of sending one of the vessels of your Squadron at a future period, how often it may be expedient to do so, and also which one of them will be best adapted for the duty.

You will make a report of your proceedings to the Department by an early conveyance.

I am very respectfully, etc.

[Samuel Lewis Southard]
Secretary of the Navy

Como. Isaac Hull
Commdg. U. S. Naval Force
Pacific Ocean.

Guayaquil 7 July 1825

Isaac Hull Esq.
Fr. *United States.*
Dear Sir

Your highly esteemed favour of the 20 ulto. was received a few days ago and I will with pleasure attend to your commission should I meet with anything that may be useful or curious.

It will afford us all much pleasure to see you at Guayaquil and with much respect I would suggest that a visit of one of our ships of war to this port would be of service to our commerce and gratify the government of the Province. There are often considerable sums of money to be carried hence to Lima and in about 6 or 8 weeks we expect to have $30 to $50,000 to send up on account of our American friends.

I beg you will remember me kindly to the ladies and your officers and when I can serve you command me.
               Very respty.
                  Your obt. Svt.
                       Edwin Bartlett.

During the next five months the *United States* was at sea most of the time. Huacho, Pisco, Valparaiso, Coquimbo, Arica, and other ports were visited. Then followed a long period at anchor in Callao. The entry in the log for July 4, 1826, is: "At sunrise fired a Salute of 24 Guns to commemorate the 50th Anniversary of the Independence of the United States of North America. . . . At Meridian fired a Salute of 24 Guns." November 19: "At 10 A.M. mustered the Crew. At meridian lowered the Flags to half mast and fired 24 minute Guns as a mark of Respect to the memories of the Ex-Presidents John Adams and Thomas Jefferson, who both departed this life on the 4th July last."

Lima, April 23, 1826

Dear Sir,

I congratulate [you] on your arrival. We have been looking out for you some days. I suppose you bring us no news from the Intermedios and here we have none later than the beginning of December from the U. S.

A few weeks since I received a letter from General LaFayette of which the following is an extract. In his answer he has blended our resolutions and a private letter which accompanied them.

Extract

La Grange Oct. 13, 1825

"My dear Sir;

The testimonies of kindness and approbation, which on the shores of the Pacific have been conferred upon me by American fellow citizens and our other republican brethren, have reached me before my departure from the United States[1] and I feel equally proud and happy in your so very honorable and affecting remembrance and in your no less gratifying manner to express it, the more flattering indeed when the illustrious Libertador[2] has been pleased to join in the marks of esteem and

---

[1] LaFayette sailed for France September 7, 1825, on the U. S. Frigate *Brandywine*.

[2] Bolivar.

friendship, and when I find in the chair of the respected meeting the gallant Commodore Hull and recognize in the secretary a friend, the son of my old friend Judge Tudor, far am I from having forgotten the times of our first acquaintance and avail myself of it to request you to become with the Commodore the gentlemen of the meeting and yourself a kind organ of my gratitude, respect and affection, the expression of which I wish by every opportunity to convey."

I hope we shall have the pleasure of seeing you and the ladies in this city, and beg my respectful compliments to them and remain

                    Yours truly

Commodore Hull                   W. Tudor

                Lima April 26th, 1826.

Dear Sir,

Captain Myrick has made a protest against the mutineers on board his vessel, and from his account, it seems to me that he would be very unsafe in going to sea with such men, as in a vessel of her description he is peculiarly exposed to danger from mutiny. The two foreigners he can turn ashore as they can have no resort to me. But as respects the Americans, I know of no middle course, either they must be discharged receiving their advance wages, as they would come on me for support and passage, or they must be taken home as mutineers. If, therefore, you will consent to keep them on board your ship, you will relieve him from considerable embarrassment, and by keeping them in irons, it may serve to repress a mutinous disposition on board our merchant ships which seems at the moment to be contagious.

>With respect I am
>>Yours truly
>>>W. Tudor.

Commr. Hull
Etc.

>Lima August 4th 1826

Sir

In a letter from Mr. Cobb, Vice Consul at Arica, of the 16th ulto. he speaks of an outrage committed by some customhouse guards in firing into a boat belonging to your ship and encloses me copies of his correspondence with the Intendente on that subject. The guards were confined for three or four days and then discharged, which Mr. Cobb thinks a punishment very inadequate to the offence. I will thank you to give me a statement of the circumstances of this affair, not for the purpose of making a direct application to the government now, but to serve as a document to shew by a collection of similar facts hereafter, that the conduct of many of their subalterns is outrageous and requires some direct and general animadversion from their government, to prevent a recurrence of acts which must be productive of very unpleasant consequences.

I tender you the assurance of my high consideration and respect

>>W. Tudor

To Isaac Hull Esq.
Comg. the Squadron
of the U. S.

Rio de Janeiro, Nov. 13, 1826

Dear Sir;

I had the pleasure to receive on 18 inst. [?] per *Andes* your friendly communication of July 17, dated at Callao, and thank you for the interesting details of the same. It is truly lamentable to reflect that notwithstanding the revolutions and changes, the sacrifices and the sufferings, of this South American Continent, the political tranquillity which has been the object of all patriotic exertion, seems to be as distant as when the Royal Authority was first assailed. That much time was requisite for the amalgamation of so many heterogenious elements, and for the consolidation of a system so different from that under which the South Americans were born and educated, was easily to be imagined, but our philanthropic republicanism of the North never dreamt that after the European sway was annihilated, dissentions amongst brethren engaged in the same noble cause would have originated, even to the extent of endangering the *liberties* of their country.

The great delay of the *Brandywine* will have prolonged your banishment, but it will have thrown you into a better season for returning to the United States. As I suppose the term of enlistment of your crew will have expired before you reach this port, I will take the liberty of mentioning to you what happened here on the return of the *Franklin* in July 1824. A number of her men presented themselves to the Commodore, as we learn, in a body and demanded their discharge. This of course was refused, but in order to avoid a repetition of complaint, the ship was actually got underway a day before the intended period of her departure, and laid at anchor outside the harbour, exposed to the danger of a storm, should one have taken place. But this was not the worst of it. This little adventure laid the foundation for a report which, after the departure of the ship, exposed us Americans here to the deepest mortification. It was stated, that the crew of the *Franklin* were in a state of mutiny, and that they wanted to enter into the Brazilian service!!! I wish our Government would observe a little more punctuality in such matters, and when you reach home I think your mentioning it would be of much service.

I cannot promise you a collection of curiosities here. Seeds and plants may be procured, and so may some specimens of natural history. But they are too expensive for my purse and I have not ventured upon them. When you arrive, a day or two will enable you to see all that may be worth your purchasing.

Mrs. Raguet anticipates with much pleasure the visit of Mrs. Hull and Miss Hart, and desires to be kindly remembered to them. Be pleased also to make my respectful regards. Enclosed herewith is a letter from Mrs. Raguet to Mrs. Hull, in which she has desired her remembrance to your good self.

   I am very sincerely and respect.
    Your friend and svt.
      Condy Raguet,
Commodore Isaac Hull  [U. S. Chargé d'Affaires].
U. S. Squadron in Pacific Ocean

                                    Lima Nov. 22d, 1826
Dear Sir

The measures of respect which you have shewn to the memory of the two great men [Adams and Jefferson], the circumstances of whose death were so peculiar, and marked by the favour of Heaven, were suitable to the occasion. I thought of calling a meeting here to pass some resolutions, but the difficulties attending it prevented. But I requested Mr. Pando to have an article published in the gazette that may perhaps be more useful than resolutions.

. . . . . . . . . .

                         W. Tudor
Commre. Isaac Hull

Log-book, Callao Bay, December 16, 1826: "At 10.30 [A.M.] hove up the Anchors, hoisted the Jib and flying jib and filled away. Returned the Cheers by the *Dolphin* and a Salute of 13 Guns by H. B. M. Ship *Eclair*. At meridian Royals in, Courses up, and becalmed." The *United States* was homeward bound. Commodore Hull's relief had arrived in the Pacific. January 6, 1827: "At 9.45 [A.M.] filled away and stood in for Valparaiso. At 10 discovered the Frigate *Brandywine* [flagship of Commodore Jacob Jones] and Sloop of War *Vincennes* at Anchor. . . . At 10.50 the *Brandywine* fired a Salute of 13 Guns, let fall her Top Sails, hauled down the Blue and hoisted the Red Pendant." On January 24 the *United States* and *Brandywine* Sailed out of Valparaiso together, but soon parted company. The *United*

*States* rounded the Horn about February 7 and anchored for several days in the harbor of Bahia March 6. On the 14th the U. S. sloop of war *Boston* came into port. The *United States* soon continued her voyage, stopping at Barbados, and arrived in the North River, New York, April 24, 1827.

## Chapter VI
## THE COMMODORE HAS ENEMIES

ASSUMING that Isaac Hull was an estimable character, well liked and respected by most people with whom he came in contact, which certainly seems to have been the case, it nevertheless would appear that he did not succeed in winning the esteem and affection of all. Some were repelled by him or disliked him. Whether it was something about his manner or personality or in his way of enforcing discipline, can only be conjectured. There is evidence that he had a temper, which he was sometimes unable to control.[1]

In 1822, when he was in command of the Boston Navy Yard, one of the officers under him was Lieutenant Joel Abbot, who had entered the navy as a midshipman in 1812 and had a fine war record. He was in the battle of Lake Champlain, was highly commended by Commodore Macdonough, and was given a sword by Congress. His later career was also meritorious. Yet he appears to have been morose and suspicious and certainly entertained animosity towards his commanding officer, whom he honestly believed to be guilty of serious misdemeanors. This opinion he freely expressed in conversation and in letters to the Secretary of the Navy. Captain Hull asked for an inquiry, but this the Secretary refused as wholly unnecessary. It became neces-

---

[1] See *Autobiography of Commodore Charles Morris,* 109.

sary, however, to take notice of the matter. Captain David Porter, Navy Commissioner, brought charges against Lieutenant Abbot and, in April, 1822, he was tried by a Court Martial. It was charged that he "scandalously attempted to take from his superior officer, Capt. Isaac Hull, his good name," making "false insinuations" that Captain Hull "had been concerned in a game of peculation," and "in fraudulent transactions against the Navy Department." Lieutenant Abbot was found guilty and was sentenced to two years' suspension.[1]

Captain Hull again asked for an investigation of his conduct as commandant of the Navy Yard. A Court of Inquiry[2] was thereupon convened in August, 1822, the court consisting of Captains John Rodgers, Isaac Chauncey, and Charles Morris. The inquiry lasted two months and was most thorough. A large number of witnesses were examined and a great amount of testimony taken. The witnesses were examined on five points: First, had any public property in the Navy Yard been converted to Captain Hull's private use; or, second, had any of the Yard laborers been employed for his private benefit; third, had he been guilty of neglect of duty; or, fourth, neglect of measures for the detection of Fosdick's fraud; fifth, was Captain Hull unjust or oppressive in his treatment of subordinates?

Benjamin H. Fosdick, clerk of the Navy Yard, by manipulating the payrolls, had embezzled a large sum

[1] *Trial of Lieutenant Joel Abbot.*

[2] *Minutes of Proceedings of the Court of Enquiry into the Official Conduct of Capt. Isaac Hull.*

of money. The most serious of Lieutenant Abbot's charges was that Captain Hull had been in collusion with Fosdick. Abbot had full opportunity in this trial to present his side of the case, and did so.[1] The testimony of nearly every other witness was favorable to the commandant on every point. It was clearly established that Captain Hull, far from being negligent in the case of Fosdick, had shown zeal, energy, and promptness in prosecuting him and had forced restitution of the stolen money.[2]

The opinion of the court was that "in his conduct towards the officers, mechanicks, and others under his command Captain Hull has been guilty of no act of oppression or unjustifiable severity; but, on the contrary, he has, so far as was consistent with his duty to the United States, granted every proper indulgence." With certain exceptions of trivial consequence, involving indiscretion, "the conduct of Captain Hull, since his command of this Yard, for strict personal attention to the preservation of the public property committed to his charge, the judicious application of the means placed at his disposal for the public service, and for the faithful performance of all his other official duties, has been correct and meritorious."[3]

Some years after Commodore Hull's return from the Pacific, his conduct on that station was made the subject of inquiry in Congress. January 21, 1833, William Hogan introduced in the House of Representatives a

---

[1] *Court of Enquiry*, 49.
[2] *Court of Enquiry*, 46.
[3] *Ibid.*, 243.

resolution which was referred to the Naval Committee. This resolution contained five allegations which were fully answered, January 24, by John Etheridge, the commodore's secretary, in a communication addressed to the Naval Committee.[1] The following brief statement of the allegations and replies will make the matter clear.

First. "It is alledged that Captain Hull, of the Navy, was improperly interested with Amos Binney or others in the private adventure and profit of the voyage of the Brig *Good Hope,* of Boston, Anthony Kelley, master, partly freighted for Government and partly for private account, which vessel arrived at Valparaiso in March, 1825." References: Captain Kelley, John A. Bates, purser of the *Dolphin,* George Beale, purser of the *United States,* affidavit of Michael Hogan,[2] United States consul at Valparaiso, now in Washington. Reply of John Etheridge: "A small shipment of stores made by Amos Binney, of Boston, to Captain Hull for the use of his private table and so applied by Captain Hull, was the only interest possessed by him, and it is utterly false that Captain Hull was in any manner . . . interested with Amos Binney or others" in the voyage of the *Good Hope.*

Second. "It is alledged that Captain Hull attempted to exact deposit money on freight payable by him." References: Samuel Swift, master of the store ship *Jasper,* Lieutenant John C. Long, U. S. N., and John

[1] These long documents containing the allegations and replies, in the handwriting of John Etheridge and signed by him, are in the Athenæum collection.

[2] Possibly a relative of William Hogan.

Etheridge. Reply: The store-ship *Jasper* was employed by the Navy Department to take stores to the Pacific squadron. The bill of lading required that freight should be paid in Spanish dollars. At the time of presentation, Captain Hull was without funds on public account, but out of his private funds offered to pay the freight bill less one per cent. Captain Swift declined. Captain Hull then directed Etheridge to pay the full amount of the bill out of his private funds.

Third. "It is alledged that Captain Hull, having on board a quantity of Spanish dollars provided by the Navy Department or its agent, the amount whereof may be ascertained by examination at the proper Bureau, sold part thereof for Gold currency of Peru at a premium and paid the officers and seamen in the less valuable currency, without paying also the premium received, until checked by the remonstrances and murmurings of his officers." References: Purser Beale and the lieutenants of the *United States*. Reply: "The charge is totally without foundation." Captain Hull managed financial affairs very judiciously. Etheridge explains this in great detail. On his return from South America Captain Hull turned into the Treasury a profit of $2,200 which he had made for the Government.

Fourth. "It is alledged that Captain Hull received $500, or some other sum of money, as an inducement to convoy a short distance from Callao an American vessel commanded by an American citizen." References: Edward McCall, of Lima, who is believed to have paid the money, and Purser Beale. Reply: "This allegation can only be met by an unqualified and positive denial."

## THE COMMODORE HAS ENEMIES 67

Etheridge and Purser Bates had entire charge of Captain Hull's money matters, public and private, and no such transaction could have occurred without their knowledge. Refers also to McCall.

Fifth. "It is alledged that Captain Hull abused the discretion vested in him and by so doing caused much of the prodigal waste and expenditure on the Pacific Station which has been erroneously and unjustly attributed to others." References: Consul Hogan, who was also navy agent at Valparaiso, and the log-book of the *United States,* showing how long the ship lay at anchor instead of cruising for the protection of commerce, the training of officers and crew, etc. Twenty thousand dollars of freight might have been saved between Callao and Valparaiso by transporting supplies, and other savings might have been made. Reply: The log-book of the *United States* shows not only the time at anchor, but the reasons for it. The disturbed condition of the country required the presence of Captain Hull at Callao and his constant interference with the authorities at Lima and the Patriot naval commanders, for the protection of commerce. It was irksome duty. Discipline and training did not suffer. Every effort was made to reduce the cost of freight, but the charges were exorbitant. Consul Hogan lost commissions through the captain's economy and for this or some other reason, was hostile to him.

The Naval Committee "made a report which was read and laid on the table."[1]

---

[1] Newspaper clipping accompanying the document.

## Chapter VII

## THE WASHINGTON NAVY YARD

IMMEDIATELY after his return from South America, in April, 1827, Commodore Hull was offered the place of Navy Commissioner, to fill an approaching vacancy in the Board, but this honor he seems to have declined. How he was occupied during the next two years is uncertain. In 1829 he was appointed to the command of the Washington Navy Yard, a post which he held for six years.[1] While on this duty the commodore became involved in a controversy with the workmen in the Yard.

[Order]

The Commandant of the Navy Yard at Washington D. C. finds it necessary to adopt the following regulations, viz.,

The mechanics (with the exception of the anchorsmiths and engineers) and laborers employed in the Navy Yard are prohibited entering the Work Shops, Ship Houses and other places where the public property, tools, etc. are deposited during the hours allotted for meals.
The mechanics and laborers are forbidden to bring their meals into the Yard either in baskets, bags or

---

[1] Hibben, *History of Washington Navy Yard*, 65, 70.

otherwise, and none will be permitted to eat their meals within the Yard unless specially permitted by the Commandant.

Persons will be selected to remain in the Yard to see that the foregoing are observed and to report all violations.

The Clerk of the Yard will give publicity to the above either by reading or otherwise so that all persons employed in the Yard may be made acquainted with the wishes of the Commandant.

Comd. Off.<br>July 29, 1835<br>Isaac Hull

[Notice]

In answer to the complaints of a number of Mechanics and Labourers at the Navy Yard at Washington, who consider the late regulations of Commodore Hull, the Commandant of the Yard, for securing the public property as an insult to them and an impeachment of their characters, I have to observe that this regulation was adopted from the circumstance that the public property was frequently purloined, and that lately a considerable quantity of copper was stolen by one of the men employed in the Yard.

This regulation is not to be considered as an insult to those employed in the Yard.

Laws against larceny are no impeachment to the community. Locking my doors to secure my property, is no insult to my neighborhood.

Commodore Hull is held responsible for the public property entrusted to his care. If he is not permitted to make regulations for the preservation of that property he ought to be relieved from his responsibility. If however, he adopts regulations which are inconvenient to those employed in the Yard, they have their remedy by refusing their services.

While the Commandant remains in charge of the Navy Yard, he must be permitted to regulate it.

3 Aug 1835          M. Dickerson
[Secretary of the Navy]

Navy Dept. 10th August 1835

Sir

The enclosed is a letter recd. today from Messrs. George Lyndall, Jn. A. Miskell and Saml. S. Briggs, with an original letter addressed to you.

The persons delivering the letters were verbally informed that the subject of employing hands rested with you, as well as the regulations and discipline of the Navy Yard.

The order of which they had formerly complained, they had been assured was not intended as any imputation on their characters, it carries with it no such imputation, and needs no explanation.

The manner in which the hands left the Yard was disrespectful to yourself and if the same disposition exists among them yet, which induced them to leave the yard, the public interest would not probably be promoted by receiving them back, as a cheerful performance of duties under the most advantageous contract can hardly be expected from those who entertain hostile feelings to their employers, or the agents of their employers.

As it is probable however that many of those who left the yard, may have been led into the measure by deceptive statements, or through a misapprehension of facts and motives, and as it appears from the letter to you that some of them at least are now satisfied of the impropriety of their conduct, it is suggested for your consideration, whether it would not be well for you to let it be known, either through the gentlemen referred to in the letter or in some other public manner, that persons who have left the yard, and against whom there may not be special objections, will be readmitted on their expressing to you the impropriety of and regret for their late conduct towards you.

With other dispositions than these they would be wrong to return to the yard and I presume would not. They perfectly well know their own rights, and will refuse any terms not agreeable to them by withdrawing entirely from the yard.

    I am very respectfully your
      Obt. and Humble Servt.
            M. Dickerson.
Commodore Isaac Hull.

      Washington, August 10th, 1835
To Com. Isaac Hull
 Commandant of the Washington Navy Yard
Sir
 We the undersigned, a committee authorized by the working men lately employed in the Yard to transact

any business that should transpire during the recess of the meetings, beg leave to state that we have had a conference with the Gentlemen who have kindly taken upon themselves the responsibility of waiting on you for the purpose of closing the breach that now unhappily exists between you and the men lately employed in the Yard; from them we learn that all the concession is to be on our part; to this we have to reply that the men can not consistently agree to, for while we acknowledge the point of etiquette we have stumbled over, we must still claim the right of being free and independent citizens which you must be proud to acknowledge.

But while you have the power to make laws for the protection of the public property, we have it in our power to refuse our services when those laws oppress us and in their nature will cast a shadow of suspicion on our characters.

And we learn also from the conversation of the Gentlemen acting as mediators that you disclaim any intention on your part of casting any imputation on our characters; but on the contrary you entertain the highest opinion of us as regards both our honesty and industry. In consideration of which we think the men are willing to make the following acknowledgements, provided on your part the Orders (which they still conceive to be offensive) be so altered that the public opinion shall be that there is nothing now in it derogatory to the feelings of any man, and that all the men who are willing shall be allowed to return to the Yard without any distinction of persons. If this be done we think the men are willing to acknowledge that they were led to the precipitant step they have taken by a sudden burst of feelings at the orders lately issued by you and that they are sorry they have so far misconstrued your intended application of said orders and also that they would be willing to withdraw the charges now lying before the Secretary of the Navy and suspend all further publications.

With the greatest feelings of respect
We are yours, very respectfully
George Lyndall
John A. Miskell
Samuel S. Briggs.

[Certificate]

We the undersigned certify that we have been authorized by the mechanics of the Washington Navy Yard to state that they have acted hastily, inconsiderately and rashly in first appealing to the Secretary of the Navy, without laying their grievances before the Commandant of the Navy Yard in the first instance, and that they regret the occurrence and hope that a better understanding may hereafter exist, ~~and that they have promised to cease all further publications and withdraw those gone forth.~~

Alex Mc. Williams
Mathew Wright

Wm. J. Belt, Lieut, U. S. N.

The erasure in the above certificate was made before it was finally submitted to Commodore Hull.

Wm. J. Belt.

August 12, 1835.

In 1827 construction of the dry docks at Norfolk and Boston was begun. These were the first naval dry docks in the country. They were finished in 1833, the Norfolk dock being opened June 17, while just a week later the frigate *Constitution* entered the Boston dock[1] with ceremony appropriate to the occasion. All the officers of the Navy Yard were in full dress. President Jackson had been expected, but was detained by illness. Vice-President Van Buren, Hon. Levi Woodbury, Secretary of the Navy, and General Lewis Cass, Secretary of War, were present. Commodore Hull stood once more on the deck of the ship he had commanded in battle, when together they "first broke the charm of British naval invincibility on the ocean."[2]

In the fall of 1835 Commodore Hull was detached from the Washington Navy Yard and given leave of absence. A little later he made a European tour, accompanied by Mrs. Hull and Miss Hart. They spent most of the time in Italy and were away altogether about a year and a half.

Navy Yard, Washington.<br>Sept. 30, 1835

Respected Sir,

I should do injustice to my own feelings if before taking your final departure, I failed to express, individually, my grateful sense of the many obligations I owe you. The uniform courtesy, kindness, and indul-

---

[1] The *Constitution* is now (1928) in the same dock, undergoing reconstruction.

[2] Paullin, *Commodore John Rodgers*, 389.

gence you have extended towards me, during your command of this Yard, have excited feelings of respect and gratitude which neither time nor distance can efface; and the remembrance of your friendship shall ever be cherished with the liveliest pleasure. Farewell! Sir, and that every blessing under Heaven may attend you and yours, is the fervent prayer of

      Your grateful S't.
         Richard Barry.
Commr. I. Hull.

     Navy Department
       October 1st, 1835
Sir,
 Commodore Isaac Hull of the Navy of the United States, now on leave of absence, may possibly desire a passage for a few days in the vessel under your command, for himself and family; if so, you are hereby authorised to accede to the request, if no inconvenience to the public service shall be likely to result from it.

     I am, respectfy, yours.
       M. Dickerson.

To the Commander
of any vessel of the
United States Squadron
in the Mediterranean or elsewhere.

     Washington July 27, 1837
My dear Sir,
 I wrote to you a few days past and have had the pleasure since then to receive yours of the 16th June

and sincerely regret the delay you have experienced in consequence of the ship in which you took passage having been run ashore, but am happy to hear that you suffered no other inconvenience than that of detention.

All your friends here are prepared to give you "welcome return" and none are more profuse in their congratulations than Commo. Patterson and his family.

I infer from your last letter that you have some desire or wish for active service and as the Big Ship *Pennsylvania* is now in the water and will probably be fitted out during the ensuing year, I know of no command which will reflect so high credit and elicit so great interest as the station to which she may be destined and I am sure no one has so great claims as yourself and should you be so disposed I do not believe any Captain Senior or Junior would stand in your way.

. . . . . . . . .

With the hearty congratulations of Comm. Patterson, his family and all your friends, I add most cordially my own and am
     With very great respect
      Yr. Obt. St.
         Jn. Etheridge.

Commo. Isaac Hull
U. S. Navy
New York.

In April, 1838, a Board of Revision was organized, at the suggestion of the Navy Commissioners, and the Secretary of the Navy appointed as members of the Board Commodores Isaac Hull and John Downes and

Captain Joseph Smith, with Hull as chairman. This body was called into existence "for the purpose of revising, under instructions to be furnished by the Board of Navy Commissioners, the Tables of Allowances for vessels of the Navy. . . . In the present Tables, the vessels of the Navy are arranged under the heads of Ships of the Line, Frigates, Sloops of War, Brigs and Schooners, dividing the first into three classes, and the second and third into two classes each, leaving the Brigs and Schooners to form one separate class. It is proposed to add separate columns for Razees and third class Sloops." Many technical details follow, including the complement of vessels, rigging, etc.[1] On this Board Hull's service was brief and a few months later he obtained a command afloat. He was ordered to the Mediterranean Station, to relieve Commodore Jesse D. Elliott.

---

[1] Chauncey to Hull, April 26, 1838, in Athenæum collection.

## Chapter VIII
## PRIVATE AFFAIRS

THERE are numerous letters, in this collection of his papers, relating to Hull's private business affairs. By care and good judgment he seems to have accumulated, by the end of his life, a reasonable competence. He was thrifty, but by no means penurious, and always lived well and comfortably. He invested principally in real estate. He bought land in Charlestown, adjacent to the Boston Navy Yard, while commandant — part of it for himself and part, at the suggestion of Secretary Crowninshield, for a needed extension of the Yard; this he held until the Government was ready to take it over.[1] His own land near the Navy Yard he improved and built upon. His agent in Charlestown took care of the property and made his reports to the commodore. By 1835 the net annual income from rents appears to have been about $1,500.

On February 25, 1818, he wrote to Senator Daggett in regard to his father's claim for services in the Revolution, then before Congress. He was sure the claim was just. "You know my father's situation — he is poor and is now supported in part by myself, and probably ere long he will be entirely dependent on me, and on

---

[1] *Court of Enquiry*, 49.

my pay I have hard work to keep along with my little family."[1]

In 1822, at the Court of Inquiry into his conduct, he testified: "My whole property, after twenty-four years of public service, does not amount to $18,000, including all my pay and prize money and every species of estate."[2]

Together with his father-in-law, he was interested in real estate in Ohio. He had a farm at Derby, Connecticut, in which relatives seem to have been concerned, which he arranged to sell before leaving for Europe in 1835. Late in life he bought a house in Philadelphia.

The commodore invested to some extent in bank stock and in mortgages, which seem to have involved him in troublesome litigation. He bought a slave while living in Washington, a man servant named John Ambler. To this man he gave his freedom just before his European tour in 1835.

Commodore Hull had a claim against the Government for pay, which he declared he had never received, on account of public services. In the matter of pay and allowances, he stood up strictly for his rights as he understood them, but the Secretary of the Navy and the Fourth Auditor of the Treasury Department did not always agree with his interpretation of laws and regulations. At all events, in his later years his income was ample.

---

[1] Yale University Library.
[2] *Court of Enquiry*, 50.

[Rough draft]

New York Sunday
Oct. 11th, 1835.

Sir

I have taken a passage for Gibraltar and should have great [pleasure?] in taking charge of any command to the Mediterranean that the Government may be pleased to trust to my care. The vessel will sail on the 18th, this day week. Will you be pleased to direct that I may receive my pay in Paris from Mr. Wells or from such person as may be the agent for the Dept. Mr. Wells will be my private agent and letters sent to him will be sure to be forwarded.

I am happy to say that Mrs. Hull is a little better and I hope the voyage will restore her to her usual good health.

With great respect
I have the honor to be
Your obt. servt.

[Hon. Mahlon Dickerson],      I. H. [Isaac Hull]
Secretary of the Navy.

[Manumission]

Whereas during my late residence at Washington in the District of Columbia, I purchased in proper form of Carey Selden of said Washington, a certain negro, or coloured man, named John Ambler, as a slave, and whereas, I have recently given up my said residence at Washington, and being about to embark for Europe — Now, Know all men by these presents, that I, Isaac

Hull, in consideration of the premises and of the faithful and highly useful services of the said John Ambler, do hereby give, grant, and confirm unto him his freedom, during the remainder of his life, and do hereby absolve him fully, and to all intents and purposes from all and every obligation to me as a slave, by virtue of the aforesaid sale from the said Carey Selden, so that he is now, and at all times hereafter, at liberty to do business for himself, and to go and come, when and wherever he chooses, free of any claim whatever of me, or my heirs. In witness whereof, I have hereunto set my hand and seal, this 17 day of October A.D. 1835

Isaac Hull

Witness
Herman Allen.

(SEAL.)

New York 18 October 1835

Dear Sir,

Wishing to sell my farm in Derby and the other Towns, prior to my departure for Europe, it became necessary for me to extinguish the claims of your wife and the other heirs of my brother Joseph, and for this purpose, Mr. Allen will go to Derby in a few days, in order to obtain the requisite releases of yourself and wife, and of Eliza, which I presume you will cheerfully give. I regret extremely that my limited time will not allow me to see you personally on this subject, but the circumstances of the case must be familiar to you, and in the event of your compliance, it is my wish and intention that you take all the crops of last season, with the furniture in the house, and the stock on the farm for the benefit of yourself and wife, Eliza and Joseph Hull, in equal proportions; also, all the farming utensils etc. to be divided in like manner. It will be necessary for me to give immediate possession of the farm, but I shall reserve the use of the house and out houses for you, until the first of April next. By this intended provision for my brother's heirs, and by other liberal advances I have from time to time made to them, I consider they will have received more than an equivalent for the conveyances now asked for, but I have no intention to charge them with any balance. I doubt not therefore, that you will at once coincide with me in this view of the case, and thus enable me to complete the sale of the farm, which I am extremely anxious to do at this time. If there are any little debts against the estate, I shall expect they will be paid out of the property now on the farm, so that no outstanding claim shall remain against me for the same.

I have duly received your several letters, but under the circumstances, it is my choice to sell the farm, and Mr. Allen is authorized to make the requisite arrangements to carry the same into effect. My feelings toward the family will not by this act have undergone any change, and on my return I hope to find you all in the enjoyment of many blessings. I pray you to give my love to Sarah and Eliza, and to believe me ever,

Your friend and servt.<br>Isaac Hull

J. L. Ufford, Esq.

[Rough draft]
New York November 12th, 1841.

Sir

I have had the honour to receive your letter of the 10th inst. and must of course submit to your decision.

It is true leave of absence had been sent to me by Mr. Badger but it was unsolicited, and notwithstanding it I was compelled to remain more than a month in Boston corresponding with the Navy Department, and every day occupied by business connected with my late command.

Those duties rendered the services of Mr. Etheridge essential to me and for which I compensated him from my private funds.

I have also to acknowledge your favour granting me leave of absence for one year for which I beg to offer my thanks.

      Respectfully
       Your obt. servt.
[Hon. Abel P. Upshur],    Isaac Hull
Secretary of the Navy.

## Chapter IX
## THE *OHIO*

THE first line-of-battle ship of the United States was the *America,* built during the Revolution. She was never in the nation's service, but in 1782 was presented to the French Government. At the outbreak of the War of 1812 there was no vessel of this class in the navy, but during the war several were authorized by Congress. About a dozen of these large vessels were built or begun during the next ten years; some of them were never finished. Most of them were rated as seventy-fours, but ships of war carried more guns than their rates would indicate. The *Pennsylvania* was the largest and mounted one hundred and twenty guns.

One of the seventy-fours, the *Ohio,* was built at New York by Henry Eckford, naval constructor, U. S. N., and was launched May 30, 1820. Her length on the spar deck was 208 feet, 8½ inches, and breadth 49 feet, 6 inches; tonnage, 2,542. For armament she carried on the lower gun deck thirty long 42-pounders, on the main deck thirty-two long 32-pounders, on the spar deck twenty 42-pound carronades and two long 32-pounders — in all eighty-four guns. Her complement of officers and enlisted men, including marines, was nine hundred and twenty.

An idea of the complexity of a ship's organization, even a century ago, and the multiplicity of duties to be

THE *OHIO*

performed, may be derived from an analysis of her personnel. Besides the commodore, captain, and commander (executive officer), she had nine lieutenants, a master and second master; thirteen passed midshipmen and ten midshipmen; a surgeon and three assistant surgeons; a purser, chaplain, and professor of mathematics; a boatswain, gunner, carpenter, and sailmaker; a captain's clerk, master's mate, master at arms, yeoman, ship's cook, coxswain, armorer, cooper, ship's steward; six boatswain's mates, four gunner's mates, three carpenter's mates, two sailmaker's mates, ten quartermasters, eighteen quarter gunners; three captains of the forecastle, nine captains of tops, two captains of the hold, two ship's corporals; two officers' stewards, two officers' cooks; one master of the band and nine musicians; a secretary, a clerk, a steward, and a cook for the commodore, and a surgeon's steward; 260 seamen, 244 ordinary seamen, 166 landsmen, and 58 boys; a captain and two lieutenants of marines, with three sergeants, four corporals, one drummer, one fifer, and forty-five privates. The yearly pay of the commodore was $4,000; of the captain, $3,500; commander, $2,500; lieutenant, $1,500; surgeon, $2,100 and assistant surgeon, $950; purser, $626; passed midshipman, $750; midshipman, $400; chaplain and professor, $1,200; warrant officer, $750. . The monthly pay of the yeoman was $40; of master's mate, $25; of petty officers, $15 to $19; musicians, $10 to $12; of seamen, $12; ordinary seamen, $10; landsmen, $9; and boys, $6. Pay in the Marine Corps is not stated.

Warships in the days of the old navy were expensive, relatively perhaps almost as costly as today. On the Fourth of July, 1845, Charles Sumner delivered an oration in Boston on the subject of "The True Grandeur of Nations," in the course of which he gives, in exact figures based on official sources,[1] the cost of the *Ohio*. These, with other interesting observations, make the passage worth quoting: "It appears from the last Report of the Treasurer [of Harvard College], that the whole available property of the University, the various accumulation of more than two centuries of generosity, amounts to $703,175. Change the scene, and cast your eyes upon another object. There now swings idly at her moorings in this harbor a ship of the line, the *Ohio,* carrying ninety guns, finished as late as 1836 at an expense of $547,888, — repaired only two years afterwards, in 1838, for $233,012, — with an armament which has cost $53,943, — making an aggregate of $834,843, as the actual outlay at this moment for that single ship, — more than $100,000 beyond all the available wealth of the richest and most ancient seat of learning in the land! Choose ye, my fellow-citizens of a Christian state, between the two caskets, — that wherein is the loveliness of truth, or that which contains the carrion death."[2] It may be hoped that eventually all statesmen throughout the world will come to Sumner's way of thinking. However, on several occasions since 1845, we have found our navy quite useful.

During the summer and early fall of 1838 the *Ohio*, under the command of Captain Joseph Smith, was fit-

[1] *Exec. Doc.* No. 132, 27th Congress, 3rd Session.
[2] *Works of Charles Sumner*, I, 81.

ting out at the Charlestown Navy Yard, preparatory to her Mediterranean cruise. Getting a ship ready for commission, making all the necessary repairs, and enlisting a new crew, is a considerable undertaking. It is a long, slow process, subject to delays. When other ships, returning from cruises, discharged their crews, their best men were reënlisted, if willing, for service on the *Ohio*. The executive officer of the ship was Commander Robert F. Stockton, who, however, by reason of his promotion to the rank of captain, soon took his leave.

As soon as it became known that Commodore Hull was to command the Mediterranean Station, he began to receive letters from officers wishing to be ordered to the *Ohio* or to other vessels of the squadron; from the parents and friends of midshipmen expressing the same wish and asking his care for their material and moral welfare; and applications for passage to Mediterranean ports on behalf of certain men of prominence. Commodore Downes, a particular friend of Hull's, was solicitous about his son, Midshipman John Downes, Jr., who was serving on the *Cyane,* one of the Mediterranean squadron. The faithful old slave, John Ambler, who after attaining his freedom had enlisted in the navy, wrote to Mrs. Hull, and later to the commodore, telling of his troubles and asking to be discharged or transferred to the *Ohio*. Commodore Patterson expressed the hope that his friend Hull would "have a respectable squadron as to numbers and force" and that he would be "permitted to take the Ladies" with him; also that he would visit the coast of Syria — a beautiful country and safe anchorage eight months in the year, and a market cheap and abundant. Mrs. Hull and Miss Hart accompanied the commodore, as usual.

Pensacola August 29th 1838.<br>
U. S. Ship *Ontario.*

Dear Madam

I take the liberty of writing these few lines to inform you that i am now on board U. S. Sloop of War *Ontario* as Captain's Cook and the galley does not agree with me, and I have not been well since i have been out here, and I hope that you will ask the Commodore if he will try and get my discharge what makes me more anxious for to leave Capt. Breese has gone home sick and since he has left i have been Confined two weeks in the brig in double irons and then taking out and was punished i am now on the doctor list i went on shore by the leave of one the Midshipmen not knowing but what he could give me permission for to go well then i went on shore after my wash Clothes and it came on to rain very heavy and i did not wish for to get wet and when i went down on the wharve the Market boat had gone of to the ship and i could not get off so i went back to a Store and waited there for another boat but they did not come till four oclock in the afternoon well when i went on board i was put under the sentry charge and in double irons and there was kept for two weeks since the captain has left the Ship Company has been so dissatisfied that a great many of them has runned away and i have been almost induced for to run myself but i thought that i would ask the Commodore

first if he would please to get my discharge which I know very well he can, madam i am sorry that i was so foolish as to ship in the State Servase but the reason why i shipped was that i was taking sick and was sick for several weeks and lost what little money i had and I thought I had better ship so i could have a little Money when i come home. Mrs. Hull it is not for my sake that i ask this favour but for them which i left behind me. no [more] at present
  But still remain
    Your most Humble and Obeident Servant
    until death   John Ambler

     New York Sept. 8th, 1838.
Commodore Isaac Hull
 Dear Sir
  At the solicitation of my friend and relation Col. Lewis Morris of S. C. I have taken the liberty of requesting your influence in having his son, a midshipman now attached to the Sloop *Levant* and lately returned from a cruise, ordered to the ships under your command. His reasons for so doing are, that he may thereby enjoy the advantages of a schoolmaster, of which he is deprived in a small vessel. Mr. Morris is a young gentleman of one of our first families, and a promising, ambitious young man, and there is no officer in our Navy under whose command it would give me more pleasure to see him than your own.
 With sentiments of the greatest friendship and respect
    believe me dear Sir
     Your obedt. servt.
      Thos. R. Gerry

Navy Yard Boston
Sept. 23rd, 1838.

Sir

Agreeably to your instructions I have the honor to report, that during the past week, the progress made in equiping the *Ohio,* has not been quite equal to my hopes. Two rainy days have somewhat retarded the out-door work. The standing rigging is in its place and has been once set up. The lower and topsail yards are aloft and toplgt mast pointed. The running rigging is ready and will be rove soon as the painters are out of the way. The caulking is nearly completed. The carpenters work is nearly finished. The sails are also nearly ready. The joiners work is backward. The magazines will be nearly, if not quite, finished the ensueing week. The necessary fixtures to accommodate the seamens bags and mess-utensils on the lower Gun Deck, as well as the state rooms, pantry, etc., on that deck for the officers, have not yet been commenced. The Captains cabin is progressing slowly and the difficulty appears to be in the scarcity of good joiners. The plummer and blockmaker are not forward in their work, the main pumps will be placed in all next week. The painters have commenced and will complete their work in about two weeks or perhaps ten days. Salt provisions are being taken on board and the shot are selecting and blacking. The Boats will be ready in two and a half weeks. The furniture in hand for the Como. and Capts. cabins, will require two and a half weeks to complete it. I observe the stores are accumulating and I presume they will be ready in two weeks. A set of copy lightning conductors, three sets of splicing tails and a mooring swivel which I have required, will occupy the same time.

I learn that one Lt. several midsh'n the Boatswain, Gunner and Carpenter have reported to the commandant for duty.

I would respectfully recommend that you ask the proper authority, to allow 60 Life Preservers of I rubber, to the ship. Also, that you write to the Commandant at N York (or authorize me to do so) and request that the gun carriages, blocks (excepting the sponge and rammer staffs) may be painted black or crow-colour, as I understand they are only primed, and that the service and marling on the foot of the topsails and courses be removed and those sails roped, and leathered in the way of the stays and braces. Also that *flint locks* be prepared for the guns (as I fear the percussion locks are not to be trusted), and fitted to them.

Taking all things into consideration, I believe that three weeks is the shortest possible time the ship will be made ready to depart hence for N. York.

     I am very respectfully
       Sir Yr. Obt. Servt.
To Como. Isaac Hull      Jos. Smith
Commander in Chief       Captain
U. S. Naval Force in
The Mediterranean Sea.
     Boston.

The *Ohio* went into commission October 11, 1838, at 9 A.M.; and 206 seamen, 258 landsmen, and 49 boys were transferred to her from the receiving ship *Columbus*. The marine guard also came on board. The log[1] relates that, October 13, "four pilots came on board"; on the 15th "at 2 P.M. the Navy Commissioners visited the ship." The next morning, "at 8.30 called all hands, made sail from our moorings, set Top Gallant Sails, Top-sails, and Jib. At 9.30 crossed Royal Yards and set the sails. . . . Standing out of Boston Harbour" with a westerly wind. The ship's first destination was New York, and the commodore joined her there. She arrived in the harbor October 23 and the next day was towed up to the Navy Yard.

A number of the *Ohio's* officers were dissatisfied with the quarters assigned them on the orlop deck. They were so placed by the Navy commissioners "for the purpose of keeping the gun decks always clear and ready for action," and it was believed that this arrangement would be more convenient for the officers. The orlop deck, far down in the ship, was dark and close, particularly in hot weather, though ventilated by windsails. The large amount of room required by the commodore caused crowding elsewhere. Before the cruise was over, this state of things brought about friction between the commodore and some of the ward-room officers.[2]

U.S.S. *Ohio*   Oct. 22nd 1838

Sir

I have received your letter of the 18th inst directing the *Ohio* to be moored in Buttermilk bay. As we are

---

[1] The log of the *Ohio* and the letters, extracts from which are quoted in the text of this chapter, are in the Athenæum collection.

[2] *Autobiography of Commodore Charles Morris,* 108, 109.

compelled to anchor and wait till tomorrows tide, I write this to say that I am fully of opinion that the departure of the Ship for her ultimate destination will be greatly facilitated by her proceeding to the Navy Yard direct. Both the F & M topsail yards are badly sprung, the latter we have been obliged to take on deck and fish and the former we fished aloft. The M yard is also very weak and limber. It is evident to me that the topsail yards are entirely too small to sustain and spread the topsails.

The Commissioners visited the Ship on the 15th in a violent rain storm. When on the Orlop deck it was apparent to them that the Ship required ventilating below and they recommended to me to write to Como. Ridgley and require ventilators to be in readiness to place in the lower deck on our arrival here. We sailed early the next morning and I had not time to write. Much other work required to be done which the 1st Lt. has a memo of.

I am sorry that I cannot speak in more flattering terms of the ship and crew than the evidence thus far will warrant. She does not sail equal to the character given her nor quite equal to my expectations. The crew are miserable, we want more seamen and must have them. 120 on the sick report. We have a good many landsmen that appear willing and are well behaved but they are lost on deck and perfectly bewildered.

I remain most respectfully and in great haste
                              Yours

To Como. Isaac Hull                 Jos. Smith.
Comr. Naval Forces of the
U. S. in the Mediterranean.

There was further delay at New York. The guns were taken aboard and mounted and stores of all sorts were received. The crew was not yet complete. November 7, Captain Smith writes to the commodore that he hopes to get some of the best of the crews of a frigate and sloop just arrived, and that he has "ordered the [rubber] submarine dress with the supplying Engine and hose, and the Life spars and life preservers." November 10: "The *United States* [recently from a cruise] has a fine crew and seventy of them are desirous to enter for the *Ohio* immediately, if they can be discharged and allowed to do so. I think it would be well to ask the Secretary to discharge them for that purpose." November 15: "The state and condition of the crew is not such as it is my wish and pride to report. There are some very good men, but the greater part of the crew are light men, wanting muscle and hardness. They are rather short of clothing and nearly all are considerably in debt. . . . Having come without their hammocks and bags, wet and cold, having nothing but the deck to sleep upon, and no clothing to change, as a matter of course more or less of them will be on the sick list tomorrow and next day. The sick list today is fifty-seven."

At last everything was ready and December 3, says the log, "at 1.30 P.M. Commo. Hull came on board, on which occasion 13 guns were fired." The next day the ship was towed to the lower harbor. On the 6th, "at 9.30 A.M. the Steam Ship *Fulton* got under way and proceeded with the Pilot to examine the water on the Bar. At 10 A.M. unmoored the Ship. At 10.40 a Signal was made by the *Fulton* that there was water enough on the Bar. At 11 A.M. got under way with Topsails, Jib, and Spanker. At 11.20 the Pilot came on board, made sail and passed through Gedney's Channel with not less than 28½ feet water, ship drawing 26 feet, 4 inches. Wind light from southward and westward."

The *Ohio* made a good passage to Gibraltar. The log relates that on December 22, at 5 P.M., "while reefing the Main Top Sail, James Morse, O[rdinary] S[eaman], was killed by falling from the weather quarter of the Yard on Deck." The next morning "called all hands to bury the dead and after the usual services committed the body of James Morse to the deep." The ship passed the Straits of Gibraltar December 29, and on January 4, 1839, arrived at Port Mahon, on the Island of Minorca, the headquarters of the United States Mediterranean Station. The U. S. S. *Cyane,* one of the squadron, was in port. The next day the *Ohio* saluted the Spanish authorities with twenty-one guns and exchanged salutes with a French and an English man-of-war.

U. S. S. *Ohio,* At Sea<br>Dec. 28th, 1838

Sir,

. . . . . . . . . .

The ship proves light, staunch, and strong, and in every way, thus far, has fulfilled all reasonable expectations, entertained of her good qualities. During a rough winter's passage she has sustained no material injury in hull, spars, sails, boats and rigging. . . .

In reporting on the sailing qualities of the ship, it

gives me pleasure to say that she performs extremely well under every circumstance in which she has been tried. In a severe gale, which continued with some violence for thirteen hours, she was scud under close reefed main topsail and foresail with perfect safety. She is stiff, lively, and buoyant, steers with ease, and is as dry as could be expected. She rolls deep but easy, straining nothing below or aloft. In a "head beat sea" she pitches quick and heavy; this I attribute to the construction of the ship, her floor being too short, and the foremast being placed too far forward, but few opportunities have offered to test her qualities in "working ship." In tacking she is rather sluggish in her movements. . . .

Of the state and condition of the ship's company, I am happy to say that perfect harmony and subordination exist, and a zeal to do their duty, each in his proper sphere, is apparent in all ranks. The officers generally are intelligent and competent, and evince a disposition to exert themselves to make the ship what it is desirable she should be. The men are well behaved and subordinate, and, with but few exceptions, are efficient. As far as can be, they appear generally to be desirous of preserving cleanliness, but in this respect much remains to be done. No good opportunity has yet offered to them to show what they can do for themselves in regard to their personal appearance. The slop clothing furnished by the Government is very much against the comfort as well as appearance of seamen. The shoes are miserable, being neither fit for winter or summer, wet or dry weather. The Marines with their stout "cowhide" shoes are dry shod, when Jack's soles are soaked and ripping from his feet. Although I am not required to give opinions, I beg leave to say that I think slop shoes should be of two kinds, thick stout shoes, and light neat pumps. . . .

The ship accommodates her officers and crew as well as ships of her class can, as far as I am able to judge. I have with Commander Stockton made enquiry of the officers occupying rooms on the Orlop deck, as to their convenience and comfort, and they stated that their apartments had been quite comfortable, and much more so than they had expected to find them. Thus far that deck has proved extremely comfortable to all whose berths are there, and much more so in my opinion than any other deck could have been made for all its occupants. The consumption of oil and candles is an objection here as it is in all ships below, but certainly not more so in this than in any other ship. The Orlop deck can be and has been kept clean, dry, and well ventilated by wind sails, and I have perceived no ill effects, and as far as I have learned I believe no instance of ill health is attributed to, or exists in consequence of sleeping or messing on that deck.

. . . . . . . . .

I am, Very respectfully<br>
Your Obt. Servt.<br>
Jos. Smith.<br>
Capt. U. S. S. Ohio.

To Como. Isaac Hull
Commander in Chief of the
Mediterranean Squadron
        Present.

CHAPTER X

# THE MEDITERRANEAN SQUADRON

DURING his stay of two years and a half on this station, Commodore Hull's squadron comprised, in addition to the flagship, the sloop of war *Cyane,* already on the station, the frigate *Brandywine,* which arrived a year after the *Ohio,* and the sloop of war *Preble,* which came two years after.

The winter climate in the Mediterranean was boisterous and the vessels of the squadron generally remained in port January and February, but during the rest of the year they were cruising most of the time. All ports and countries bordering on the sea, from Spain to Syria, required attention at one time or another. The rights and interests of American citizens — seamen and others — must be protected and supported by a show of force, if necessary. The Barbary States, after centuries of piracy, were quiet, but pirates still plied their trade to some extent in the Levant. The condition of American commerce in the various ports was inquired into and reported upon. The interviews and correspondence with United States ministers and consuls were constant and voluminous. A naval station was maintained at Mahon and the consul, Obadiah Rich, acted as United States Naval Storekeeper. The financial agent of the Government was a firm of bankers in Marseilles — Fitch Brothers & Company.

The commodore received periodical and occasional reports from the commanding officers of his squadron,

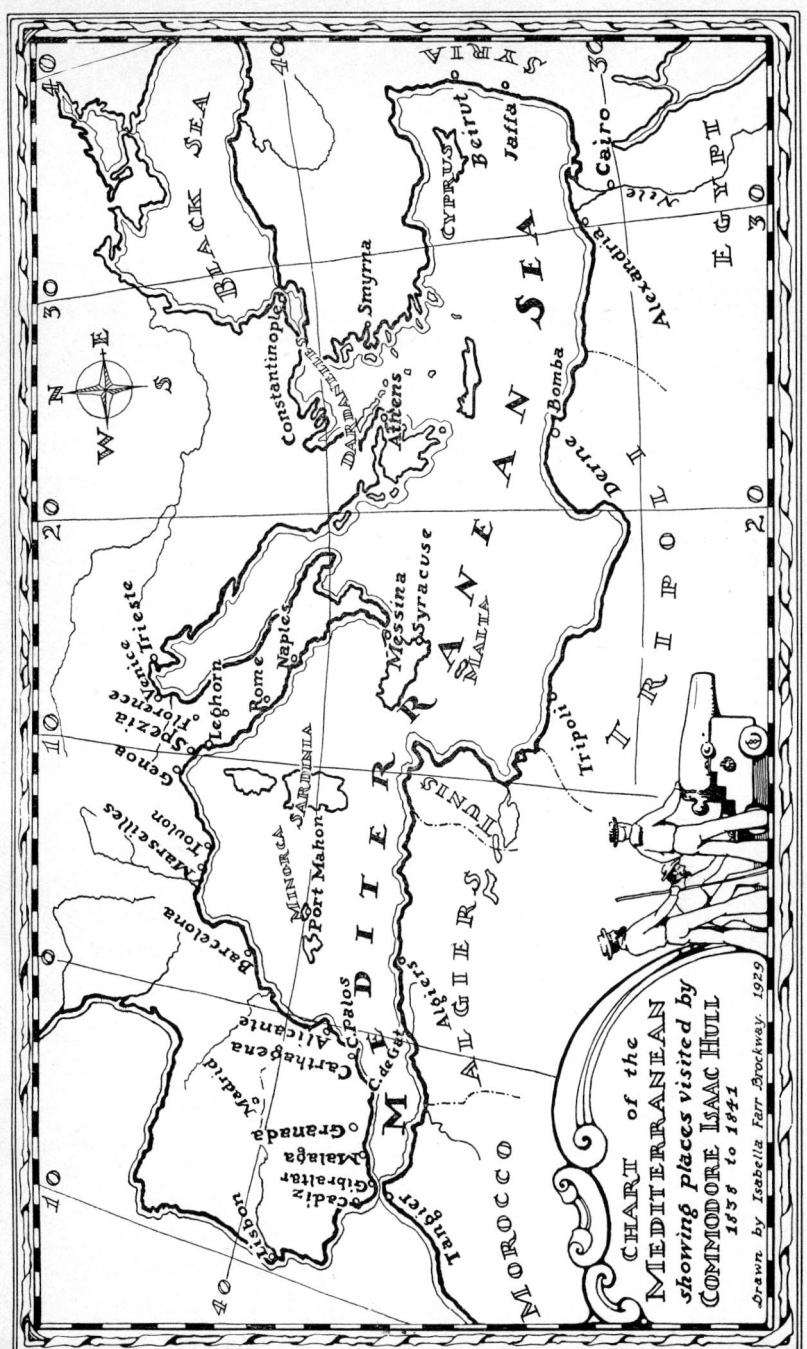

Scale, 405 English statute miles to one inch.

each on the condition of his ship and her stores, the welfare and health of his officers and crew, their competency and conduct. The sailors transgressed as sailors do — they sometimes got drunk and occasionally committed worse offenses, such as fighting and theft. When called to account, they took their punishment stoically. One of the evils widely practiced by both officers and men, productive of much scandal, was the contraction of debts in foreign ports. When a ship left port, some of these obligations would remain unpaid. At this time a special effort was made to abate this wrong. One of the passengers on the *Ohio* was a resident of Mahon, who had come to the United States for the purpose of collecting some of these old debts.

Captain Joseph Smith remained in command of the *Ohio* until the summer of 1840, when he was relieved by Captain Elie A. F. Lavallette, who reported his arrival at Marseilles July 3. Extracts from the ship's log and from letters will give some idea of naval routine.[1] On January 7, 1839, Captain Stockton — with Captain Gosselman of the Swedish Navy, a passenger — left the ship. After this, Lieutenant Garrett J. Pendergrast acted as executive officer of the *Ohio*. On January 12 the ship was visited by the governor of Mahon. February 22: "At Meridian hoisted an American Ensign to the Fore and Mizen and fired seventeen Guns, it being the anniversary of the Birth of General George Washington. The French Sloop of War saluted with the same number of Guns."

---

[1] The log, which is missing from December, 1839, to October, 1840, and the extracts from letters quoted, unless otherwise noted, are in the Athenæum collection.

On April 16 the *Ohio* sailed on a cruise. She visited Gibraltar and Lisbon, and later, with the *Cyane* in company, Marseilles, Leghorn, Naples, and Athens, returning to Mahon in September. Another cruise in October took her to the Canary Islands, to inquire into the case of a slaver.

On May 5, 1839, the *Ohio* being at sea, Commodore Hull communicated the following order to Captain Smith: "You will be pleased to prepare and submit to me a report of the sailing and working qualities of the U. S. Ship *Ohio,* under your command — the state of efficiency of the several Divisions of the Ship's battery, particularly of the Lower Gun deck, whether the Guns of that Deck can be used with certainty in an Ordinary Sea and whether they can be used at all in a rough sea, also as to the degree of proficiency which has been attained by the men at the Guns, stating your opinion, generally, of the *Ohio* as a man of War, and particularly, any defects which you know or believe to exist. You will be pleased to call upon the first and other Lieutenants of the *Ohio* for written reports on all these points. You will also report to me the condition of each of the Departments of the Warrant Officers of the *Ohio,* whether every thing in relation to them is in readiness for a time of War, whether deficiencies exist in either, and if so, to state particularly what those deficiencies are. You will call upon the Gunner, Boatswain, Carpenter, and Sailmaker for written reports in relation to their Departments. I request that the written reports of the Lieutenants and Warrant Officers may also be submitted to me."[1]

---

[1] MS. copy, Boston Public Library.

In compliance with this order Captain Smith submitted a very long report, accompanied by reports from all the lieutenants and warrant officers, giving the information required in great detail. In the course of the captain's report he says "that, of the sailing and working qualities of the *Ohio,* I have very little to add to my last report to you on that subject, dated Dec. 26th [28], 1838. Full opportunities have not yet occurred to test the sailing qualities of the *Ohio* in different trims or in company with other vessels, and, of the few opportunities that have occurred since that report, nothing has transpired to give me a more favorable opinion of her sailing than I then expressed. Within the last few days an opportunity has offered of trying the qualities of this ship in lying to. Under close-reefed Main topsail, reefed Spanker, Fore and Main spencers, and Fore-storm staysail she lies to steadily, coming to and falling off but little; she rolls very easily and but little in comparison with other vessels, is remarkably easy upon her rigging, and she is dry and comfortable; but at the same time, she drifts very fast to leeward and makes much leeway, carrying a lee helm and requiring the after sails to be trimmed very sharp. But it is to be observed that she steers easily under all circumstances and, in a smooth sea, stays surely but slowly.

"The batteries of the Ship are in as good condition as the outfits allowed will permit. The Guns are worked with rapidity and general correctness, according to the mode of exercise prescribed by regulations. On the Main and Spar decks there is ample room for every exercise and evolution of the batteries. The Lower Gun

Deck is, undoubtedly, too near the water. With all the appointments of the Ship on board, with 80,000 gallons of water and five months' provisions, the Lower Gun Deck battery does not swim over five feet five inches above the load water line amidships; and with the lower battery of a heavy two-decked ship so near the water, it cannot be presumed that the Guns can be worked in anything of a rough sea, but with an ordinary topgallant breeze and a smooth sea, they can be used with certainty and effect."

Speaking of the ward-room officers' complaints of their quarters on the orlop deck, the captain observes that "it would be difficult whilst so many Officers are put on board our Ships, to satisfy all with their accommodations. It would therefore, in my opinion, be better for the Service if there was more duty to be done and fewer Officers to perform it."

Log-book, May 21, in the River Tagus: "Commo. Hull visited the French corvette and was saluted on leaving with eleven Guns, which were returned by the *Ohio*." May 24: "At 8 o'clock hoisted the English Ensign at the Fore, it being the Birthday of the Queen of England. . . . At 12 saluted with 21 Guns in honor of the Queen's Birthday." August 31: "William Somers, apprentice boy, fell overboard. Brought the Ship up in the wind, cut away the Life Buoy, hauled up the Mainsail, took in lower Stud'g sail and Flying Jib, lowered the lee Quarter Boat, and picked him up."

In his report of December 1, 1839, Captain Smith writes: "On our passage from Gibraltar to his place [Mahon] we had a severe gale from the North which lasted four or five days. This afforded a good opportunity for testing the Ship's qualities in such times and I am happy to say that she behaved remarkably well. She rolls easily, strains nothing below or aloft. . . . I would also remark that I deem it of the utmost importance to the Navy, in these days of improvement, that an officer of the rank of Lieutenant should be appointed to each ship for the special purpose of attending to the drilling and exercise of the great guns, to ascertain the best device by which to aim cannon at sea, to devise plans and try new methods of mounting and operating with cannon and to report thereon."

On May 1, 1840, Lieutenant Samuel Mercer, who was acting as executive officer of the *Ohio*, then lying in the Bay of Spezia, wrote to the commodore: "In reporting upon the State and condition of the crew generally, it affords me great satisfaction to commend them for the alacrity and cheerfulness with which they perform their several duties. I have not to report a single act of insubordination, on the contrary they are always obedient and respectful." Log-book, Mahon, November 18: "At 3.10 [P.M.] George Fountain (O. S.) departed this life. . . . 8 A.M. [November 19] Hoisted the Spanish Flag at the fore in Honor of the Birthday of the Queen. Threw overboard the Bedding of George Fountain (Deceased). . . . At 1.30 [P.M.] Called all hands to Bury the Dead and sent the Body of George Fountain (O. S.) to the Lazaretto for Interment. At 3 the U. S. Ship *Cyane* went to Sea." Mahon, February 1, 1841: "At 11 half masted our Colors to a Funeral Procession from the French corvette." Toulon,

May 1, 1841: "At 8 [A.M.] hoisted the French Flag at the Fore in Honor of the Fete day of the King of France. . . . At Meridian fired with the French Fleet a National Salute of 21 guns, which was returned with the same number from the Admiral's Ship." Mahon, May 5: "At Sun Rise hoisted the colors half mast and fired a Gun every half hour in Honor to the Memory of General Wm. H. Harrison, late President of the United States." Officers wore crape on the left arm for one month. May 30: "Made sail and stood down the harbor. The French corvette *Victorieuse* sent her boats to assist in towing." The *Ohio* was now homeward bound. Gibraltar Bay, June 13: "At 1 P.M., H. B. M. Ship *Hastings* saluted Commodore Hull's Flag with eleven guns, which was duly returned from this Ship. The United States Consul came on board, saluted him on leaving with nine guns. H. B. M. Ship *Thunderer* arrived and anchored."

The *Cyane* was commanded by Commander John Percival. He was one of the notable characters in the old navy and was known as "mad Jack" Percival. The *Cyane* was a second-class sloop of war, of 792 tons, rated 18 but carrying twenty guns; a new ship, having been built at Boston in 1837. She had been cruising during the fall of 1838, before the arrival of the *Ohio*, and in November was at Messina. On May 25, 1839, being then at Lisbon in company with the *Ohio*, Captain Percival wrote to Commodore Hull that the *Cyane* had only two-thirds of her complement and that many were unfit for service by reason of injury or disease. "I have no hesitation in saying . . . that this crew is

## THE MEDITERRANEAN SQUADRON 105

without exception the most inferior and indifferent ever attached to a vessel of this class which ever left the United States."

In the following summer Percival was relieved, at his own request on account of ill health, by Commander William K. Latimer, who reported his arrival at Marseilles early in August and took command of the *Cyane* in October. This delay was due to the difficulty of getting passage from Marseilles to Mahon. All steamers had been requisitioned by the French government and were crowded with troops going to Algiers. Latimer was obliged to proceed by way of Barcelona. The *Cyane* was soon cruising again and before the end of the year visited Toulon, Genoa, Spezia, Leghorn, and Naples. December 23 Captain Latimer reported on the facilities and accessibility of these ports, enclosing reports of United States consuls on the condition of American commerce.

After a few weeks at Mahon the *Cyane* was at sea again in February, 1840. On her return to port, March 19, Captain Latimer reported: "I have the honor to acquaint you of the arrival of this ship, and in obedience to your orders of the 15th ulto. I proceeded to Gibraltar and arrived at that port on the 24th and as directed by you I delivered the letter bag of the *Ohio* to Horatio Sprague, Esq., [United States consul], with a request he would give it an early conveyance to the United States." On this cruise the *Cyane* also visited Malaga and Cartagena. October 29, 1840, Latimer made a long report of a cruise of several months in the Levant, on business suggested by Commodore David

Porter, United States minister at Constantinople, to Commodore Hull, in a letter of January 23, 1840. This related to conditions and American interests in that quarter, and the security of American citizens. Between June and September the *Cyane* visited Athens, Smyrna, Samos, and Beirut, and had returned as far as Malta by the middle of October. The danger to American lives and property was due to a serious revolutionary upheaval in Syria. The governor of Beirut gave assurances to Captain Latimer of his ability to protect Americans. Piracy was not a menace. During the two previous years United States consuls at Constantinople and Saloniki had reported on the doings of Greek pirates, which, however, were not alarming. Late in the year, orders came from the Navy Department for the return of the *Cyane* to the United States and she sailed in January, by way of Teneriffe.

The frigate *Brandywine,* of 1726 tons, rated a 44 but carrying fifty guns, was built at Washington and launched in 1825. Under the command of Captain William Compton Bolton, she came to the Mediterranean in the fall of 1839. In 1840 she sailed on a cruise, visiting Genoa, Leghorn, and Lisbon.

The *Preble* came out in the early spring of 1841, to replace the *Cyane.* She was a third-class sloop of war of 566 tons and sixteen guns. She also was a new ship and was launched at Portsmouth in 1839. She was commanded by Commander Ralph Voorhees. The *Preble* was with Commodore Hull a few months only, but remained on the station after the *Ohio* and *Brandywine* had returned home.

U. S. S. *Cyane*
Messina, November 22nd, 1838.

Sir,

. . . . . . . . .

While lying at Naples Her Britannick Majesty's Line of Battle ship *Hastings* arrived, bearing the Royal Standard of Great Britain, having on board the late, but now dowager Queen of England — Adelaide. I felt it proper to shew every mark of respect to so distinguished a personage, and on passing this ship on her way to the landing from the 74, I manned the yards, fired a salute of 21 guns and gave three cheers. I felt, to have neglected this mark of distinction, where all the world that was present were shewing every mark of respect, would not read well for our national gallantry. On the following day, the British Minister called on our Charge des Affaires, Mr. Throop, by the request of Her Majesty, to express the great satisfaction she had received from the mark of respect shewn her, where she had no claim to expect it, by the ship bearing the flag of his country, and on the same day the Captain of the *Hastings* came on board, by the command of the Queen, to express her personal thanks for the courtesy shewn her by me.

I hope this course I have pursued, will meet the approbation of the President and the Department.

          I have the honor to be
              Very respectfully
                Your obt. Servant

Hon. James K. Paulding          J. Percival
    Secretary of the Navy          Commdr.
    Washington City.

Consulate of the U. S. of America
Tripoli in Barby. Feby 15, 1839

Sir

While on a short visit at Malta a few days since I had the honor to receive your dispatch of the 30th ultimo informing me of your arrival in the Mediterranean, upon which occasion permit me to offer you my cordial and respectful congratulations.

Our relations with this Regency continue upon the most friendly footing and as long as the general peace remains undisturbed among the principal European Powers, there is little to fear of the resumption of the piratical habits of the Barbary Regencies, yet the display of a naval force by our Government in these seas must in any event be attended with important advantages in case of a rupture and though there has not been for many years any absolute necessity for the visit of our men-of-war here at this port, still the good effects of an occasional visit are too evident in impressing these powers as well as others with a just idea of our maritime strength and preparations to redress insults and aggressions. This leads me to regret that the limited force of the Commander in Chief in the Mediterranean has not permitted our ships of war visiting this more frequently, as since November, 1836, we have not had the pleasure of seeing one. Should more important services for the force under your command also deprive us of the pleasure of a visit from you, I would have much satisfaction in going over to Malta to communicate with you personally, should you visit that port and be able to give me timely notice of your intentions.

The quarantine from this port at Malta is reduced

to 12 days for ships of war, from thence the ship will be in free pratique in all the ports of Europe.

With sentiments of distinguished<br>consideration and respect<br>I have the honor<br>to be Sir<br>Your mo. obt. servt.

| | |
|---|---|
| Commo. Isaac Hull | D. Smith M'Cauley |
| Commander in Chief of the | U. S. Consul near the |
| U. S. Naval Forces in the | Regency of Tripoli |
| Mediterranean. | |

[Rec'd at Naples per Steamer from Marseilles July 14, 1839.]

Navy Department<br>February 28th, 1839

Sir,

Your despatch No. 56 dated the 28th Decr. '38 accompanied by a report from Captn. Smith of the qualities and conditions of the Ship *Ohio,* and one from Surgeon Ticknor on the general health of the officers and crew, has been received.

It is gratifying to learn from these that the utmost harmony prevails among the officers of that Ship, such as might have been anticipated from their high character for good sense, patriotism, and devotion to the service; and that the apprehensions at first entertained that the position they occupied on the Orlop Deck might be prejudicial to their health, have not been realized.

In the instructions received from the Department it was earnestly recommended to you that you would use all the authority of your station to discourage and discountenance the officers of every rank and degree, as well as the crews of the vessels under your command, from incurring debts at Mahon, or any other port they might chance to visit during their cruise.

The Department has learned from sources which cannot be questioned, that debts to a large amount were left unpaid by the officers and crews of some of our ships that have lately returned from the Mediterranean. The fact, if true, is calculated to degrade the character of the individuals, as well as that of the service, and to inflict a stain on the reputation of the Country, which is judged by the standard of its representatives abroad. It is also, in the opinion of the Department, a virtual violation of the law for the better government of the Navy, which enjoins a correct and gentlemanly deportment on every officer, since nothing can be more directly inconsistent with both, than a disregard to the obligations which every man incurs by contracting a debt to another. The word of an officer should be sacred, whether pledged to a superior, an equal, or an inferior, and that pledge is always considered as given when a debt is contracted.

The pay allowed by the liberality of the Government, to every grade of Junior Officers, naval and military, is sufficient to enable them to sustain their rank and supply the means of every rational enjoyment, if not wasted in dissipation and extravagance. There is then no cause for incurring debts for any purpose whatever, nor can any officer plead a necessity for such an imprudence.

It is confidently expected that you will set your face firmly and sternly against such practices, should they be indulged in by any officer under your command. You

## THE MEDITERRANEAN SQUADRON 111

are authorised to do this under the injunction to take care of their habits and morals, and the Department enjoins on you the performance of this important duty.

Should any officer abuse the liberty allowed him of going on shore, by running in debt, that liberty should be withheld from him until he has discharged the obligation, and a repetition of the offence visited by a refusal of such an indulgence in future. It is left to your discretion whether in case of an officer being arrested and detained on shore by a process sanctioned by the laws of the Country in which the debt is incurred, it might not be well to refrain from all interference a sufficient time to afford adequate punishment to the offender and an example to others.

Some delay has occurred in making up the complement of the Squadron under your command, as originally contemplated, in consequence of the Frigate *Constitution* having been ordered to replace the *North Carolina* in the Pacific Ocean, the latter ship being on her way home. The *Brandywine* is now preparing with all despatch to join you in the Mediterranean and will either be accompanied or followed by a Brig or Schooner, as soon as one shall be at the disposal of the Department for that purpose.

With the best wishes for a successful and honorable cruise to yourself and all on board

    I have the honor to be
        Very respecty. yours,
            J. K. Paulding
        [Secretary of the Navy]

Como. Isaac Hull
Condg. U. S. Squadron
Mediterranean.

U. S. S. *Ohio*
At Sea. April. 17th 1839.

Sir.

I duly received your order of the 15th inst. directing me to proceed with this Ship to the mouth of the Straits, and stating that the *Cyane* would probably come out of Mahon and try her sailing with this Ship. The *Cyane* did come out and we sailed for about three hours together "close hauled" on a wind; the wind was light and she rather got the better of us, but my opinion is that, in most circumstances in which ships sail, this Ship will spare that more or less canvass. However, I have never thought this ship equal to the reputation she gained from the officers who sailed in her from New York to Boston, more especially upon a wind.

      Very Respectfully
       Yr. Obt. Servt.
       Jos. Smith

Com°. Isaac Hull.    Capt U. S. S. *Ohio*.
Commr. in Ch'f of the
U. S. Naval Force in the Medn.
    Present.

      Marseilles
       August 10th, 1839.

Sir

I have the honor to inform you that I arrived here on the 5th inst.

I have been directed by the Honorable Secretary of the Navy, to report to you for the Command of the Ship *Cyane*. Having understood on my arrival here, that you had proceeded to the Levant and not being able to learn anything definite as to your movements, or at what point it was probable I should meet with you, I have considered it most safe to remain here and await your instructions.

If it will not interfere too much with your arrangements, I would esteem it a particular favour, if you will permit the *Cyane* to proceed to this port, where I may be instructed to relieve Captain Percival in the Command.

I have the honor to be<br>
with great respect<br>
Your Obt. Servt.<br>
W. K. Latimer.

Comre. Isaac Hull
Commanding U. States Naval
Forces in the Mediterranean.

Navy Department<br>
25th Sept. 1839.

Sir;

The United States Frigate *Brandywine* under your command being presumed to be ready for sea, you will proceed with her to the Mediterranean and report to Commodore Isaac Hull for duty in the Squadron under his command.

You will in the first instance, after your arrival in the Mediterranean, proceed direct to Mahon, where it is probable you will either find the U. S. Ship of the line *Ohio,* or instructions from Commodore Hull for your government until you can fall in with him.

Should he not be there nor have left such instructions,

you will proceed thence to the point where, from the best information you may be able to obtain, you shall think it most likely to meet with him.

As it appears from advices recently received at the Department, that the early presence of the *Brandywine* in the Mediterranean is of importance, you will expedite her departure from Norfolk with all the means in your power.

You have permission to touch at the Island of Madeira, should you deem it advantageous to our commercial interests in that quarter that you should do so, and should it not occasion a delay of more than a few days on your passage out.

Wishing you a pleasant cruise

    I am very respectfully

        Your Obt. Servt.

Capt. Wm. C. Bolton     I. Chauncey
U. S. Ship *Brandywine*    Acting Secy. of the Navy
Norfolk.

Circular

      Navy Department
       28th Octr. 1839

Sir,

The Department having been apprised that His Majesty, the King of Sardinia is preparing the Frigate *La Reine* for a voyage of discovery round the world, in the course of which you may probably fall in and have intercourse with her, I have to direct that in such an event you will offer her every assistance and afford every facility to an enterprise so honourable to the Sovereign by whom it was directed, and which is due to the friendly relations subsisting between the United States and Sardinia.

  I am Sir, very respectfully yours,

        J. K. Paulding.

Come. Isaac Hull
Comg. U. S. Squadron
Mediterranean.

     United States Ship *Cyane*
      Port Mahon December 23d, 1839

Sir,

 From the very indifferent material of which the crew of this ship is composed, I feel called upon to represent to you its inefficiency and the necessity of filling, if possible, the complement of *Petty Officers* and *Seamen* both of which are now short. With truth, I may say, that with the exception of two Boatswain's mates, three Quarter Masters, one Quarter Gunner, the Captains of the Fore and Main Tops and some half a dozen seamen, the balance of the crew are the most inferior and inefficient men I have ever known on board a ship. There are only *forty two Seamen* on board, and as an instance of their condition, more than one *half* have been *constantly* on the sick report since I have commanded the ship, leaving but very few to perform the duties of the ship, and those of a very inferior order of men. If I had encountered weather such as would be expected at this season of the year on our coast, I really believe there would not have been a sufficient number of well *Seamen* left to have performed the duties of the ship.

The Gunner is a very infirm man and is so very deaf, that it operates seriously against him in the performance of his duties; besides he does not profess to be a Seaman, consequently that part of his duties are in a great measure neglected or performed by the Boatswain; and the Gunner's Mate is ignorant of his own duties or that of the Gunner's. You will therefore see how badly I am off in that important department of the ship.

I would respectfully recommend that the Gunner be permitted to return to the United States and recommended for some situation on shore, where he could be usefully employed and rewarded for the services he has rendered to the Government, and that his situation may be filled by an appointment from your ship.

Your compliance with my wishes will confer a particular favor, if in your power to grant them, and I hope you will believe they are not made without a firm conviction of the necessity of my doing so.

I have the honor to be
>With great respect
>>Your obt. Servt.
>>>W. K. Latimer

Commodore Isaac Hull  Commander.
Commanding U. S. Naval Forces
in the Mediterranean.

>U. S. S. *Ohio* Mahon
>>April 10th 1840

Sir

Your letter of yesterday's date enclosing the surgeon's certificate in my case, I have received.

The flattering manner in which you have noticed my services whilst acting under your orders, and the regret and sympathy you evince at the cause for, as well as the circumstances under which we are about to separate have filled me with emotions which I cannot now express.

To give up my command, so honorable, at this stage of the cruise, and to part with a Commodore with whom it is my pride and my pleasure to serve, have caused me a struggle, which I will not attempt to describe.

I feel that I have not done my whole duty to my own satisfaction for a long time; still, with your ready assistance I fondly, but vainly, hoped to hold out to the end of the cruise.

In now resigning the command of this ship and taking leave of you, I part not only with my Commodore but with my friend.

My warmest thanks you have for your kindness to me and mine. May health be continued to you. May the remainder of your cruise be prosperous and happy, and may He who has our destiny in keeping at last receive you at his right hand.

I remain Most<br>Respectfully and Truly<br>Yours

To Como Isaac Hull            Jos. Smith
Comr in Ch'f of the U States       Captain
Naval force in the
Mediterranean
    Mahon

Consulate of the U. S. of America
Tripoli Barby, May 10th, 1840.

Sir

I have the honor to acknowledge the receipt of your despatch of February 19th last.

The hostilities between the Arabs and the Bashaw still continue and although the latter gained some temporary advantages over the former in the month of March and succeeded in advancing his troops nearly as far as Benioleed [Beni Ulid], in the interior, yet his forces have lately been driven back and it is probable that his troops will again soon be confined to the fortresses of the seaboard.

There does not appear the least inclination on the part of the people of this Regency to resort to piratical depredations. Small Christian vessels visit all parts of the coast without further molestation than occasionally some arbitrary and illegal exactions by the authorities under pretext of custom house duties.

. . . . . . . . . .

Noticing your information to me of the number of midshipmen on board of the ships under your command being short of the compliment allowed by the regulations of the service induces me to ask the favor of you to take my son Edward on board as a volunteer.

I have applied this Spring to the President to obtain a warrant for him and hope that the consideration of upwards of 20 years in the service of the government and the exertions of my friends in the U. S. may obtain it in the course of the year and should you take him on board it would bring his application more forcibly under the notice of the government, and you would be conferring on my family a favor for which I shall indeed feel most gratefully indebted. Edward is nearly 14 years of [age], talks fluently Italian, French and Arabic, and sufficiently of Turkish for the ordinary use of communication, is tolerably well advanced in his English education and evinces talents that I flatter myself may lead him to be a distinguished officer.

With sentiments of distinguished consideration and respect

     I have the honor to be
       Sir
     Your most obt. servt.

To Commodore Isaac Hull    D. Smith M'Cauley
Commander in Chief of the
U. S. Naval forces in the
Mediterranean.


     U. S. Consulate
      Athens June 22d, 1840.

Sir

I have the honor to inform you that the vessel you were pleased to promise me in your favour of Feb. 19th reached the port of the Piræus on the morning of the 18th inst. But I regret to say that my expectations of aid and support which I was [to] receive from the presence of a Man-of-War and the counsels of its Captain, have been frustrated: and the conduct of Commander Latimer has been such as to occasion sincere regret and call for particular notice.

On the morning of the 18th inst. the U. S. ship *Cyane* entered the port of the Piræus: and shortly after I was informed of its arrival by common report, but no official communication having reached the Consulate through the day, I could not, of course, visit the ship or pay my respects to the commander and officers; unwilling, however, to consider the omission intentional and desirous to come in communication as soon as possible, I waved the usual etiquette and on the morning of the 19th addressed to the Com. of the *Cyane,* a friendly note, the object of which was to ascertain the hour when I could visit the ship and pay him my respects; instead of meeting my advances in the spirit in which they were made, he informed me through an official communication dated the 19th but forwarded the 20th, that he would be happy to see me on board; omitting, however, to mention the hour or offer me a boat, the first of which was directly and the second indirectly requested. This though a violation of duty and breach of that courtesy known and practised by none so well as the officers of our Navy, was neither so marked nor so public an insult as to satisfy Com. L., accordingly at the same time with his dispatch to me, he left his ship and repaired to Athens, where he called upon other Am. citizens but avoided the U. S. Consulate, and acted as if his visit had no other object but to insult the Consul of his Nation.

In neglecting to apprise me of his arrival and give me a passage to his ship, Com. L. acted in direct violation at once of duty and etiquette. He may justify himself on the plea that there being no Consul at the Piræus, he was not obliged to send after one, but the visit of the ship being to Athens and not to the Piræus, and commanders of higher grade than himself having acted in conformity with this regulation, he cannot be permitted to make rules for himself. Admitting, however, the validity of this plea, or supposing that he acted in ignorance of regulations which he ought to know, still when I requested the honor of paying him my respects, was there any reason for refusing me a favour to which I was entitled by right and treating my civilities in a manner so unbecoming the dignity of his station? Can he find any plea in his instructions from the Navy Department, or in the code of politeness for such conduct? I wish it were in my power to find some plausible excuse for an occurrence calculated to prejudice the interests over which I preside. Indeed, Sir, the rights of the U. S. Citizens in Greece have not as yet enjoyed due deference, and the various things which deserve remonstrance. The real property of Mr. Hill and Mr. King has been taken, the one for the palace, the other for the National Church, without the consent or knowledge of the proprietors, and without indemnification. The U. S. Consulate has been broken open and robbed by soldiers in the service of the King without my having been able to obtain the least indemnification or satisfaction. The U. S. citizens have been threatened with assassination by one of His Majesty's Aides-de-Camp, and though, in consequence of my remonstrance, the offender has been reproved, the reproof has not been in the way of his promotion. This in short is the consideration we enjoy in King Otho's dominions, and the visit of the *Cyane* has not altered things for the better.

Com. L. was not probably aware that his marked disrespect to an accredited officer of the U. S. Government was calculated to compromise his own honor, and prejudice our relations with Greece.

Having never had the honor of an acquaintance with Com. L., it is not to be supposed that he can have any personal pique against me, and I do not like to give credence to the report that he cherishes a peculiar dislike to Consuls. Suppose, however, either of these causes to have operated, can this be considered as a justification? Has he been commissioned to these seas for the sake of gratifying his personal caprices, to the sacrifice of sacred duties? He ought to rise above personal feelings and discharge his duties with a dignity and equity proportionate to the high interests entrusted to his hands. He must have better reasons than I can assign to justify himself in the eyes of the Am. nation for insulting not only Am. citizens but U. S. officers and thereby weakening the influence he should strengthen, exposing to danger the interests he should protect, and trifling with the honor he is bound to defend even with the cannon that girt the sides of his noble ship.

In communicating the above I perform a duty and I hope you will give to my statement the attention it may deserve.

      I have the honor to be, Sir,
      Your Hbl. and Obt. Servt.
      G. A. Perdicaris

To Com. Isaac Hull    U. S. Consul
Comr. in Chief of the U. S.
Naval Force in the Medr.

U. S. Ship *Cyane*
Port Mahon, Novr. 10th, 1840.

Sir,

I have received and read with attention, the statement of Consul Perdicaris, bearing date 22nd June 1840.

To this communication I am called upon to reply, not however from any respect I can entertain for an individual who would knowingly misrepresent occurrences and indulge in personal remarks; but from a desire to place matters before you in their proper light, and to convince you that so far from neglecting any etiquette towards the Consul at Athens, I was treated by him with the most marked disrespect and slight; he evinced no disposition to waive etiquette, nor can I admit it was neglected by me.

If he felt that great desire to come in personal communication with me, and which he now seems to think was of such moment to the interest of the country, why did he not avail of the opportunity which presented itself, when I was in Athens, where I remained more than twenty four hours at an Hotel, within a short distance of his residence, and which it appears he was fully acquainted with? I would beg to enquire, what prevented our interview at that time? I was a visitor to the place of his residence, and the established rules of polite society entitled me to a call from him, which would have been appreciated and returned in the same polite manner as a visit of a portion of the American Citizens residing at Athens had been, and which was the object of my visit to that place. Or, does Consul Perdicaris presume to think I am unacquainted with the rules of etiquette and willing to yield to him what I, as the stranger and visitor, had first a right to expect, had not my official situation required it of him.

He was not, therefore, desirous to come in communication with me, as stated in his complaint, for, by my visit to Athens, I had made more than half the advance, and opened the door to a personal acquaintance, if he was desirous of making it.

In my letter to him of the 19th June, I expressed the pleasure it would afford me to see him on board the *Cyane,* which letter was in his possession many hours before I reached Athens, and consequently was informed of the feelings entertained towards him. I was not out of my ship from the morning of the 18th, the day of my arrival, until I went on shore about the noon of the 20th; which I considered ample time for the Consul to have made his visit, if he had intended so to do. He was not at the port when I sailed, nor do I believe he was there at any time during the visit of the *Cyane;* at least, I never was informed of it.

I arrived with the *Cyane* at Port Piræus on the morning of the 18th June; immediately on anchoring I despatched a Lieutenant to obtain pratique, and to call upon the American Consul and the authorities of the Port, and to offer the former a passage on board the *Cyane.* On the return of the boat, Lieutenant Dove, the Officer sent on shore, informed me, the ship was in pratique, and that he had called upon the captain of the Port, as the highest officer in rank present, and as well as I recollect, was informed there was not an American Consul or agent residing there.

On the next morning the Revd. Messrs. King, Benjamin and Houstin from Athens came on board to pay their respects to me, and in the course of conversation, I remarked to Mr. King, that I believed he had been a long time a resident of Greece, and had officiated as the Consul of our country, which induced me to suppose he was well acquainted with the political affairs of that Government, and had taken the liberty to write to him, requesting to be informed on that subject and of all other matters that would be interesting to our Government and proper they should be acquainted with.

This he replied, he would do most willingly, but that there was a Consul at Athens, and mentioned his name. This was the first intimation received of there being a Consul at that place, and I said I would address myself to him. I had then been at anchor in the Port more than twenty four hours, and it seems strange that Consul Perdicaris should have been ignorant of my arrival at the Piræus, as there was hourly communication between that and Athens, as the American citizens whose interests he was there to protect and with whom it is supposed he was on terms of friendship, found their way on board the *Cyane* for the purpose of welcoming the arrival of the ship, and to extend to their countrymen an invitation to visit them at Athens, where Consul Perdicaris resides.

It, therefore, must be inferred that the Consul has been guilty of a gross subterfuge or wilful misrepresentation in the friendly note addressed to me, wherein he says he has just that moment been informed of the arrival of the ship, and which letter reached me on the afternoon of the day the American gentlemen paid their visit, and upwards of thirty hours after my arrival.

I beg to call your attention to my letter to Consul Perdicaris of the 19th June, wherein I invite him to communicate fully with me on all subjects, and why he failed to advise me then that the U. S. citizens in Greece had not enjoyed due deference; that the real property of Messrs. Hill and King had been taken without indemnification; that the U. S. Consulate had been broken open and robbed; and that the U. S. citizens had been threatened with assassination, is yet to be explained to me, and never remotely hinted at by an American citizen during my visit there.

I feel Sir I am incapable of neglecting the interests of the citizens of the United States and my duty, as my late cruise will show, when called upon to protect them, and how is it possible I could be acquainted with those circumstances, except through themselves or the Consulate at Athens, as full time and opportunity was afforded them to have informed me officially by letter. The Consul, therefore, has been guilty of a neglect of his duty and properly chargeable with it.

The concluding paragraph of his letter is unworthy of an official reply from me, and therefore can take no notice of it.

I have the honor to be
    with great respect
      Your obt. Servant.

Commodore Isaac Hull    W. K. Latimer
Commander in Chief of the U. S.    Commander
Naval Force in the Medr.

United States Consulate
Beyrout, 3d July 1840

Sir:

Our situation in Syria and most particularly here in Beyrout is daily becoming more unpleasant and unsafe. In such a small town as this we have now not less than about 25 thousand troops composed of Egyptian regulars, the Sultan's Regulars, that were at Alexandria and a number of Albanians and though so many, they dare not shew their faces out, such being their panick fear of the Mountaineers.

The insolences and atrocities committed by them, they are beyond description; the houses and churches round the gardens of Beyrout have been all plundered and destroyed by them; many poor Christians wounded and murdered and their women insulted.

Many of the Franks[1] (who by the bye are detested by the soldiers) have had also much to suffer, and particularly so the French, of whom several have been beaten; others fired at; one or two wounded and one, three days since, stabbed and killed, for which the French Consul, not having been able to obtain satisfaction, was obliged to strike his Flag and send a deputation of three French Gentlemen to Alexandria with his Despatches.

The English Consul has had his share too, on account of the murder of a servant under the British protection and as yet he obtained no satisfaction.

We have also in our port a fleet of 16 large frigates, and line of Battle Ships and several others cruising, partly Egyptian and partly of those of the Sultan.

[1] Europeans living in the Orient.

Many of the Frank families are leaving this place for Cyprus and three of our American families, Mr. and Mrs. Beadle, Mr. and Mrs. Keyes and Mr. and Mrs. Thomson, left also yesterday for Jaffa, hoping to be safe there and for the others who remain here, I sent each one of my Cavasses[1] and got them also a Guard from the Bashaw for their better security, and I have been obliged also to reinforce our Consulate with two more Cavasses.

Your Excellency will judge by all this, in what state of anxiety and fear we live in here and how happy we would be to have some American ship of war stationed here for our safety. The Sardinians have a Corvette in port and an English Frigate is just arrived. If your Excellency will deem it proper to transmit an extract of my present letter to Commodore Hull, perhaps the Commodore might be kind enough to take some steps towards our safety.

We continue still in a state of siege; the insurgents in large numbers occupy the pines to the south of Beyrout about 15 minutes from the city, and the river of Beyrout to the east about half an hour distant, so that we can hardly find any meat, bread or vegetables of bad quality and at enormous prices.

The troops made a few attempts out, but they were always beaten and obliged to retreat; even while they were ten to one, say 8000 of our troops against 800 Mountaineers.

Excuse my writing on this paper as I have no foolscap, nor can I get any in town.

---

[1] Turkish police officers.

I have the honor to remain with great respect
Your Excellency's most obdt. humble servt.
                                            J. Chasseaud

To His Excellency Commodore David Porter
Envoy Extraordinary and Minister Plenipotentiary
for the United States of America at the Sublime Ottoman
Porte, Constantinople.


                    U. S. Legation
                Constantinople July 6th, 1840.
Sir,
   I have had the honor to receive your letter of the 2nd inst. informing me of your arrival in the Levant, and the object of your being there. It would afford me much pleasure to see you in Constantinople, but the existence of a treaty between the Porte and Russia, would render it improper for me to ask a firman for any of our ships of war to pass the Dardanelles, without some urgent public necessity for my doing so.
   I have heard of no cases of piracy in this quarter for a year past, and it is not probable that there will be any, while the English, French and Austrians keep up such large forces, and they and the Greeks are so active in keeping it down, yet the visit of our ships of war to the different ports in the East formerly most frequented by them, may have, by example, a good effect and give confidence of protection to our merchants.
   Should I have occasion to avail myself of your offer of services, I will take advantage of it, and in the meantime, I beg leave to return to you my thanks and to

offer to you assurances of my high respect and great consideration.

Your very obt. humble servt.<br>
David Porter

Captain W. K. Latimer
Commanding the U. S. Ship *Cyane*
now at Smyrna.

Circular

Navy Department<br>
July 16th, 1840

Sir

The practice of allowing the mechanics employed at the several Navy Yards and on board ships on foreign stations to repair vessels belonging to the merchant service of the U. States, will in future be limited to cases where a refusal to do so would of necessity impose injurious delays or greatly increase the expenses upon the merchant vessel. In such cases the mechanics shall make no demand for any compensation, but receive only such as the owner, assignee, or master of such merchant vessel shall choose to give and their Commander is willing they should take. Officers of the Navy, in like cases, shall neither claim or receive any compensation whatever.

In all cases of distress, gratuitous assistance is to be given as heretofore, to the fullest extent practicable.

I am very respectfully<br>
Your obt. servt.<br>
J. K. Paulding.

Com. Isaac Hull
    Comdg. U. S. Squadron
        Mediterranean.

U. S. Ship *Ohio*
Port Mahon, August 1st, 1840

Sir,

As soon as the *Brandywine* is prepared for sea, you will proceed with her to Marseilles for such Funds and Stores as may be required and cannot be procured for that Ship at this place. Strict economy must be exercised and no larger sum of money drawn than will probably be required to last through the fourth quarter of the present year. You will then proceed to the Italian Coast, touching at Genoa, Spezia, and Leghorn, remaining at each only sufficiently long to make the usual enquiries as to the security of the Commerce of the United States and to render any assistance or protection it may require; you will then return, running down the Spanish Coast, calling off Barcelona, touching at Alicante, Cartagena and Malaga, after which you will resume your late cruising ground between Cape de Gat and Lisbon.

You will be governed by the extracts of instructions from the Navy Department in your possession, as well as by my orders of 17th April last, as to the objects of your cruise.

Should political changes or public events occur during your absence from my flag, which you deem essential to be conveyed to the Government, you will be pleased to communicate them immediately and directly to the Navy Department, reserving a copy in your possession for my use.

You will continue to cruise between Cape de Gat and Lisbon as long as your provisions will enable you to do so, of which you will be pleased to take on board a full supply. You will return to Mahon to replenish the same.

 Wishing you a pleasant cruise
   I am
    Very respectfully

Captain W. C. Bolton   Yr. Obt. Svt.
Comg. U. S. Frigate    Isaac Hull
*Brandywine*, Port Mahon.   Commr. in Chief of U. S. Naval Force in the Medr.


    U. S. Ship *Ohio*
    Port Mahon, August 1st, 1840.
Sir,

 I have received your report dated Smyrna June 29th 1840 of the progress made by you in the execution of my instructions of the 3d of May, containing interesting information which I have deemed it important to transmit to our Government, and I have to request that, on your return to this place, you will communicate immediately and directly to the Navy Department, any political changes or public events you may have collected and which you deem of sufficient moment, leaving at Mahon a copy of your letter for my use.

 On arriving at this place, you will be pleased to use all despatch in preparing the *Cyane* for Service, and, without loss of time proceed to Marseilles for such funds and stores as may be required for your Ship, taking care to exercise economy and to draw no larger amount of money than will probably be required to last through the fourth quarter of the present year. You will then proceed to the Coast of Italy and the Levant, touching at Leghorn and Naples, Sicily and Malta, and if you deem the letter of which the enclosed is a copy of sufficient importance to take you to the Archipelago, you will visit Athens and Smyrna, and any other ports therein you may think proper; you will however be careful so to regulate your movements as to enable you to return to Mahon by the middle of December next. Should you prefer performing your quarantine at Syracuse or any other port to the eastward of this, you have my permission to do so.

You will be governed by the extracts of instructions from the Navy Department in your possession, as well as by my orders of the 3d of May last as to the objects of your cruise.

I request you to prepare and leave at this place for my use a report of your whole proceedings etc. under my orders of the 3d of May, with the Monthly Returns, Reports, etc. since you left my flag.

Hopes are entertained that Lieutenant Ellison on reflection returned to duty and that his difficulty has been reconciled; should this not be the case, you will be pleased to allow him to remain at Mahon, if he wishes it, until legal proceedings can be instituted.

With our Consul here I leave all letters and papers that have come to hand for your Ship, together with such orders etc. to yourself as are necessary to enable you to carry out the views of the Government, to which I ask your particular attention and strict compliance. Wishing you a pleasant cruise

I am, very respectfully
Yr. Obt. St.
Isaac Hull
Commander in Chief of the U. S.
Naval Force in the Mediterranean

Commander W. K. Latimer
Commanding U. S. Ship *Cyane*
Port Mahon

U. S. Ship *Ohio*
At Sea   August 4, 1840

Sir,

As you have been invested with the command of the U. S. Ship *Ohio*, Flag Ship of the U. S. Squadron in the Mediterranean, I have the pleasure to hand you a Book containing copies of Circular Letters and Extracts of Instructions from the Navy Department with copies of such General Orders as I have found it necessary to issue from time to time, which are intended for your observation and guide.

The Orders in relation to the internal police of this Ship will be subject to your revision or alteration whenever circumstances may render it necessary.

The Book of Expenditures of Stores on board this Ship will also be put in your possession.

No Lists of Cabin Furniture, Books or other matters contained in the Captain's Cabin of this Ship having been left with me by the late Captain, I am unable to furnish you with any account thereof, but should you deem it necessary that an examination, for the purpose of preparing such Lists should be held, Officers will be ordered to attend to that duty on your application.

Any other information you may desire in relation to the Ship, her Officers and Crew, Stores, etc. etc., will be cheerfully furnished.

  I am
   Very respectfully
    Yr. Obt. St.
     Isaac Hull
     Commander in Chief of U. S.
     Naval Force in the Mediterranean

Captain E. A. F. Lavallette
Commanding U. S. Ship *Ohio*
   At Sea


     U. S. Ship *Ohio*
     Trieste Sept. 1st 1840

Sir

In compliance with your order, requiring a monthly report showing the employment of the ship under my command, the work done on board, and generally the state and condition of the Ship and Crew, I have the satisfaction to state that in compliance with your order, the ship departed from Mahon on the 3rd inst: and having passed to the southward of the Island of Sardinia and Sicily through the Malta Channel thence into the Adri'c. after a passage of eighteen days protracted by head and light winds, we anchored in the Port of Trieste.

 . . . . . . . . .

The state and condition of the ship is such as might be expected from the most perfect ship of war and I am most gratified to say that the harmony and good will amongst the Officers, the obedience and praisworthy conduct of the Crew, is highly creditable to all. No impropriety having been committed, nor public punishment taken place since I have had the honor to Command.

. . . . . . . .

I have the honor to be, Sir,
Yr. Obt. Serv.
E. A. F. Lavallette
Captain.

To Commodore Isaac Hull
Comr. in Chief of the U. S. Naval Forces
in the Mediterranean.

U. S. Ship *Ohio,* at Sea
October 1st 1840

Sir,

In making my report showing the employment of the Ship under my Command, the work done on board, and generally the state and condition of the Ship and Crew, I have to state for your information, that the early part of the Month of September was passed in the Port of Trieste where we had Anchored on the 22nd of August, and from whence we sailed on the 11th of Sept., passing down the Adriatic in contention with constant head and light winds, on getting within the entrance of the Archipellago, again meeting with head strong Gales from the Northward and Eastward, and current seting in the opposite direction, which lengthened our passage thus

# THE MEDITERRANEAN SQUADRON 137

far to an unusual degree. We were enabled however to test the good qualities of the Ship, from the variety of winds, weather and currents through which she has passed, and to speak of her admirable qualities in the highest terms.

. . . . . . . . . . .

I think the state and condition of the Ship is in as complete order as could be expected: of the Officers I am able to speak in the most favourable terms, and of the Crew and Marines, in terms of much commendation; there were some acts of misconduct amongst a few of the boats crews, but upon the whole the orderly behavior of the Ships Company while at Trieste must have left a favourable impression of the Character of American Seamen. . . .

     I am very Respectfully
      Yr. Obt. Servt.
       E. A. F. Lavallette, Captain.
To Com[r] Isaac Hull, Commander in Chief of
  Naval Force in the Mediterranean.

      U. S. Ship *Ohio*
       Smyrna, Oct. 18, 1840

Sir,

Having understood, at this place, that you were detained on the Coast of Egypt, in the performance of important services, much longer than was contemplated by my orders to you of May 3d and August 1, 1840, and believing that the appearance of the *Cyane,* under your Command, on the Coast of Spain will be more useful than a compliance with my orders of August 1st, I have to direct that, instead of again visiting the Coast of Italy, the Levant and the Archipelago, you proceed to Marseilles or Toulon for such funds, etc., as your Ship may be in want of, and then proceed to Barcelona and such other ports on the Spanish Coast as, in your judgement from the state of that Country and the Commerce of the United States, may appear to be necessary. You will be pleased to return to Mahon from the first to the middle of December next.

    I am, very respectfully, Sir
     Yr. Obt. St.,
      Isaac Hull
       Commander in Chief of the U. S.
       Naval Force in the Mediterranean

Commander Wm. K. Latimer,
Commanding U. S. S. *Cyane,*
Mahon.

P.S. Be pleased to forward to the U. S. Consul at Athens, the letter enclosed in my orders to you of the 1st August directed to him.

      Isaac Hull

    U. S. Ship *Ohio*
     At sea Nov$^r$ 2nd 1840.

Sir.

My Report of September left us at sea in the Archipelago on our way to Smyrna, before passing into the Gulf, we anchored at Vourla and filled up the water which detained us until the 7th of October, when getting underway we proceeded up the Gulf and at noon of the 8th anchored off the City of Smyrna, and remained there until the morning of the 18th when we sailed and proceeded through the passage of the Grecian Islands: thus far there were no peculiar circumstances which could develope any other quality of the Ship than had already been observed and noted, except that of sailing, which we have reason to believe is improved by the Ship being lighter some inches by the consumption of stores.

The State and Condition of the Ship in all the departments is what might be desired; the Officers are in the most perfect state of harmony and good feelings amongst themselves, evincing a strong desire to preserve the good order and discipline which now exists thruout the Ship, and which is so necessary for the perfection of a Ship of War. Of the Crew, it affords me pleasure to speak in the most favourable terms, being orderly, respectful and obedient, and perform their duties generally with alacrity and cheerfulness; the moral character of the persons comprising this Ship's Crew appears to me to be of a higher standard than that of any other Ship's Crew I have ever met with, their general good conduct may be mainly ascribed to the small quantity of Ardent Spirits which is consumed by them, there being only one hundred and forty out of Eight hundred and fifty, who draw their Grog, and I think it must be evident, that if Sugar and Tea were made a part of the Ration, and a reduction made of one half the allowance of Grog, the condition of Seamen would be much more improved.

. . . . . . . . . .

<blockquote>
I am Very Respectfully
Yr. Obt. Servt.
E. A. F. Lavallette
Captain
</blockquote>

Commodore Isaac Hull
Com<sup>r</sup> in Chief of the U. S.
Naval Force in the Mediterranean.

<blockquote>
U. S. Ship *Ohio*
Port Mahon December 1st 1840.
</blockquote>

Sir,

In reporting to you the employment on board, and generally the state and condition of the Ship and Crew, for the Month of November.

I have to state that after a passage of twenty days from Smyrna, we anchored in the lower harbour of this port, subjected to a quarantine of Fifteen days.

. . . . . . . . . .

Of the Officers, it affords me great pleasure to speak, in the most favourable terms, harmony appears to prevail among them, and I trust, and confidently believe, from the ready obedience to orders and gentlemanly bearing of them all, that we may anticipate a continuance of such conduct as will contribute to the prosperity of the service; Lieut's Pendergrast and Missroon reported themselves for duty on the 28th ult, Lieut. Dupont on the 2nd inst; the two former have been on duty since, and thus far I have been pleased with their prompt and ready obedience; the latter has not yet entered upon duty.

Of the forward Officers, Boatswain, Gunner, Carpenter and Sailmaker, I cannot speak in too much praise, prompt and ready in obedience and skilfull in the performance of their duties.

The Crew merit a continuance of my approbation, and altho now placed where temptation asail them in the manner most likely to cause disorder and insubordination, there could scarcely be a more orderly Ships Company; from fifty to seventy of them have had daily liberty on shore, and there has not been a complaint made of misconduct, since we have been in the port; to render the service more popular with Seamen however, Sir, I think it necessary that some regulation should be made which would cause uniformity in the kind and quality of slop clothing, matrasses and shoes which are furnished, those which are now on board, and all which have been served, have given general dissatisfaction. Seamen generally, will give double the price for a good suit of cloths, than a moderate one for inferior articles.

The Ship may be considered in as perfect a state as a Ship of War may well be, and will require no more than the ordinary supply for wear and tear, for a length of time, and could be continued in the active service of any other cruise with less expense probably than any other ship of the line.

I herewith enclose the Pursers monthly returns and recapitulation of the Ship company's term of service togeather with the deaths

        I am     Very Respectfully Yr. Obt. Servt.
Commodore Isaac Hull     E. A. F. Lavallette,
Comr. in Chief of the U. S.     Captain
Naval Force in the Mediterranean.

Sir,
U. S. Ship *Ohio*
Port Mahon Jan'y 1st 1841

. . . . . . . . . .

Of the Crew, their general conduct has been good, some irregularities growing out of intemperance have occurred, which rendered some severity of punishment necessary; a report of the offences committed and punishment inflicted since Nov. is herewith enclosed; it will be observed that the greater number composing it are old offenders, and who have been punished more than once during the quarter, and also that nearly one half are foreigners. I beg leave to report that my attention has been called to the condition of the Salt Beef which we now serve to the Crew, by the offensive smell arrising from it while being cooked, and I am surprised that complaints have not been made by the Crew of its unfitness to be eaten, it appears to be sound but from age and the frequency of resalting has become hard, tasteless, and I think unfit to be eaten, the brands of 1836 particularly.

Very Respectfully
Yr. Obt. Servt.
E. A. F. Lavallette
Captain

Commodore Isaac Hull
Comr. in Chief of the U. S.
Naval Force in the Mediterranean.

Sir,
U. S. Ship *Ohio*
Port Mahon March 10, 1841

The U. S. Sloop of War, *Preble,* under your Com-

## THE MEDITERRANEAN SQUADRON 143

mand, being ready for sea, I have to direct that you proceed with her to Toulon without unnecessary delay, for the purpose of communicating with the Agents of the Navy Department, Messrs. Fitch Brothers & Co'y. and to procure funds for the Squadron under my Command.

Mr. Purser Sinclair of the U. S. Ship *Ohio* has been entrusted by me with the Requisitions, and for whom I ask a passage in the *Preble,* he will proceed from Toulon to Marseilles, and I think it will be well for the Purser of the *Preble* to accompany him to attend to his own requisitions. Purser Sinclair has been directed to seek at Marseilles the latest information relative to the exciting subjects pending between the United States and Great Britain, and if it should appear that serious measures are likely to ensue, he is to be governed solely by your judgment in the matter of receiving the money. Should there however be nothing to prevent the closing of the business on which Mr. Sinclair has been instructed, you will be pleased to receive the money with any other matters for the Squadron under my Command, on board the *Preble,* and return to this port as speedily as possible.

Any Stores or parts of the Ration of which your Ship is in need, and cannot be supplied from the Stores on hand at this place, you had better procure at Toulon.

The Revd. Mr. Wilmer, Chaplain of the U. S. Ship *Ohio,* and Lieut. Vail, attached to the Squadron are at Marseilles and Toulon, and for whom I ask facilities for their return in the *Preble* to this place.

Wishing you a pleasant trip and a speedy return,
    I am Sir

                    Very Respectfully
                        Yr. Obt. St.
                    Isaac Hull
                    Commander in Chief of the U. S.
                    Forces in the Mediterranean.
Commander Ralph Voorhees
Commanding U. S. Sloop of War *Preble*
Port Mahon.

                U. S. Ship *Ohio*
                    Port Mahon March 19, 1841
Sir,

As the Vessels of the Squadron under my Command will shortly leave Mahon, and may not again return, I desire to call your attention to the Extracts of a letter bearing date February 28th 1839, from the Navy Department (copy of which has been furnished you) in relation to discouraging and discountenancing the officers of every rank and degree as well as the crew of the vessel under your command from incurring debts at Mahon or any other port; and you will carry into effect the orders of the Navy Department in case of officers "running in debt."
                    Very respectfully
                        I am Sir,
                        Yr. Obt. St.
                        Isaac Hull
                        Commander in Chief of the U. S.
                        Naval Force in the Mediterranean
To Officers Commanding
Vessels of the U. S. Squadron
in the Mediterranean.

U. S. Ship *Preble* [at sea]
April 1st, 1841

Sir:

In compliance with your order requiring a monthly report of the employment of the vessel under my command, her general condition and the state of the crew, I have the honor to state: after landing the Honble. Edward Kavanagh, Charge d'Affaires to the Court of Portugal, whom I have brought from the United States, I left Lisbon on the twenty third of February. On the twenty fifth of February I anchored in the Bay of Gibraltar and after communicating with the American Consul and receiving on board a quantity of stores for the squadron, sailed for Port Mahon on the twenty sixth of February and arrived there the sixth of March. On the twelfth of March I left Mahon for Toulon where I arrived on the fourteenth. I left Toulon on the twentieth of March and arrived in the Harbor of Mahon on the twenty third. I left Mahon on the twenty-fifth of March and am now bound to Malaga.

The ship requires caulking. She has a leak forward which lets considerable water into her store rooms. One suit of sails require a thorough repair. She also requires a new set of hammock cloths and an overhauling of the rigging generally. The hold has become very offensive and requires breaking out.

The crew are all in good health.

Very respectfully
I am Sir, Yr. Obt. Svt.

Isaac Hull, Esqre.           R. Voorhees.   Com.
Commr. in Chief of the U. S.
Naval Forces in the Mediterranean.

U. S. Ship *Ohio*
Harbour of Toulon May 1st, 1841

Sir.

In reporting to you the employment of the *Ohio* under my command, the work done on board, and generally the state and condition of the Ship and Crew for the month of April, I have to state, that, in persuance to your orders, The Ship proceeded to sea on the 25 of March and worked down to Malaga, speaking and boarding several vessels for the purpose of getting inteligence in relation to the difficulties existing between the United States and England; we arrived off the Port of Malaga, where the *Preble* had been previously despatched, and received papers brought out by Captain Voorhees, containing such information as rendered it very certain war was not to be anticipated immediately. Your further instructions were complied with by returning up the Mediterranean communicating with Mahon by Boat, on the 15th, thence proceeding to this port where we arrived on the 21st ult.

. . . . . . . . .

Of the Crew, I regret to say, I am much disappointed, much insubordination has been evinced since the new mode of punishing offenders have been introduced, the first Lieut. being deprived of the authority of starting [flogging] men, it has rendered them careless and slovenly; the Officers of the Watch have much trouble in carrying on the duty, or in getting the men up in their watches quickly. The near approach to a termination of their service has shown itself in the application of nearly the whole Crew again for their Grog, which has greatly changed the character of men from quiet to noisy, and it is much to be desired, that authority may be given ere long, to reduce the allowance to one half the quantity, and allow tea and sugar as a part of the ration.

Enclosed are the returns of the Purser and Report of the Surgeon.

      Very Respectfully
       I am Sir
        Yr. Obt. Servt.
         E. A. F. Lavallette
           Captain.

Commodore Isaac Hull
 Comr. in Chief of the U. S.
 Naval Force in the Mediterranean.


       U. S. Ship, *Ohio*
       Port Mahon May 15, 1841

Sir,

I am extremely anxious that the U. S. Ship *Ohio* under your command should be in readiness, in every respect, to proceed to sea on her return passage to the United States on the 28th of the present month. With this view I have given directions to close our Hospital on shore, all the sick from which you will be pleased to receive on board the *Ohio,* and have directed the U. S. Consul and Store Keeper at Mahon to cause all the Accounts against the Ship to be prepared for settlement. I have further to request the particular attention of all Officers and others under your command to my wishes. You will be pleased to cause an account rendered to me, of all articles belonging to this Ship which it may be deemed adviseable to leave behind.

Lieut. R. S. Pinckney and Surgeon Greene have been directed to report to you for passage in the *Ohio* to the United States, to whom you will be pleased to afford the necessary facilities and accommodations.

>Very Respectfully
>I am
>Sir, Yr. Obt. Svt.
>Isaac Hull
>Commander in Chief of the U. S.
>Naval Force in the Medn.

Captain
Elie A. F. Lavallette
Commanding U. S. Ship *Ohio*
Port Mahon.

>U. S. Ship *Ohio*
>At Sea June 2nd 1841.

Sir.

I have the honor to submit the following report of the employment of the U. S. Ship *Ohio* under my Command, the condition of the Ship etc etc during the month of May.

On my last report we were at Toulon, from whence we sailed on the 8th of May, arrived at Mahon on the 10th, and again sailed on the 29th. On arrival at Mahon there were discovered secreted in the Ship, Three Seamen, who had clandestinely got on board in the night, prior to leaving Toulon; on being discovered and by your instruction, an examination of them was had in the presence of Mr. Rich our Consul, togeather with the French Consul and an Officer of the French Corvette *Victorieuse;* the men professed to be Americans, but from their language, and the inconsistency of their stories, they proved to be Frenchmen, and are probably deserters from the French Navy. Altho. it was evident they had no claim upon us, yet all the circumstances of their case was by your order enclosed to our Consul at Toulon, they were sent over to the French Steamer by the Capt. of the Corvette *Victorieuse* who gave a receipt for them and his concurrence to sending them back to Toulon for their further examination.

Your order of the 15th May, to prepare the Ship for sea on her return passage to the United States, was complied with by taking in provisions for Three months and a half, receiving also the various articles which had been required in the different departments, calling in and setling all debts and accounts and it is with great satisfaction I can state, that with the exception of two or three of the Midshipmen every debt which came to my knowledge, was paid by the Officers and Crew, and the Midshipmen aluded to made satisfactory arrangements for liquidating theirs, and I believe few ships have left this station under more favourable circumstances in this particular than the *Ohio.* On the 29th ult. we left the Harbour of Mahon and proceeded down the Mediteranean. The Officers perform their duties promptly and cheerfully, the Crew perform theirs satisfactorily; much severity was found necessary when in port to keep proper discipline, but which at sea is rarely found requisite, and I think we may now look forward to a happy termination of our Cruise.

I herewith enclose the Pursers monthly returns, and the Surgeons Meteorological Journal.

I am Sir Respectfully<br>Yr. Obt. Servt.<br>E. A. F. Lavallette<br>Captain

Commodore Isaac Hull
Comr. in Chief of the U. S.
Naval Force in the Mediterranean.

Consulate General U. States,<br>Tangier, June 13th, 1841.

Sir:

Understanding that you purpose leaving Gibraltar by the first wind for the U. States, I should be most happy if in passing this place, you could make it convenient to run the *Ohio* in sufficiently near to be seen from the town. For the past two years, much curiosity has been expressed by the Authorities and others, to see a vessel bearing the high reputation of the one under your command, and should it not meet your purpose to come to anchor in the bay, I hope the Moors may have their wishes gratified by a passing sight of the *Ohio,* before leaving the Mediterranean. It is now three years since this place has been visited by an American Vessel of War.

With sentiment of high respect<br>I am your obt. svt.<br>Thomas N. Carr.

Commodore Hull

## Chapter XI
## THE OFFICERS OF THE SQUADRON

OFFICERS on board ship are happy and contented, or otherwise, according to their relations with each other and with their commanding officers. A congenial mess and a captain who wins the respect and liking of his subordinates make things agreeable. Men of varying temperaments in the close contact necessary on shipboard, month after month, easily develop antipathies. The ancient method of settling quarrels was passing away. Duelling was forbidden by navy regulations, and although it was perhaps not quite extinct, there were apparently no instances of it on the Mediterranean station at this time. Instead of this, charges were brought against an offending messmate before the captain or the commodore or a court of inquiry, and later, in aggravated cases, before a court martial.

On the flagship, dissatisfaction with the living quarters on the orlop deck was an unfortunate circumstance. The irritation aroused in the commodore led to his sending several officers home. Nevertheless, the *Ohio* seems to have been, on the whole, a rather happier ship than either the *Brandywine* or the *Cyane*. The officers of the *Brandywine* were particularly disputatious, especially the medical officers, who quarreled among themselves and with others. Charges and countercharges were of frequent occurrence. It was the same, though to a lesser degree, on the other ships. Sometimes officers brought charges against their captains. When the *Cyane* was at Spezia, some of her officers visited Carrara. There was a misunderstanding as to their leave of absence from the ship, or the length of their leave, and this gave rise to an amount of discussion apparently out of all proportion to the offense, which was unintentional. Horatio Bridge, the purser of the *Cyane*, who was a friend of Nathaniel Hawthorne, sometimes found it hard to get on amicably with his shipmates and with his captain.

Officers coming out from home under orders to join the squadron were sometimes delayed in finding their ships. It was often difficult to get transportation to Mahon, and furthermore the ships might be cruising and out of reach. Officers under these circumstances sometimes seemed to give the commodore the impression that they were in no great haste to report on board and were obliged to render a strict account of their movements.

Yet after making every allowance for shortcomings, it must be admitted that these men were good average specimens of the American naval officer, and there is none better.

"Private"
          U. S. S. *Cyane*
                Port Mahon Feby. 1st, 1839.

Dear Sir,

I apprehend, from a remark I have heard, that you have the impression that I am disposed to multiply correspondence on the subject of duty, and thereby evincing a litigious disposition. Allow me to assure you, with great frankness, that I have never written you a letter but for the purposes of information or explanation; that I have no object but to know your views distinctly, wherever and whenever there is no discretion allowed me, that my actions may correspond with your instructions. I could have no object, apart from duty. I had no object, apart from a sincere desire to do my duty correctly and obey your instructions, when once possessed of them. I have no petty ambitions to subserve, or little envies to satisfy, or paltry little vanities to gratify. On the contrary, I feel as little desire to increase documents as you can possibly wish me. I assure you, after an acquaintance of twenty four years with you, one third or more of that period under your command, my friendship is unabated and my esteem and respect increased for you and Mrs. Hull, and that I have always felt a desire, when under your command, to the utmost of my feeble abilities, to sustain the honor of your flag, and carry into execution your instructions promptly. I again reassure you with that blunt frankness of character and profession which is my lot, that with an untiring zeal I shall continue to devote my little abilities to the completion of your wishes, but, Sir, you must allow me, for I shall certainly practice it, when enquiries are made of me relating to this ship or the service, generally to state facts and opinions as they bear on my mind, without consulting the feelings or wishes of any one. Were I not to do so, whatever the opinions might be, they would not be mine. Permit me again, with the seriousness that my time of life gives to protestations and assurances, to assure you of the sincere good feelings and good wishes I feel for your present prosperity, health and future happiness, and am as ever

Very respectfully, Sir<br>
Your obt. Servant<br>
J. Percival

Commo. Isaac Hull
   U. S. S. *Ohio*
      Port Mahon.

U. S. S. *Ohio*<br>
At Sea July 28th, 1839.

Gentlemen,

I received your communication of yesterday, last evening. I regret extremely that you find your Orlop rooms untenable from the suffocating closeness and the extreme impurity of the atmosphere there. I have transmitted a copy of your communication to the Commander in Chief, and requested instructions respecting it. The Commodore says in reply, "I do not feel myself at liberty to authorize any alterations in the Ship under your Command in relation to the accommodations of the Officers, but I repeat that your (my) suggestion in relation to a part of the Officers berthed on the Orlop removing their cots and hammocks to the ward room and main deck during the continuance of the warm weather, meets my approbation." Therefore no permanent alterations can be made until the pleasure of the Government is known and instructions received upon

## THE OFFICERS OF THE SQUADRON 155

the subject; but I will direct the 1st Lieutenant to have temporary rooms made for your accommodation during the continuance of the warm weather.

Very respectfully<br>Your Obt. Servt.<br>Jos. Smith<br>Capt. U. S. S. *Ohio*.

Lieuts.
    Samuel Mercer
    S. F. Dupont
    Wm. L. Howard
    R. L. Browning
    J. S. Missroon
    Jno. W. Cox
    S. W. Godon
    Alfred Taylor
    Guert Gansevoort
    John W. Grier
        Chaplain
U. S. S. *Ohio*
        Present.

U. S. S. *Ohio*. July 29th 1839 (At Sea)

Sir:

As it is my intention to decline occupying one of the places which you have directed the first Lieutenant to dispose of, for temporary sleeping accommodation to those officers who have complained of the suffocating state of the atmosphere in their rooms on the Orlop, and as I should greatly regret if my so doing were attributed to an improper spirit, I beg leave to say a few words in reply to your communication of yesterday, which you were pleased to address in answer to one signed (among others) by myself on the 27th inst. I shall speak freely, but with feelings of the very highest respect for my superiors.

   I am one of those Sir who believe that a Lieutenant is as much entitled by regulation, by usage, and by military propriety to a permanent and fixed apartment, suitable to his rank and few personal wants, as the captain of a ship is to his cabin, and that a ship of this class is capable of affording such a one at least as he would occupy in a Frigate or Sloop of War. I signed the letter of the 27th inst. representing the present state of the Orlop rooms under the impression that if the complaints contained in it were found to be well grounded, other permanent and usual accommodations would be given me, particularly as it had been generally understood, if not officially stated, that the present arrangement of berthing very nearly all the officers of the ship on the Orlop was merely an experiment. But the Commander in Chief having decided that he is not authorized to make any permanent change, of which he is of course the sole and proper judge, I prefer remaining where the Navy Department have placed me, as long as my health will endure it, rather than occupy quarters which I deem unfit for an officer holding the third rank known in our service, and from which he may be ejected at any moment.

   I trust Sir however that you will not for a moment suppose, that I do not fully appreciate the consideration which induces you to do all that you conceive being in your power, to alleviate the present state of things.

I have the honor to be Sir
with very great respect
Yr. Obt. Servt.
S. F. DuPont
Lt. U. S. S. *Ohio*.

Capt. Joseph Smith
Comdr. U. S. S. *Ohio*.

U. S. S. *Ohio*.
At Sea   July 30th, 1839

Sir,

I have received from Lieut. Dupont a very, as I think, extraordinary and uncalled for communication, which I think it is proper, as well as it is a duty, to enclose to you.

The true military course for me to pursue would be to *compell* him to occupy the apartment assigned to him in addition to that which he has so much complained of, and which he says is untenable. But under the present state of excitement upon the subject of the accommodations of the Ward Room Officers, I do not deem it expedient to take such a course, but to allow the gentleman to remain in the apartment assigned to him by the Navy Department, which he prefers to that prepared for and appointed to him by myself and which was certainly intended by me to relieve him from what he complained of in the other. The tenor and character of this communication, as well as the course he has taken — first, in making the complaint referred to, and then declining to accept the accommodation offered as a remedy for the evil — develope a spirit of dictation in its author too clearly, to my view, to require comments from me.

Respectfully, Your Obt. Servt.
Jos. Smith

Como. Isaac Hull          Capt. U. S. S. *Ohio*.
Comr. in Ch'f of the U. S.
Naval Force in the Medr.
    At Sea.

Marseilles
August 10th, 1839.

My dear Percival,

    I arrived here on the 5th inst. and hasten by the first opportunity that I think a letter will reach you, to say that I have been directed to relieve you, as you requested, in the Command of the *Cyane*. Do, my dear fellow, endeavor to get the Commodore to permit the Ship to come here, as it would be a mutual convenience, and to land you at any port that it would be most convenient for you to embark for the United States. I have written to the Commodore reporting my arrival here and informing him I could learn nothing definite relative to his movements and should await his instructions. I have also requested him as a particular favour to permit the Ship to come here and take me on board. I hope you have recovered your health. I heard indirectly from Mrs. Percival before my departure, she was quite well. I have not brought a clerk with me and if the gentleman you have is desirous of remaining and you can recommend him, I should be happy if he would do so.

                  In haste
                     your svt. and friend
                            W. K. Latimer.

U. S. Ship *Ohio,* Port Mahon
Sept. 14, 1839

Sir

I am induced by reasons of a domestic nature to sollicit very respectfully permission to return to the U. States.

It is with reluctance that I thus ask to be relieved from duty; and though the circumstances which lead me to do so touch me very nearly, I should not perhaps have yielded to them, had I not already seen a fair portion of active service and if Captain Smith had not officially informed the Officers in June last, that he had one more Lieutenant in the Ship than he required.

Trusting Sir that it may accord with your views to grant this request,
    I have the honor to be
     with great respect
      Yr. obt. Servt.

Commodore Isaac Hull    S. F. DuPont.
Comr. U. S. Naval Forces    Lt.
Mediterranean.

U. S. Ship *Cyane*
Port Mahon Jany. 8th, 1840

Sir,

I have to request that you will order another Lieutenant to this ship.

The duty required of the Watch Officers allows but a short recess from duty, and the indisposition of one frequently imposes additional duties upon the Master of the Ship whose proper duties already occupy him closely.

I must also request that four Passed or Senior Midshipmen be ordered to the ship in exchange for four now on board. My reason for asking that an exchange may take place is that the Midshipmen now attached to the ship want that experience which is necessary a portion should have.

The names of those I request may be detached, are Midshipmen McDonough, Williamson, Downes and Tattnall.

I would ask as a particular favor that the two last named young gentlemen may be ordered to the ship *Ohio,* as it is my object in making this request in their behalf, that the balance of their cruise should be performed on board a larger class of vessel.

I have the honor to be
    With great respect
      Your obt. Servt.

Commo. Isaac Hull    W. K. Latimer
Commdr. in Chief of the U. S.    Commander
Naval Forces in the Mediterranean.

      Boston, July 5th 1840
Dear Sir

I yesterday heard that the officers which were ordered home from the *Ohio* are ordered back — to report for duty on board the *Ohio,* how true I do not know but the information comes tolerably straight.

I regret you should have ordered them home, more particularly after they made the disclaimer of never having intended to treat you with disrespect, unless you had authority from the Dept to do so.

It will be placing you very unpleasantly. If it is true they are ordered back, it must have, I suppose, originated from the fact that the Secty of the Navy viewed it as an act on your part as conflicting and countermanding an order of the Dept which attached them to that ship. But I do not pretend to know anything on the subject.

Matters in the U S are all absorbed in politics. Will you please present my respects to your family and be assured I am

      Respectfully,
Com'dore I. Hull   Your friend
        J. Percival

    U. S. Ship *Ohio*
   Port Mahon, Nov. 9, 1840

Sir,

I have received your communication of the 7th inst. requesting "that the truth of the charges alleged against you by Commander Latimer may be investigated" before the departure of the *Cyane* on the contemplated cruise; assigning the following as reasons, which I quote from your letter, viz, "as there is now a sufficiency of Officers of Superior rank to myself present in the Squadron, and there can be no reasonable pretext why such investigation should any longer be with-held." To this I am impelled by a sense of duty to the Naval Service, before giving a definite answer to your request, to suggest to you the propriety of recurring to the spirit which dictated those reasons, as well as to a revision of the language giving them form. I also advise you to refer to an "Act for the better Government of the Navy of the United States" under the head of "Naval General Courts Martial" for information as to when and by whom Courts Martial may be convened. The spirit of dictation which your letter carries upon its face and the implied charge against the Commander in Chief of the Mediterranean Squadron, viz., that "pretexts" have been resorted to, to with-hold an investigation into the charges upon which you are now under arrest, might be the basis of further charges against you. I deeply regret to find you laboring under a state of feeling which can neither aid your cause nor facilitate my movements.

A further letter is before me of the same date in which you request to be detached from the *Cyane* and permitted to remain on shore until a tribunal can be assembled to investigate the charges upon which you are deprived of your rank and station in the Navy and you assign as reasons for asking this indulgence (and I again use your own words) "as since my arrest I have been constantly subjected to the mortifying and degrading position of a prisoner and at times placed under the orders of a Junior Officer."

That you have thus been "subjected" I truly regret, but it has been the consequence entirely of your own election. At the very inception of your difficulties at Spezia, I endeavored to point out to you a course which I thought was for your welfare, due to the Naval Service and which would have relieved you from the position in which you were placed; but to my surprise my efforts were repulsed with a temper and a manner which convinced me that your own will was not to be interferred with, and that advice from your Senior Officer was not acceptable to you. Since then, however, I have given unusual scope to Commander Latimer in your case. At the time of your arrest I wrote to him as follows, "As I would gladly avoid bringing that Officer (Lt. Ellison) to trial, I hereby empower you to annul the charges and restore him to duty, should he at any time during your absence, make such concessions as to you may appear satisfactory," and again afterwards a letter was addressed to him of which the following is an extract: "Hopes are entertained that Lieut. Ellison on reflection returned to duty, and that his difficulty has been reconciled; should this not be the case you will be pleased to allow him to remain at Mahon, if he wishes it, until legal proceedings can be instituted." In these attempts to relieve you I have also been disappointed and to my great astonishment I have seen a most solemn protest signed by you "against being sent on shore in a foreign port", in consequence of which I withdrew the permission for you to remain at Mahon.

The other branch of your reasons for requesting to be detached from the *Cyane,* viz., that you are "at times placed under the orders of a junior Officer", is not admissible; because the functions of an Officer whilst under arrest cease, no matter what his rank, he is then specially bound by the terms of his arrest, and if on board ship must observe the internal rules and police of the Ship, no matter whether executed by a senior or junior Officer, and further because I am informed by Commander Latimer "that Lieut. Ellison was never placed under the orders of the Officer who was temporarily in charge of the Ship during my (his) absence, and repeated instances occurred of his having received my (Com. L's) permission to visit the shore, returning on board and leaving the Ship again under the same permission when I (Comr. L) was absent from the Ship, without reference to the Officer in charge and his return always reported to me (Comr. L) in writing and to no other Officer", and that Lieut. Ellison "has had privileges and indulgences extended to him far beyond what is customary in the service to Officers under arrest."

Your letter of the 8th inst. I have also received, but as you do not refer to any instance in which you were actually placed under the orders of a junior Officer but simply that you conceived yourself "at all times" when the Commander was out of the Ship "to have been actually placed under the orders of the Officer who was left temporarily in Command", I do not think it has the slightest bearing in the case.

I have no wish to confine you to the *Cyane* and I will repeat, I would gladly avoid bringing you to a Court Martial; but I shall in all my proceedings be governed by what I conceive to be the "public interest" and the "good of the service", and, in convening General Courts Martial, the necessity of the case and the proper time must be left to my judgment when in command of a Fleet or Squadron out of the United States.

    Very Respectfully
    I am, Sir,
     Yr. Obt. St.

Isaac Hull
Commander in Chief of the U. S.
Naval Force in the Mediterranean

Lieut. Francis B. Ellison,
U. S. Ship *Cyane*,
Port Mahon.

U. S. Ship *Ohio*
Harbour of Boston
July 27, 1841.

Lieut. Henry B. Watson
U. S. Marine Corps,   Dear Sir,

The cruise of the *Ohio* having ended, we are about to separate, to devote ourselves perhaps to more pleasureable pursuits; before we do so however, I must indulge in a gratification in the performance of a duty which adds much to the satisfaction I have enjoyed in your attention to duty whilst under my command. It is due to you that I should bear testimony to your correct conduct and to the soldier-like manner in which you have attended to the duties of your proper office, as well as to your gentlemanly bearing, which have met my entire approbation.

Accept my best wishes for your welfare and happiness and may your most ardent wishes be gratified in advancing in your profession.

I am

Very Respectfully,
Yr. Obt. St.
Isaac Hull.

## Chapter XII
## MIDSHIPMEN

MIDSHIPMEN sometimes entered the service at a very early age. Farragut was less than nine and a half years old when he began his remarkable career in the navy. Although as a rule considerably older than this, acting midshipmen were yet mere boys. If they passed successfully through a period of probation, they received warrants dated back to their first appointment. After about six years' service, if all went well, they became passed midshipmen, equivalent to the present grade of ensign. Under the apprentice system established in 1837, — unfortunately of short duration, but later reëstablished — a superior class of boys were enlisted and the brighter ones were occasionally able to get appointed midshipmen.

Instructors were furnished for the training of midshipmen. The education of the young officers was doubtless inadequate and a few years later was greatly improved, upon the establishment of the Naval Academy.

Together with the instincts and overflowing spirits of youth, the midshipmen were conscious of their importance as officers of the navy, keen to resent any slight and impatient of restraint. Consequently they sometimes found themselves in hot water, often as a result of their boyish behavior.

When the *Ohio* was lying in the Bay of Spezia, June 29, 1840, Lieutenant Mercer transmitted to the commodore certain reports of other officers. One lieutenant complained that his sleep had been disturbed "by some of the Midshipmen blowing upon Instruments of Music belonging to the Band. It is with regret that I state the frequent occurrence of profane language and boisterous conduct of the Midshipmen upon the Orlop." The surgeon's "notice was attracted by a noise and upon looking up I discovered" a number of midshipmen "passing forward with several instruments of the band. They were very soon put in action in the most discordant strains."

Midshipmen sometimes reported or brought charges against their superior officers. March 28, 1840, at Mahon, Midshipman Fox of the *Cyane* complained to his captain of his arbitrary treatment by the first lieutenant, in not allowing him shore leave and forbidding his appeal to the captain. In this difficulty Captain Latimer took the part of the midshipman.

At the end of the cruise Commodore Hull wrote personal letters to several midshipmen commending their conduct and wishing them health, happiness and speedy advancement in their profession.

United States Ship *Cyane*<br>1st October 1838

Sir

I have the honor to submit to you the report from the Mathematical School of this ship, for the quarter ending 30th September 1838. The names of the young gentlemen are written in the order of merit, commencing with the attentive and studious and ending with the careless and indifferent.

Respectfully<br>Your Most Ob't Servant.<br>James Major

To John Percival Esq.
  Commander, U. S. S. *Cyane*

Report

Mr. Archibald McRae. This young gentleman has been very industrious and persevering. He has gone through an elementary course of Algebra, commenced the elements of Euclid and is now in the fourth book.

Mr. Reed Werden. Commenced Bowditch's Practical Navigator and learned the following subjects as treated in that work, viz: Geometry, plane trigonometry, plane sailing, parallel sailing, middle latitude and Mercator's sailing, and is now learning the application of plane trigonometry to the mensuration of heights and distances, surveying coasts and harbours, etc.

Mr. Gustavus V. Fox. Commenced algebra and has advanced as far as quadratic equations. Mr. Fox is a very intelligent student.

Mr. George B. Balch is reading simple equations and the second book of Legendre's Geometry. He is attentive and studious.

Mr. David Williamson is learning algebra and geometry. He has been attentive and persevering from the commencement and very successful in his studies.

Mr. Charles W. Place is learning algebra and geometry. He is a pretty good algebraist for his time, but rather behind in geometry.

Mr. John Downes is reading an elementary course of Algebra. He has learned the fundamental rules, the theory of the greatest common divisor, and algebraic fractions. He is now solving simple equations and is rather idle.

Mr. Edward F. Tattnall has learned algebraic fractions, and is now in simple equations. He is not sufficiently industrious. Disposed to be idle.

Mr. Fredk. W. Colby was a pretty attentive student during the first two months, but he has done very little during the last month.

Mr. Chas. H. B. Caldwell is learning very slowly. He possesses some talent for mathematics, but is rather indolent.

Mr. Robert A. Knapp is learning algebra and geometry. He does not bestow sufficient attention to his studies. He is [in] simple equations.

Mr. John L. Worden attends the school very irregularly and consequently has not gained much mathematical knowledge. He learns plane trigonometry and algebra.

Mr. Edward Allen is learning arithmetic only. His knowledge of this subject was very limited. He has learned the doctrine of fractions and is now commencing decimals.

Mr. Henry A. Wise, owing to sickness or some other cause unknown to me, seldom attends the school. He has learned very little indeed from this school.

James Major<br>Prof. Math.

U. S. Ship *Cyane*
Messina, Novem. 22nd, 1838.

Sir.

Since the date of the above mathematical report I have felt it proper to extensively curtail the liberty of those young gentlemen whose names are noted in said report, of not having manifested that attention and energy in their studies which the Government had a right to expect, and for whom its paternal solicitude had so judiciously procured the means of improvement, by placing on board this ship a talented, attentive mathematical instructor. I apprehend no unfavorable result to the *health* or the *morals* of young midshipmen on this station being limited to the duties of the ship and their studies, and in fact it is the only coercive power which a Commander of a Ship can wield with any effect on an idle Midshipman, and an indulgence to visit the shore on liberty, from the limits of these restrictions, is one of the greatest incitements to study and duty.

All of which is respectfully submitted.
I have the honor to be
Very respectfully
Your obt. Servt.
J. Percival
Commdr.

Hon. James K. Paulding
   Secretary of the Navy
      Washington.

Navy Yard Boston
22d. Novr. 1838

My dear Commodore

I have received your favour of the 17th and with Mrs. Downes, offer you many thanks for your kind offer to take anything she may have to send to her boy. Mrs. D., as well as myself, hope that if Capt. Percival should leave the *Cyane* that you will have the kindness to take our boy on board your own ship, but so long as there is a good teacher on board the *Cyane* and Capt. Percival keeps the middies under rigid discipline, I think my son had better remain where he is. If however you should see anything which might lead you to suppose that he would be the better for a change, I trust that you will, as my friend, take him from the *Cyane*. The frigate *U. States* has brought home a fine crew. I wish you had them on board your ship, they will be discharged tomorrow and I have no doubt many of them will go to New York for the purpose of joining your ship. I hope you will take them without the formality of their shipping at the Rendezvous.

There is a man here by the name of Amstead belonging to Mahon, he came out in the *United States* for the purpose of collecting money owing him from the crew of that ship, he has succeeded in getting his money and now wishes to return to Mahon. I hope you will give him a passage in your ship, he is a very respectable man at that place and has rendered good service to our officers in the Mediterranean for many years past, and if you require his services I have no doubt he will give you perfect satisfaction in whatever he may undertake.

I am dear Sir<br>
Very sincerely<br>
Your friend and servt.<br>
Jno. Downes

Commre. Isaac Hull
New York.

U. S. S. *Ohio*
Mahon   Feby. 14th, 1839

Sir

I am under the painful necessity of presenting to you herewith charges and specifications of charges against Acting Midn. A. C. Rhind of this ship.

The case seems to me to be of such a character as to demand serious notice. I have suspended the accused from duty and informed him that I should submit charges to you against him as soon as I could prepare them.

Very respectfully<br>
Your obt. Servt.<br>
Jos. Smith<br>
Capt. U. S. S. *Ohio*

Como. Isaac Hull
Commr. in Chief of the U. S.
Naval Force in the Medn.
Present.

Charges and specifications of charges preferred by Joseph Smith, a Captain in the Navy of the United States and Commanding the U. S. Ship *Ohio*, against

A. C. Rhind, an Acting Midshipman in said Navy and serving on board said ship, and preferred to Commodore Isaac Hull, Commander in Chief of the United States Naval Forces in the Mediterranean.

Charge 1st.

Quarrelling and using profane, provoking and reproachful words.

Specification.

In that the said A. C. Rhind, on the thirteenth day of February, A.D. 1839, on board said Ship *Ohio,* lying in the Harbour of Port Mahon, and in the Midshipmen's mess-room, did without cause or provocation, call Henry S. Newcomb, an Acting Midshipman aboard said Ship, a *damned liar,* and did repeat it by calling him a *damned infernal liar,* and did, then and there, in the most provoking and tantalizing manner, dare him the said Newcomb to report him the said Rhind to the first Lieutenant for so insulting him and did offer to give to him the said Newcomb money, to wit fifty cents, if he dared to, or would, report him the said Rhind to the first Lieutenant for thus addressing the provoking and reproachful language, before recited, to him the said Newcomb. Thereby knowingly and wilfully, coolly and deliberately violating the Laws and regulations of the Navy, and especially the third and fifteenth articles of an Act for the better government of the Navy of the United States.

Charge 2nd.

Unofficerlike and ungentlemanly conduct.

Specification,

In that the said Rhind, at the time and place named

in the foregoing specification, did, without cause or provocation, call the said Newcomb a damned liar, and did, shortly afterwards, at the place before mentioned, coolly and deliberately use unofficerlike and ungentlemanly language by calling him the said Newcomb a *damned infernal liar* and did meanly and contemptuously dare the said Newcomb to report him the said Rhind to the first Lieutenant, and did meanly offer the said Newcomb money, to wit, fifty cents, if he would so report him. Thereby setting an example totally unworthy and unbecoming the character and conduct of an Officer and Gentleman, and thereby setting at defiance the exercise of the right and duty of an Officer to report another to the proper Authority for unofficerlike and ungentlemanly conduct, and thereby vainly and arrogantly insinuating that the said Newcomb dare not report him the said Rhind for such unofficerlike and ungentlemanly conduct, and thereby violating the Laws and regulations of the Navy, and particularly the third and fifteenth articles of an Act for the better government of the Navy of the United States.

Jos. Smith.

U. S. S. *Ohio*.
    Port Mahon, Feby. 14th, 1839.

U. S. S. *Ohio*   Mahon<br>Feb'y 18th 1839

Sir

I have been under suspension for several days for improper language made use of to a mess-mate.

It was under aggravating circumstances and I am

very sorry it should have occurred. I beg you would overlook it and restore me to my duties.

Yours very resp.

Capt. Joseph Smith                A. C. Rhind.
U. S. Ship  *Ohio*.

U. S. S. *Ohio*  Mahon<br>Feb'y 18th, 1839

Sir

I have just received your letter of this date. A day or two ago I submitted charges and specifications of charges against you to Como. Hull for an alledged violation of the Laws and Regulations of the Navy; and, having done so, the power to release you from your suspension has passed from me. If, in a proper spirit and under a conviction of your error and a promise to avoid a repetition of the offence in this ship, you appeal to the Commander in Chief, I doubt not that your petition will be respectfully considered and liberally acted upon.

Respectfully<br>Yr. Obt. Servt.<br>Jos. Smith.

Acting Midn.
A. C. Rhind
  U. S. S. *Ohio*.
    Present.

U. S. S. *Ohio* Mahon<br>Feb'y 21st 1839.

Sir

I have the honor to hand you herewith copies of two letters, one from acting Midn. Rhind to me and my answer.

Mr. Rhind stated to me this evening, that he had addressed a note to you, based upon my letter to him, requesting to be released from suspension.

If his note to you had passed through my hands, I should have added to it what I will now say, that, he having expressed to me deep regret for his fault, I do not wish to prosecute the charges and request that you will allow the gentleman to return to his duty, if he shall satisfy you, and those to whom you think he should make acknowledgments, as he has me, that he is really sorry at the occurrence and will restrain himself in future.

Very respectfully<br>Sir Yr. Obt. Servt.

Como. Isaac Hull                                        Jos. Smith
Comr. in Chief of the
U. S. Forces in the Mediterranean.

U. S. Ship Cyane,<br>Port Mahon March 1st, 1839

Sir

I have the honor to solicit orders to the U. S. Ship *Ohio*.

Very respectfully<br>Your obedient servant<br>Gustavus V. Fox<br>Act'g. Midn.

To
    Commodore Isaac Hull,
    Commander in Chief of the U. S. Naval
    Forces in the Mediterranean.

U. S. Ship *Cyane*
At Sea March 26th, 1839.

Sir,

The father of the above applicant made a personal appeal to me, to watch over his child and enforce on him a strict moral conduct and to guard him against the licentious and libidinous practices which surround a youth, and prevalent in the most of the cities in the Mediterranean.

I respectfully solicit that unless the public service requires it, you will not grant his request, as I apprehend his principal cause for the application grows out of the fact that I will not let him visit the shore but once a week and then only until sundown, and not then unless he has attended properly to his studies and other duties. I am not desirous to obtain the popularity of midshipmen at the expense of discipline and their moral benefit.

Very respectfully, Sir<br/>Your obt. Servt.

Commo. Isaac Hull        J. Percival, Comdr.
Commander in Chief of the
U. S. Naval Forces
in the Mediterranean.

U. S. Ship *Cyane*
Port Mahon March 1st, 1839.

Sir,

I respectfully request orders for duty on board the U. S. Ship *Ohio*.

I am very Respectly.<br/>Your Obdt. Servt.<br/>John Downes Jr.<br/>Act. Md.

To   Commodore Isaac Hull
     Commander in Chief of the U. S.
     Naval Forces in the Meditr.

U. S. S. *Cyane*<br>At Sea, March 26, 1839

Sir,

The above application is from the son of your friend Commo. Downes, who requested I would keep a vigilant watch over him and to prevent, by every means in my power, his being transferred, *unless you* or who might be the Commander in Chief should deem it, *for the public interest,* but if I should leave the ship, he hoped you would let him be placed under Capt. Smith. Since your arrival I have received two letters from Commo. Downes urging upon me a vigilant care of his son, and to keep him strictly to his studies and duty and allow him to visit the shore but seldom. I therefore respectfully solicit that you will not comply with his request, as the wish is created from the fact that he is compelled to attend school regularly and not allowed to be out of the ship after sundown and thereby guarded from the temptation which lurkes in wait with the lust of interest for the unwary, vain and thoughtless.

Very respectfully, Sir<br>Your obt. Servant

Commo. Isaac Hull            J. Percival   Comdr.
Commdr. in Chief of the
U. S. Naval Forces in the Mediterranean.

U. S. Ship *Ohio*
Gibraltar Bay April 25th 1839.

Sir,

I have the honor herewith to hand you a report of the character and condition of the Apprentice boys on board this Ship.

Believing as I do that the system of enlisting apprentice boys, if properly carried out, is of the utmost importance to our Navy, and as I take great interest in it, I respectfully request that you will forward this report to the Navy Department with such remarks as you may think the subject merits.

The Apprentice boys on board this Ship, without exception, have conducted themselves with great propriety, exhibiting on all occasions a commendable ambition and a desire to excel in every thing they are directed to do; crime is not known among them, and the slightest degree of correction is seldom necessary; they evince an elevation of character and respect for themselves entirely different from boys not under the special care of the Government.

I beg the indulgence to say that, in my opinion, the system of enlisting apprentices is of vital importance to the Naval Service, and if the three Receiving Ships at our principal Naval Stations can keep up the number of two hundred apprentices to each, with a proper school and under proper discipline, for two years, in a very short time there could be transferred six hundred apprentices in the course of each year to our sea-going Ships. By such a system, in a few years there would exist a class of Seamen peculiar to our Navy and of a character entirely different from those at present employed, who are on an average more than one half foreigners.

Permit me also to remark that I find it impossible to educate Midshipmen on board a cruising Ship, and my opinion is that, instead of permitting them to remain idle after their appointment, they should be ordered immediately to one of those Receiving Ships, where they should be kept to their studies under a Professor of Mathematics and a teacher of languages, to which might be added a drawing and a fencing Master, with the usual duties attended to, morning and evening, of a Ship equipped; and a regular tour of Watch duty once a week, all under proper regulations, with a proper Officer at their head. By such a course in two years they would become efficient Officers for active sea service, and as it is, probably, the intention of Government to send the Receiving Ships to cruise a couple of months in the summer, such advantages would prove of the utmost importance to our Country and to its Navy.

Very respectfully
I am
Sir
Yr. Obt. St.

Commo. Isaac Hull
Commr. in Chief of the U. S.
Naval Force in the Medr.
  Gibraltar Bay.

Jos. Smith
Capt. U. S. S. *Ohio*

U. S. S. *Cyane*
Port Mahon Sept. 28, 1839.

Sir,

The report of Acting Midn. Downes, I send in *consequence of the regulations* of the service.

I consider the report exaggerated and made by the complainant under excited feelings, pushed on by his associates in insubordination. I investigated the affair and found to my satisfaction that the complained was passing with an officer's of the wardroom breakfast, while the Midshipmen were sky-larking and rioting (inconsistent with gentlemen), they ran against the complained, trod on his feet and otherwise hurt him; interrupted him in the execution of the duty on which sent by the Officer on whom he attends. The boy admits that, after having passed forward, he, under the agonizing pain, exclaimed, "God damn it, or my Soul! I wish you would let me pass without being trod upon or run against."

I very respectfully represent, that for several months past there has been evinced a spirit of insubordination tending to *rowdyism* among the Midshipmen, and but for the peculiarity of my situation, I would prefer charges against them. Some strong expression of disapprobation of their conduct might, with the papers returned to Mid. Downes, operate beneficially. In fact there appears something little short of mutiny in the service among the Acting Midn.

Very respectfully, Sir
I have the honor to be
Your obt. Servt.
J. Percival, Commdr.

Commo. Isaac Hull
Commng. U. S. Naval Force
in the Mediterranean.

U. S. Ship *Cyane*
Port Mahon Nov. 14th 1840

Sir

I have the honor to inform you that in obedience to your verbal order of yesterday, I have restricted Midn. Shields from visiting the shore, and now enclose you a communication from him with assurances that he will not be engaged in any difficulty involving personal contest while under your command.

I hope the long cruise this ship has had will be duly considered by you and that he will again be allowed to visit the shore, as I feel convinced that the assurances which he has given you will be fully complied with.

    I have the honor to be
     With great respect
      Your obt. servt.
       W. K. Latimer
Commodore Isaac Hull     Commander
Commander in Chief of the U. S.
Naval Force in the Medr.


U. S. Ship *Cyane*
Port Mahon. Nov. 14th 1840

Sir

As I am confined to the ship by your orders, under suspicion of being the principal in a difficulty now existing, I promise you, should you remove the restriction, that I will not act as principal in any difficulty, while under your command.

I hope you will be satisfied with my promise, and in

consideration of the long cruise from which I have just returned, you will grant me the privilege of visiting the shore.

    I have the honor to be
      Most respectly.
        Your obt. servt., etc. etc.
          W. Shields

To Commodore Isaac Hull
Commdg. U. S. Naval Force in the Mediterranean.

## Chapter XIII

## THE MAN BEFORE THE MAST

THE enlisted men of the navy today — fine young fellows, nearly all American citizens — are of a very different class from those of 1838. The naval seaman and the merchant seaman of that day were more of the same sort than now, — men of all nationalities, shipped in various seaports, who had roamed over the world all their lives, many of them hard characters, some of them fugitives from justice, perhaps men escaping from family cares, or boys who had run away to sea. "A sailor's life is at best but a mixture of a little good with much evil, and a little pleasure with much pain. The beautiful is linked with the revolting, the sublime with the commonplace, and the solemn with the ludicrous."[1]

In early times the lot of the naval seaman was hard, and some of the abuses to which he was subjected are now scarcely credible, but by the middle of the nineteenth century amelioration of earlier conditions had begun to come about. On board ship the welfare of the sailors was looked after by the chaplains, to the best of their ability, and on shore by philanthropic citizens and societies. In such ways attempts were made to improve the character and education of naval seamen.

The captain of a ship was something like the father of a very large family of children, many of them way-

---
[1] Dana, *Two Years before the Mast,* ch. VI.

ward, unruly, and irresponsible. In managing them there were many problems to solve, many appeals to human sympathy to listen to and decide. Such cases were referred to the commodore. September 18, 1839, Captain Smith reports that one of the steerage stewards wishes his discharge in order to enter business with his brother. The captain is willing to let him go, but considers the reason insufficient. Captain Percival enlisted five married seamen at Mahon on condition that they should be discharged on request. He was short of men and it seemed necessary, and the same thing had been done on the station before. They have behaved well and now ask their discharge, and the captain feels in honor bound to grant it. He hopes Commodore Hull will allow the discharge. The commodore received a letter from the United States consul at Mahon with a complaint against a young man, a native, who had got a girl into trouble and had fled and taken refuge on the *Ohio*, where he was concealed. The governor wishes him delivered to the local authorities.

Captain Bolton wrote to Commodore Hull, March 18, 1840: "I find myself much plagued by the Musicians (Mahonese) whom I entered here shortly after my arrival, under your verbal permission." The local authorities will not confirm their engagement, therefore they are beyond the reach of our martial law. It seems best to get rid of them and with the commodore's consent Captain Bolton will discharge them as "triflers and worthless." He hopes no other captain will be imposed upon. May 23, 1841, Captain Lavallette reports that three seamen have been discovered secreted on the *Ohio*, evidently Frenchmen. They came aboard the ship at Toulon. All have American protections, they give American names, and claim to be American citizens. These men turned out to be deserters from the French navy.

Portland, November 1st, 1838.

To the Honble
  J. K. Paulding,
    Secretary of the Navy:

The undersigned, Citizens of Portland, Maine, respectfully represent that William Emerson, a respectable Ship master of this place, having been unfortunately wrecked in a Brig he commanded and his mind disordered, as they fear, by stimulants, although he has ever been a man of good habits, he enlisted into the Navy of the United States, at Boston, and is now on board the United States Ship *Ohio,* at New York.

Captain Emerson has a wife and two small children, aged two and four years, in this City, who are solely dependent on him for support, and we earnestly request that he may be discharged from the service and returned to his agrieved and suffering wife and helpless children.

We are, Sir, with great respect, Your Obt Servts
John Anderson<br/>[and thirteen others]

U. S. S. *Cyane*<br/>Messina, November 20th, 1838.

Sir,
  I would respectfully ask your decision on the following subjects.
  I am frequently applied to, by our consuls at the

ports I visit, to receive on board *destitute American Seamen*, who have been left on shore sick, or otherwise have become a charge on their hands and consequently on the Government. Many of those men are truly just objects of commiseration, deserving but unfortunate; in a great degree meriting the fostering care of a paternal and humane Government. Others are requested to be taken on board who have become insubordinate and mutinous to their Commanders; of this class I have no doubt about receiving and furnishing a ration to them, until an opportunity offers of sending them to the United States; but how are they to make a decent and proper appearance during this period on the deck of a Ship of War, without some pay to procure seamen's clothing, for they are generally more or less destitute. An American Seaman in a foreign country applies for an asylum under his country's banner; says, "I am an American Seaman in distress. I have long served my country and now solicit shelter and protection under its flag." What am I to do under such an appeal? Refuse the poor boon? On a verbal application to a former Secretary on this subject, he observed that "the commerce sustained the Navy and the Navy should and ought to protect it and succor those who carried it on; that they were hand-maidens and commerce the elder sister." I would be the last to intrude an opinion on the Department and hope I shall not give offence by suggesting what I have long felt convinced of, that by receiving our distressed Seamen, abroad, on board our ships of war, it will save an expense to the Nation and will create a love for the service and their Country.

Sailors, as far as practicable, should be rescued from the rapacious fangs of landlords, who are ever ready, abroad as well as at home, to seduce them from their duty and plunder them of what little they may possess. I have always heretofore received them on board, and thus far the Department have not offered any objection, but not knowing the views of the Department at present on this point, I respectfully solicit your direction.

With very great respect,<br>I have the honor to be<br>Your obt. Servt.

Hon. James K. Paulding           J. Percival
   Secretary of the Navy            Comdr.
   Washington City.

P.S. Since writing the above, a case not unsimilar to those represented has taken place here. I anchored here last night; this morning an application was made to me through the Consul, to receive an unfortunate seaman, who during the night had fell and broken his arm. I directed he should be received on board, surgical assistance afforded him and a ration supplied him. The Consul has stated to me that had application been made to the authorities, to have taken him into a hospital and retained him until he was so far recovered as to be proper to put him on board a ship, as the one to which he belongs is to sail in a few days, it would have cost probably over $100.00, a pledge for which he must have given before they would have received him. This seaman had but a small sum ($15.00) due him.

I thought this a case in point and not improper to bring to your notice.

J. Percival.

Port Mahon April 1st, 1839.
Respected Sir,
Having served in the Navy for the period of twelve Years, honorably and faithful, and finding myself becoming old and feeble, caused by Sickness, pains &c, To You my Commander I appeal to for my *'discharge.'* I have no other reasons for asking this favor, only I know full well that I am unfit for duty, and have an ardent wish to join my friends relatives once more, before my final exit from this life. . . .

I sincerely hope that You Sir will Grant my request, and by so doing You will oblige Your humble Servant.
William Hudson.
To Capt.
    Joseph Smith Esq.

Captain Smith, in forwarding this letter to the commodore, expresses the hope that the request of Hudson, a musician, will be granted, although he still has twelve months to serve. "His health is poor and his performance ordinary."

Dover    June [17] 1839
Honerble Comodore
  Hon Sir    I set down to write a fieu lines conserning my Husband, James Quimby who listed under your command and it is my priyer and desire, for you to discharge him and send him home, for I am in grate need of his assestenc an can not do with out unless I suffer  no one can tell  how much I suffer for the want of his assestence  my health is so that I am not able

to work but a little of my time and I hope Sir you will discharge him if I was able to work and if my health was good I should not expose my poverty to you for I have no one to help me in my distress I have no farther nor mother nor no one to help me and my child and Sir I hope you will sent him home as soon as poseble for I dont think I ever shall see him unless I see him soon if you are the man that you have bin represented to us you will discharge him; doutless you will, and if Sir you do this you will releive the distresst an ther may be a time when you will have your reward for the good act please to inform my Husband of this and abowt my health an so discharge him if it is in your power

   This from Clarisse Quimby wife of
    James Quimby of the United State Ship
              *Ohio*

      U. S. Ship *Ohio,* Mahon
       March 30th, 1840

Sir,

I have to report that George G. Shurtleff, a Seaman belonging to this ship, was found drowned in this harbor this morning. He was picked up by one of the *Cyane's* Boats, carried on board that ship, and afterwards removed to this. His body was examined by the surgeon, and no marks of violence were found upon it. He was on board at quarters at sunset, and was last seen by one of the Captains of the Forecastle between 7 and 8 o'clock. It is supposed that he was drowned in attempting to swim ashore. He will be interred this day at 4 o'clock, with appropriate services, at the usual burying ground.

Very respectfully<br>Your Obt. Servt.<br>Jos. Smith<br>Captain.

Como. Isaac Hull
Comr. in Chief of the U. S.
Naval Forces in the Medr.
Mahon.

Connecticut Milford, April 27th, 1840

Sir,

Though I once had the pleasure of an introduction to you at the house of Mr. E. Jacksons, of Middletown in this State, still the circumstance may not be recollected by you and probably I now am unknown to you, and unknown as I am I should not address you at this time but for the following reasons.

In the fall of 1836 my son Charles Carrington left home and from that time until a day or two past I have heard nothing direct from him, and of course you can judge in some measure what my feelings have been. A few days past his sister received a letter from him dated U. S. S. *Ohio,* Port Mahon, stating where he now is and his present employment. Well as I recollect hearing of your appointment to the *Ohio* and of her sailing, but then little thought my son was aboard of her, and it is now matter of consolation that you are her commander. Like other youths, Charles is often thoughtless and inconsiderate, and far from a father's eye and surrounded with many temptations, may need advice, counsel and admonition, and Sir, as I once heard Capt. Warrington say, that parents would often beg of him to look to their sons, permit me to ask of you the favor, as far as circumstances allow, to speak to Charles of the propriety and necessity of a manly and virtuous course of life. If, Sir, you will have the goodness to do this, your kindness will lay an anxious parent under lasting obligations to you and his prayers shall ascend to heaven for your happiness here as well as hereafter. Charles has had golden offers made to him, but he has preferred to wander about the world; on his return it is my earnest desire he would visit his home and enter upon some business for life. Believing that you will oblige me in my request, I am Sir

Respectfully your<br>
Obt. Svt.

Isaac Hull, Esq.            Abijah Carrington.
Commander of U. S. S. *Ohio*.

United States Consulate<br>
Marseilles, May 4th, 1841.

Commodore Isaac Hull,
Commanding U. S. Naval
Forces in the Mediterranean.
Sir,

There are six or seven seamen of the U. States here on my hands whom I wish to send home. They evince no disposition to get employment and seem to rely on my supporting them in idleness. I paid the passage of one of them to Capt. Swan, of the Barque *Elizabeth*, but he remained on shore and permitted the vessel to sail without him. This morning I called at their boarding house and told them that your ship was going directly home, after touching at Mahon, and that it was their duty to repair at once on board and ask your permission to embark, offering to pay their expenses to Toulon on the Diligence. All, except Chas. Brown, were unwilling and Davis expressed his dissent pointedly. I then informed them that as they were living on the Government money and I was directed by law to send all such seamen home, I should employ the police to convey them on board your ship. Some of them still persisting in their refusal, I directed the police officers to take them in charge. These men are destroying their health, causing much trouble and vexation to me, and some expense to Government. Under these circumstances I feel it my duty to resort to strong measures to have them conveyed home and I have to ask you to receive them on board to that end. I may not have an opportunity to send them by a merchantman for many weeks. This request is official and if there is any responsibility it rests on me. I act under my sense of the law in the case. They are making debts without any means of paying and I am constantly being called on to pay for them.

With great Respect I have the honour to be, Sir,
yr. obt. servt.
D. C. Croxall
U. S. C.

Names of the Seamen referred to.
James Stepto
Henry Blair

John Mitchel
David Hazleton
John Gero
Chas. Brown
E. Davis

P. S. After the foregoing was written Capt. Winship of the *Carrier* came to my office and said that he had discharged two foreigners, and would take Mitchel and Davis on board his Brig to work their passage to N. York. One of the Colored men (Blair) has absconded and lies concealed. The others (three) now make no objection to go to Toulon, and I pray you to receive them.

     Yours with respect, etc.
        D. C. Croxall.


    U. S. Naval Hospital
     Mahon, May 17th, 1841.
Sir.

William Perry, Seaman, from the *Brandywine,* who died in this Hospital on the 22nd ulto. made a will a few days before his death, in which he bequeathed all his clothes to Marcus Kean, Seaman of the *Brandywine;* twenty dollars to James Gomila, Steward of the Hospital, and the balance of pay due him to be divided equally between Andrew Nicholls, Seaman, and John Collins, Seaman, now aboard the *Ohio,* as a mark of gratitude for their kindness and attentions to him while in the Hospital.

I will be pleased to receive your orders in relation to the will and effects of deceased.

I have the honor to be
>Very respectfully
>>Your obedt. Servt.
>>>James M. Greene
>>>>Surgeon.

Commodore Isaac Hull
>Commander in Chief
>>of U. S. Naval Forces
>>>Mediterranean.

>>>New York 26th July 1841

Dear Sir,

I receive from Government a Pension of Three Dollars per month (for injuries received, while with you in the U. S. Ship *Ohio* in the service of the United States, as Capt. of the Hole) which will not in my advanced age support me.

The Collector of New York has promised me a situation in the Custom House as Night Watch at $45 Dollars per month, providing you will give a certificate as to my character, etc.

If you will be so kind as to grant this request and send it to me, to the Care of S. Spencer, Pension Office, No. 16 Wall Street, New York,
>>You will oblige
>>>Your most Humble Servt.
>>>>J. Matzen.

Com. Isaac Hull
>Boston.

U. S. Ship *Columbus,*
Boston, July 28, 1841.

I hereby certify that John Metzer [Matzen] was a Petty Officer (Captain of the Hold) in the U. S. Ship *Ohio* under my command for a year or more in 1838–9, and that he was then a sober, steady and industrious man and was discharged at his own request on account of a disability received in discharge of his duty.

Jos. Smith, Captain.

[Certificate]

Jeremiah Buell has served faithfully on board the U. S. Ship *Ohio* as Gunner's Mate during the entire cruise in the Mediterranean. He has served he says on board of different Vessels of War since the year 1812, viz; he was on board the Frigate *Essex* with Commo. Porter, on the Lakes with Commo. Chauncey; afterwards on board the *Independence,* the *Washington,* the *Guerrière* and the *Potomac,* he has also served at the Navy Yard, Charlestown, and is still anxious to be employed in the Naval Service where he can be useful. The undersigned knows him to be honest, capable and deserving and therefore recommends him to the Commanding Officers of Navy Yards, Stations and Vessels of War and trusts they will extend to him that care which a faithful and diligent seaman deserves.

U. S. Ship *Ohio*
Harbour of Boston
July 27, 1841
Isaac Hull.

Rec'g Ship *Columbus*
Boston July 28, '41.

Sir,

I respectfully beg leave to state that in September of the year 1821, while under your command at the Boston Navy Yard I received an injury to my leg while stowing Mast Timber in the ship house now occupied by the *Vermont* and that the injury being repeated several times during the time I was attached to the Yard, I have not since been free from inconvenience and sickness at various periods.

Whilst attached to the Sloop *Erie* in 1838 and 9 on the W. I. Station I was for several months on the Sick List unfit for duty and finally was sent home on a Sick Ticket. Having been thirty years in the service and endeavoured to perform my duty faithfully and diligently as far as I have been able, I would respectfully request if consistent with your views and knowledge of my case, that you would be pleased to give me a certificate whereby I could procure a Pension for the above reason.

  I have the honor to be, very respectfully
    Your Ob't Serv't
      John Morris Boatswain.

Captain Isaac Hull
U. S. Navy
Boston.

      Boston July 29th, 1841

Sir,

I have received your letter of yesterday asking of me a certificate of injuries received by you, as you say in

September of the year 1821 whilst under my command at the Boston Navy Yard, and enclosing copy of a representation of your case by Surgeon John C. Spencer of the U. S. Navy.

The injuries which are the cause of the disabilities represented by Dr. Spencer I regret to say I have no record or recollection of, so much time having elapsed it would be difficult if not impossible to recollect the circumstances. It may be, however, that the Journal kept in the Yard at that time may shew the facts.

I should be glad to serve you, but in this matter I have no power.

Very Respectfully<br>I am Yr. Obt. St.<br>Isaac Hull

Boatswain John Morris
U. S. Ship *Columbus*
Boston Harbour.

## Chapter XIV
## HEALTH AND SANITATION

THE health of the squadron was naturally a most important consideration and was attended to with all the care and skill available at a time which, with the progress of medical science, now seems remote. The fleet surgeon was Dr. Benaiah Ticknor, who made periodical and special reports to Commodore Hull. He had three assistant surgeons with him on the *Ohio* and of course the other ships had a full complement of medical officers.

On January 17, 1839, Surgeon Ticknor reported that there were five or six incurables on board the *Ohio* and that this number would probably increase to twenty. They should be sent home or be provided for on shore. He strongly recommended that a hospital for the treatment of such cases should be established at Mahon. This recommendation was adopted. A building in the town was taken, cleaned and fitted up as a hospital and put in charge of Surgeon Jonathan M. Foltz. Advantage was taken of such opportunities as offered to send chronic cases back to the United States, and vessels were sometimes chartered for this purpose. Officers returning home, for the same or other reason, accompanied them. The hospital was closed shortly before the *Ohio* took her final departure from Mahon.

Surgeon Ticknor made his first quarterly report March 1, 1839. Since December 1 there had been 426 men on the sick list of the *Ohio*, a daily average of fifty-four.

There had been two deaths, one due to a fall from aloft and one to congestion of the lungs. One of the assistant surgeons, Dr. Edward H. Van Wyck, had been stricken with apoplexy and two lieutenants had suffered injuries. Catarrh, congestion of the lungs, and rheumatism especially prevailed. "Much the greater part of the crew of this ship have ceased to draw their allowance of spirits, the effects of which cannot be otherwise than beneficial."

When a ship entered port it was necessary to obtain pratique, or permission to communicate with the shore. If she had come from an infected port she must first, of course, be detained in quarantine. This was the case with the *Ohio* in September, 1839. On the 27th, at the end of her quarantine, she "sent a boat with the Surgeon to the Pratique Office; at 9.30 the boat returned, having obtained pratique for the Ship."

Tea was an important article on board ship. The Navy Department, April 25, 1840, ordered that tea and sugar were to be classed as comforts, and no longer as luxuries, and were to be sold at a profit of twenty-five per cent. Tobacco was to be regarded as a luxury and sold at a profit of fifty per cent. Captain Lavallette suggested that tea should be issued as a partial substitute for grog.

The provisions and other stores on board the ships and in the naval store house at Mahon were inspected from time to time by boards of survey appointed by the commodore. It always happened that some articles of food were found to be spoiled and unfit for use, and were condemned. The following entries in the log-book of the *Ohio* are examples. October 22, 1839: "A survey was held on 36,422 lbs. Bread, all of which was filled with various insects and was musty. The dust and small pieces, amounting to 3,612 lbs., was thrown overboard, the remainder condemned as unfit for use and subject to the disposal of the Commander in Chief." November 18, 1840: "We have held a strict and careful survey on Nine hundred and forty five pounds of fresh Beef, we find it putrid and unfit to be served out to the crew." January 19, 1841: "We have carefully surveyed a Quantity of Salt Beef, Flour, Cheese, Rice, and Raisins and found the whole, Viz. Two hundred and twenty two pounds of Cheese, ninety-eight pounds of Flour, two barrels of Rice, two barrels of Salt Beef, and two boxes of Raisins unfit for use; we condemned the same and had them thrown overboard."

[Charter Party]

Know all men by these presents, that we Obadiah Rich, Consul of the United States, on the one part, in behalf of the Navy Department of the United States, and Samuel Allen, master of the brig *Sarah and Esther,* on the other, have this day agreed as follows, viz. that the said Samuel Allen shall furnish good and sufficient accommodation for three officers and seventeen or more seamen belonging to the U. S. Navy and take them from this port of Mahon to Boston in the United States in the aforesaid Brig *Sarah and Esther,* and that he shall furnish them with a sufficient quantity of fuel for cooking and fresh water for the time the passage may last. And the said Obadiah Rich agrees to pay to said Samuel Allen the sum of fifty dollars for each of the officers, and twenty five dollars for each of the seamen, and to furnish the Navy ration or its equivalent, for each person.

In witness whereof we have signed the present in Mahon this 8th day of June 1839.

      O. Rich, Consul
      Samuel Allen, Master.

    U. S. S. *Ohio*
Sir.   At Sea September 1st 1839

. . . . . . . . . . . .

Among our men we have a few bad ones and one or two acts of flagrant insubordination have occurred. Strong suspicions rest upon one man, who is said to have been a disorganizer in other Ships; and I would recommend that he, and all such as may be found out, be discharged.

Great pains have been taken to preserve health on board and to keep the men from unnecessary exposure, and I believe, so far, there has never been a Ship in this Sea whose crew has been more healthy during the hot season (and it has been extremely so) than the crew of this Ship. We have but one man on board (excepting two we have taken from the *Cyane*) unable to do his duty at quarters if necessary. The crew improve in appearance and, during the latter part of the month, they have improved in their movements and conduct.

I regret to be obliged to state that much fault has been found with some parts of the ration by the men, and justly too. The bread being, I believe, two years old before it was taken on board at Mahon, and originally made from inferior material, does not stand the heat of summer on board Ship; it has become wormy and somewhat musty. The flour also has become musty, and the rice is so wormy that some of the men will not use it. The oldest beef is getting black, hard, and dry; but little of it has yet been condemned, but I fear that nearly all the bread and rice, and some of the beef will be condemned.

. . . . . . . . . .

Very Respectfully<br>Yr. Obt. Sv.

| | |
|---|---|
| Como. Isaac Hull | Jos. Smith |
| Comr. in Chief of the U. S. Naval Force in the Medr. | Capt. U. S. S. *Ohio* Present. |

Translation

Consulate of the United States for the Balearic Islands.

The United States Ship of War *Ohio*, having arrived at this port from a cruise in the Levant and having been twenty days at sea since she left Smyrna, from which place she brings certificates of health, and not having lost a man nor had any sickness on board, altho her crew consists of near a thousand men, since she left this place, and moreover being provided with able medical officers and every necessary means for preventing any infection, it does not appear that she is in the same case as a merchant vessel with goods on board susceptible of contagion; for which motives I trust that your Excy. will direct that this ship be subject to the shortest quarantine possible, it being of great importance that she should get ready for another cruise before the bad weather commences.

God preserve Y[our] E[xcellency] many years.

Mahon Sept. 12, 1839.<br>O. Rich, Consul

For Don Manuel Lebron
  Governor and President of the board of health in Mahon

Superior board of health of Minorca.

This board having attentively examined, in a session of this day, your official letter of the 12th has directed me to say that they deeply regret their want of power to alter the sanitary regulations of their institution, in virtue of which they are obliged to place the ship *Ohio* under twenty days quarantine, being the shortest period corresponding to vessels coming from Smyrna. Notwithstanding you will please to assure the Commodore that he will always find this corporation desirous of obliging him in whatever depends on their powers and faculties.

God preserve you many years.
To the Consul of the United States

Mahon Sept. 16, 1839
Francis Sequi, In absence of the President

U. S. Ship *Ohio*
Port Mahon Nov. 30th, 1840

Gentlemen

As there are many perishable articles belonging to the Government of the United States in store at Mahon, under the charge of O. Rich Esq. U. S. Consul and Naval Store Keeper, I have to require and direct that you carefully examine and survey every description of Provisions, Slop Clothing, Stores and other articles so belonging to the Government of the United States and in store at Mahon, commencing with the provisions and proceeding with the slops, etc. etc.

## HEALTH AND SANITATION

You will report to me in writing the result of your proceedings; of the Provisions you will be pleased to state the quality and condition, brands etc. You will also see that the salted provisions are properly preserved, barrels in good order and filled with strong pickle; that the Slops are in good and proper packages (which are not to be opened, but the marks and numbers and descriptions of clothing to be noted) and all other Stores and Articles in good, tight Barrels, Casks, Boxes and Packages.

You will be pleased to designate such articles as you find unfit for use and report separately on those which are good and fit for use and I desire that your report should embrace every article (shewing kind and quality) good and bad on hand at Mahon in charge of the Naval Store Keeper and belonging to the Government of the United States.

You will be pleased to call on the Naval Store Keeper at Mahon and show this order; and he is hereby requested to afford you all necessary facilities.

Such assistance as you may require will be furnished from the United States Ship *Ohio* on your application to Captain E. A. F. Lavallette and requisitions must be made in the usual form for such articles as you may require to carry out this order.

                Very respectfully
                I am, Gentlemen,

| | |
|---|---|
| Lieut. S. Mercer, | Yr. Obt. St. |
| U. S. Ship *Ohio* | Isaac Hull |
| Lieut. George Adams, | Commander in Chief of U. S. |
| U. S. N., Mahon | Naval Force in the Medr. |

Lieut. R. B. Hitchcock and
2nd Master Wm. D. Hurst.
   U. S. Ship *Ohio*.

U. S. Ship *Ohio*<br>
Mahon Feby 5th 1841

Sir

I have respectfully to inform you that the Squadron is entirely destitute of Tea and other stores required for the comfort and health of the Crews. A supply is deposited at Gibraltar with Mr. Sprague, and it was expected that the *Brandywine* on her passage from Lisbon, would have touched at that place and brought them up; but in consequence, as I am informed, of the very unfavorable state of the weather when she reached the Straits, she was compelled to pass through. In several instances on this station, when it was inconvenient to send a public vessel for supplies, a small Spanish vessel has been chartered with the consent of the Custom house authorities at this place, and sent to Gibraltar with one of our officers on board, and no duties have been exacted on her return. I therefore take the liberty to request that Purser Cooper and myself may be allowed to adopt similar measures, if the consent of the Custom house authorities can be procured, to obtain the supplies at Gibraltar.

I am very respectfully Sir<br>
Your very obt. servt.<br>
Wm. Sinclair

Capt. E. A. F. Lavallette                      Purser
Comg. U. S. Ship *Ohio*
Present.

## Chapter XV
## PORT MAHON

MAHON, on the island of Minorca, the best harbor in the Balearic Islands, was conveniently situated for the headquarters of the Mediterranean Station. It was well known to navy men, having been frequently visited by our frigates and other vessels during the Barbary Wars. The United States squadron spent two winters there — 1815 to 1817 — and later it became the regular headquarters of the station.

No doubt the squadron was very welcome and the Mahonese rejoiced when they saw the ships sailing into their harbor and thought of the money that the free-handed sailors would leave behind them. At the same time, with swarms of these sailors roaming about the streets, carousing and bent on enjoying their shore liberty, there was bound to be friction at times.

Mahon April 4, 1839.

Sir

I have this day received an official communication from the Acting Govr. of this place, Don Jose de Bejar, stating that in consequence of the frequent infraction of the law prohibiting racing or galloping through the streets and on the roads or walks in the neighborhood of this city, he has ordered the fine established by that law to be encreased to Five Ducats, and that whoever is found guilty will be ordered to dismount and pay the fine in the act, or otherwise be detained until complaint is made to the authority to whom they may be subject. The excesses which have led to this determination have been carried to the extreme of nearly trampling upon the late Govr. Brigadier Don Manuel Obregon, on the road to Georgetown; and as it has been remarked that the persons who most frequently commit the excesses belong to the American Ships in this port, he requests that I will communicate the circumstances to you, feeling assured that you will take the necessary measures to prevent his being under the necessity of having the penalty inflicted on any of the persons under your orders, who might also be made liable to a criminal process in case of any person being injured.

I have the honor to be, very respectfully

Your humb. servt.

O. Rich, Consul.

Isaac Hull Esq.
Comg. U. S. Forces
in the Mediterranean.

[Translation]

The Constitutional Alcaldes of the city of Mahon and its district, do hereby make known to the inhabitants of the same: that in consequence of the complaints made by the Consul of the U. S. by direction of the Commander in Chief of the Naval Forces of that Nation in this port, and in compliance with the directions of the Governor of this island, they have determined:

1st. That no person whatever, shall furnish the sailors or marines of the U. S. Squadron with any article whatever on credit, and whoever does so shall lose any right he may allege, as manifested by the aforesaid Consul by direction of the Comr. in Chief aforesaid.

2d. That no person shall purchase from the aforesaid individuals, nor take from them in payment for food or drink or for any other motives, any article of uniform or military clothing, or take the same in pawn, under the fine of two dollars.

3d. That any person in whose possession may be found any of the articles mentioned in the foregoing clause shall be prosecuted according to law.

And in order that the same may be known and nobody allege ignorance, the present is fixed in the customary places of this city.

Mahon Jan. 6, 1840

Signed  1st Alcalde    Bartolome Olivies [?]
        2nd    "       Juan German
        3d     "       Juan J. Sancho

[Translation]

Signor Commodore

My dear Sir

I have been informed that the Corvette is under orders to sail tomorrow, and I would wish to ask the favor of you, if her commission is not very urgent and important, that you would permit her to remain until Wednesday next, in order that her officers may assist at a Ball to be given by the Gentlemen of this place on Tuesday next, provided the service of the Government does not require her sailing before.

I trust that you will excuse this small liberty, assuring you that you may count upon me in anything in which I can be of service to you.

Very sincerely yours<br>Manl. Lebron.

Mahon Feb. 15, 1840

U. S. Frigate Brandywine<br>Port Mahon, Feby. 29, 1840

Sir,

A verbal report was made to me yesterday by the first Lieutenant of this Ship, of an outrageous indignity offered to her by a portion of the Crew of the *Ohio,* whilst on liberty ashore on that day. I have had his statement, as well as that of the Officer of the Deck reduced to writing, and now submit the original to you, confident in the expectation that you will take exemplary notice of the flagrant conduct alluded to, unprecedented as I believe it to be in our Navy.

I am aware that greater freedom of intercourse with the shore is extended to the crew of the *Ohio* than I have thought adviseable and useful, at this early stage of a cruise, to allow the men of the *Brandywine,* and that odious comparisons have originated therefrom, and that some restlessness manifested itself, in consequence, on the part of my crew, which, however, has been quieted. *One general liberty* has been allowed to the people here; and I contemplate giving another on some future day. In the meantime, the crew of the

*Ohio,* I am informed, go daily in Divisions on shore and remain for the night; which indulgence the *Brandywine* are carefully advised of and taunted with the irritating idea that they are less indulgently treated than the men of the *Ohio.*

I sincerely wish that undue distinction could be avoided and most deeply lament the occasion for bringing this subject to your notice, but my ship has been happy and in good discipline, heretofore, and I earnestly desire to keep her so.

I am, Sir, very respecty. your obt. servt.

W. C. Bolton

Como. Hull
Commander in Chief etc. etc.

     U. S. Frigate *Brandywine*
      Port Mahon, March 4th, 1840.

Sir;

I have the honor to acknowledge the receipt of your letter of the 3d instant, conveying to me a copy of the investigation entered into of the grounds of complaint made by me against some of the liberty men of the *Ohio,* and the result thereof. I cannot withhold the expression of my satisfaction at the prompt official notice taken of the affair, and am pleased to find that any plausible supposition can be entertained, that the conduct alluded to may not have been intended as so offensive as it was regarded to be. The impression on the minds of the officers of the *Brandywine,* and also on some of the crew, was at the time such as I represented. Surely, nothing could be more galling and of greater pernicious tendency than the momentary belief, that a consort ship had been ironically and deridingly cheered at. If it is ever tolerated, that men-of-war's men have a right to cheer, without the direction or countenance of their officers, they will soon usurp the privilege of groaning or hissing also, as their ignorance or stupid prejudices may prompt.

When I alluded to Divisions going daily from the *Ohio recently* my belief was that *general* liberty had already been gotten through with, and that additional shore recreation or indulgence followed it, dictated by what consideration I could not tell. It is certainly true that the longer period which the *Ohio* has been in commission warrants greater latitude, because the people are supposed to have money due them, and their merits ought to be fully understood by the officers. The reverse is the case in the *Brandywine,* and it is almost impossible to bring such consideration and distinctions satisfactorily to the comprehension of reckless sailors, especially if we suppose for a moment that a spirit of discontent is latent.

I certainly understood Lieut. Kelly to convey to me the idea that the *Ohio's* had had the accustomed *general* liberty, and the *Divisional* liberty, spoken of, was *extra* and *gratuitous.* Such was, I believe, his understanding from Lieut. Pendergrast, when these two gentlemen spoke together on the subject.

I have studiously abstained from making any partial difference among our crew and knowing your wishes, before I engaged Musicians having families here, I was careful to place them on the footing with the men brought from home. I do not now regret the incident having occurred, as the quickened feeling and high displeasure which you have, in so marked a manner, shewn on the occasion, cannot fail of being most salutory.

I have the honor to be, Sir,<br>
Very respectfully<br>
Your obt. Servt.

Como. Isaac Hull      W. C. Bolton, Captain.
Commander in Chief of the U. S. Naval
Force in the Mediterranean.

U. S. Ship <i>Ohio</i> Pt. Mahon<br>
January 7th 1841

Sir

I have the painful duty to report to you that on the evening of the 6th inst, about six oclock, Henry Dunn, a landsman belonging to this Ship, being landed at the usual landing place of the Ship Boats, he was followed by a person in the garb of a soldier, and it is alledged that he was assaulted by the soldier who plunged a knife or other sharp weapon into his back which is said to have penetrated his lungs and endangered the life of the said Henry Dunn; he was conveyed to a Hotel and every surgical and other aid rendered him.

I am very Respectfully<br>
Your Obedt. Servt.<br>
E. A. F. Lavallette<br>
Captain.

Commd. Isaac Hull
Commander in Chief U. S. Naval Force
in the Mediterranean.

Translation

On the evening of the 6th instant at about 7 o'clock, I received a verbal communication from the Acting Consul of your nation of the atrocious deed committed on the person of the seaman of the Ship *Ohio* Henry Dunn, and agreeable to the information which the aforesaid person gave me I ordered to appear instantly before me the Commandante of Marine and the Judge of 1st Instance of this district whom I directed to take the necessary measures, the Judge of 1st Instance to whom it corresponds to take the preliminary steps has not ceased in his examinations to discover the agressor, who will suffer the punishment established by the laws of the nation either Military or Civil, assuring you that not only by myself but by the Judge, every measure will be taken to discover the criminal, as it is due not only to the good administration of justice but also to the preservation of social order. With which I have the honor of answering your communication of the 8th inst. which I received yesterday. God preserve you many years.

Mahon 10th of January 1841.<br>
The Governor<br>
Manl. Lebron

The Commodore, Commanding in Chief the United States Squadron in the Mediterranean.

U. S. Ship *Ohio*,<br>
Port Mahon Jan. 11th, 1841

Sir,

I have received a communication from His Excellency the Governor of Mahon in which he says:

"An Officer of justice has given me notice that some Officers and Midshipmen belonging to the Squadron under your command are in the habit of coming on shore with Pistols, Sword canes and other weapons, the use of which is prohibited in this Country, not only to foreigners but to citizens, the law imposing severe punishment to those who use them and are found with them in their possession, without any consideration to the most privileged persons."

In consequence of which and to carry out the Instructions of the Navy Department, viz., to prevent all persons under my command from violations of the laws in my intercourse with foreign ports, I deem it proper to issue the following general order.

### General Order

All Officers and others under your command when visiting the shore, are hereby expressly prohibited from wearing upon or about their persons any other *arms* than those particularized in the "Naval General Order" of the Navy Department in relation to "Navy Uniform" without the order or permission of the Senior Officer present.

   Very respectfully
    I am, Sirs,
     Yr. Obt. St.
      Isaac Hull,
       Comdr. in Chief of the U. S.
To Officers Commanding   Naval Force in the Medr.
Vessels of the U. S. Squadron
in the Mediterranean.

Consulate of the United States of
America for the Balearic Islands
Mahon, 20 Jany. 1841.

Sir

I have the honor to acknowledge the receipt of your communication with the date of today enclosing an official letter from his Excy. the Governor with a complaint against me.

To which I beg leave to reply, that being requested by the first lieutenant of the *Ohio*, I gave to a police officer a list containing the names of four seamen of said ship who had overstaid their liberty and requested him to apprehend them, offering him the customary reward. When an officer of the *Ohio* went to the prison to take them on board ship he found two of them were not on the list which I had given to the police officer, but had been imprisoned before their term of liberty had expired and without any cause whatever. I then requested a policeman to give orders for the liberation of those two, but finding afterwards he had not done so I sent to the Alcalde requesting he would order their release and I received for answer that I had better arrange the matter with the prison keeper by satisfying his demands, after hearing which I presented myself before the Alcalde to learn how it was that I was to pay for the liberation of two men who had been imprisoned without any cause whatever, the amount of which interview was that the Alcalde concluded that the two men should be liberated on my paying the prison keeper half a dollar for their maintenance whilst in prison, to which I acceded and repaired to the prison to pay it and procure their release; on my offering the prison keeper the half dollar and telling him it was the Alcalde's decision that he should release the two men on my paying that sum, he replied that he should not release them for less than a dollar and a half; after expressing my astonishment at his want of respect to the Alcalde's orders, I concluded, in order to avoid further annoyance, to pay him his demand, which I sent to him a few minutes afterwards. These are the circumstances that took place; as to my threatening with a stick or maltreating with words the keeper of the prison, I have not the least doubt that any of the persons who happened to be present at the time will vouch for the contrary, as it is not my custom to treat with disrespect any person, whether holding a situation under government or not. I beg leave very respectfully to state that the imprisonment of these two men, without any cause whatever, was an act of most unjust and wanton nature, and the consequences to the perpetrators of it would be of a most serious nature if a formal notice were taken of it.

    I have the honor to remain
      Sir, with great respect your
        most obt. servt.
          J. H. Rich

Commodore Isaac Hull       Acting Consul
Commanding United States Naval Forces
in the Mediterranean.

Consulate of the United States
of America for the Balearic Islands,
Mahon 27 Jany. 1841.

Sir

I beg leave to lay before you the following communication.

Very respy. your obt. servt.

Commodore Hull
Commanding U. S. Naval Forces
in the Mediterranean.

J. H. Rich
Acting U. S. Consul

---

Mahon 25 Jany 1841

Sir

On Sunday the 17th inst. as John Pearson, seaman of the Squadron of the United States, was descending the hill which leads down to the point, he took it into his head to walk on the parapet which lines the road, and losing his balance which he could hardly keep on level ground on account of his being considerably intoxicated, he fell on to the roof of the store which I own at the waterside No. 100, and destroyed part of it. This however was not all the damage done for a large party of seamen also Americans ascended to the roof for the purpose of rescuing their companion and broke almost all the tiles on it.

With this view and it not seeming just that I should suffer so great a loss, I have taken the liberty of addressing myself to you, hoping you communicate the present to whom it may be expedient.

Very respty. yr. obt. servt.

To the Consul of
the United States
of America.

Migl. Vicens y Andreu

[Endorsement: "House to be repaired"]

U. S. Ship *Ohio*

Sir,   Port Mahon   Feb. 13th, 1841

I hereto annex copy of a communication from the Acting Consul of the United States at this place, which embraces copy of a translation of an Official letter from His Excellency, The Governor of Mahon, giving notice that a regulation has been adopted "to insure the preservation of order in this City", by which "it is not allowed to have music about the streets at night without permission from one of the Alcaldes."

You will, therefore, be pleased to inform all under your command of the existence of this regulation and require strict compliance therewith.

    Very Respectfully
     I am, Sir
      Yr. Obt. St.
       Isaac Hull
    Commander in Chief of the U. S.
    Naval Force in the Mediterranean

To Officers Commanding
Vessels of the United States
Squadron in the Mediterranean.

     [Translation]

The Alcalde says to the Military Commandant that "an American sailor whose name written by himself he encloses, in company with others of his class, infringed openly yesterday morning the police laws of the country and thanks to the zeal of my subalterns that no blood was spilt. Not only this but they also entered the house of John Maurant, ill treated his son and carried off a new hat and I know not what other articles. It is impossible that the Republicans of North Amca. are not aware of the individual security so explicitly expressed in their Constitution, and they not only break but too often their fundamental laws but are wanting in all the social respect and consideration due to a people who is giving them so many proofs of their benevolence. The aforesaid sailor is a prisoner by my orders and from the verbal information I have taken condemned to pay to said Maurant 24 dollars. His companions could not be taken, but I trust that the Commodore who has given so many proofs of his inflexible justice, will take care to have them discovered and punished, to prevent any future offences. At the same time I would notice the impropriety of allowing so many men to land at one time, as with the few subalterns at my disposal I am unable to exercise that exquisite vigilance which I could wish."

The Military Commandant says to the Commodore, that he communicates to him the foregoing with a request that he will have the goodness to order the payment of the foregoing sum and take measures to have the men punished.

He also requests that the Commo. will allow in future but 80 men to land at a time, and moreover that as a battalion is to arrive today to be billeted in private houses, that during the time they are here, he will not allow any of his men to come on shore, and that he will inform him when they leave, which will probably be between Wednesday and Friday.

[Endorsed: Governor of Minorca, Complaint, 16 Mar. 1841.]

## Chapter XVI
## A RIOT IN THE THEATRE

To His Excellency
The Governor of Mahon.

I have the honor to place before Your Excellency a statement, made by Lieutenant Pendergrast, the first Lieutenant of the United States ship *Ohio* and Flag Ship of the United States Naval Force in the Mediterranean under my command; by which Y. E. will be informed that a complaint is made to the following effect viz., that the American Officers who attended the Theatre on the night of the 3d instant were maltreated and abused shamefully by a Guard of Soldiers, acting under the orders of a Spanish Functionary; the conduct of the Soldiers on that occasion towards the Americans is stated to have been of a most flagrant character and seems to call for a correction which will insure that protection and friendly treatment which the existing treaties between Spain and the United States extend to the Citizens of both Countries.

"The misunderstanding between the Citizens of Mahon and the Officers of the American Squadron is one which the Civil Laws of Mahon, it is presumed, are sufficient to correct, but the outrage complained of by the American Officers, committed by an armed band, at a place of public amusement, sanctioned by the authorities of Mahon, upon Officers of a foreign friendly Government, who had complied with the restrictions placed upon persons visiting the Theatre, by divesting themselves of their side-arms, is one which Y. E. cannot fail to see requires the intervention of the Authority of Y. E. to prevent in future.

I regret exceedingly the necessity of troubling Y. E. in a matter of this kind, but feel myself impelled by a strong sense of duty to my command and to my Country to lay this matter before Your Excellency.

With considerations of high respect<br>I have the honor to be<br>Y. E. Most Obt. Servt.

| | |
|---|---|
| U. S. Ship *Ohio* | Isaac Hull |
| Port Mahon | Comr. in Chief of the U. S. |
| March 6, 1840 | Naval Force in the Medr. |

[Translation]

Military Command of Minorca.

With deep regret I have made myself acquainted with the contents of your official letter of the 6th instant accompanied by a copy of the statement made to you by Lieut. Pendergrast, in which he complains of the bad treatment and shameful insults experienced by various American Officers from a Guard of Soldiers under the order of a Spanish Authority on the night of the 3d inst. at a Masquerade ball, which took place in the Theatre of this City, and that the Soldiers behaved towards the Americans in so notorious a manner, with other circumstances, that it is grievous to me to relate. As your communication is the first official notice I have had of this fact, I wrote immediately to the 3d Alcalde, who presided at the Theatre on that night, the Note

CAPT. ISAAC HULL.

No. 1. that he might inform me of the behaviour of the Commandant and Soldiers of the Guard which I had officially facilitated to him as an auxiliary to his authority. His answer, marked No. 2, justifies the good conduct of the armed force, and the good opinion I have, as well of the Officers as of the soldiers of the Garrison of this place. Under these circumstances you will perceive that there is no motive for further proceedings in a case in which I am officially informed that they have fulfilled their duty, but notwithstanding, if any of the Gentlemen under your orders will point out any military individual who has insulted him or given him offence, he shall be chastised with the utmost rigor of military law.

Now that I have the pain for the first time of having a complaint made from your authority to mine, I will enter into some details perhaps unknown to you, having for object a desire on my part to prove to you that I wish to preserve by all the means in my power, a good intelligence with the allies of my Government, ceeding even my rights as far as decorum will permit to secure it, and more particularly with you, whom I esteem for personal and military sympathies.

In all public diversions, whoever frequents them subjects himself to observe the rules of good order established by the authorities, and in such cases there are no privileged persons of any class or condition whatever, and particularly so in the case of Masquerades which only by special favour have been conceded to some towns and corporations for beneficent and local purposes; under these circumstances, whoever commits any disturbance in them is subject to whatever measures may be taken by the presiding authority to preserve order. It frequently happens, unfortunately, that the voice of the authority is unheard and its passive agents are disobeyed, in which case, to prevent greater evils, it is under the grievous necessity of employing an armed force, when it is well known that the persons most active in endeavoring to re-establish order and tranquility may suffer more than those who have been the cause of the disturbance, because in a large company when the confusion is complete, who can determine the person that commits or receives injury? If I myself had been present in my individual capacity, I should naturally have taken part in restoring tranquility, and should not have thought it strange to have received a blow from a soldier or from any other person, because in the heat of the moment it is not easy to foresee who may suffer. During the whole of the Carnival, it is well known to you as well as to me, that the public as well as private diversions have been infinite, and it is very certain that during that period there have been no complaints by any of your subordinates, nor that any of mine have received any offence from anyone, which certainly proves that the greatest harmony reigned among them, and that the affair in question was entirely unpremeditated. Particularly I have learned that there are Citizens who have been injured by blows, and I am certain that they do not know who injured them, nor if they injured others.

Not to molest your attention further, I shall conclude by saying that in my opinion the fact in question was caused by the imprudence of all the persons present and was momentaneous, and with respect to the manner of acting by the escort, I beg you to believe that it was in conformity with the directions of the presiding authority, which I beg you to have the goodness to make known to the Gentlemen Officers who complain and that they will lay aside any prejudice which they may have against them, assuring you that it would be a source of the deepest regret to me, if this incident should weaken the friendly relations between us, which I trust from your uprightness and the good sense of your subordinates will not be the case.

God preserve you many years.

Mahon March 8, 1840<br>Manl. Lebron.

U. S. Ship Ohio<br>Port Mahon March 9, 1840

Sir,

Your letter of the 5th inst. with a statement drawn up by Lieut. Pendergrast in relation to the disturbance which took place at the Theatre on the night of the 3d inst. were duly received and acted upon.

A representation was made by me to the Governor of Mahon, founded on that statement and calling upon the Governor to apply the necessary corrective, which has drawn from him the enclosed reply. It is a matter of exceeding mortification to me that a disturbance should have occurred in which American Officers were in any way interested or concerned, particularly as the scene and circumstances from all I can learn, will not bear examination.

The reply of the Governor is so conciliatory and to my mind so full and satisfactory that I desire you to say to Lieut. Pendergrast that further measures in this matter in my opinion are unnecessary, unless he can in accordance with the suggestion of the Governor point out some "military individual who has insulted him or given him offence"; to any such the Governor says "he shall be chastised with the utmost rigor of military law."

I take this occasion to require you to direct the Officers under your command to abstain from any violation of the peace or laws of Mahon and they should be reminded that they are not only amenable to the Laws of the Navy for offences committed on shore, but may be held to answer to the Laws of the Country in which offences may be committed.

You will require that all Officers under your command, when on shore, appear in their proper uniform, no change of dress by throwing aside their uniform and assuming plain clothes will be sanctioned.

     Very respectfully I am
      Sir
       Yr. Obt. Svt.

Captain Joseph Smith   Isaac Hull
Com'g. U. S. Ship *Ohio*   Comr. in Chief of the U. S.
Port Mahon.       Naval Force in the Medrn.

     U. S. Ship *Ohio,* Mar. 10th, 1840
      Harbour of Mahon.
Sir,

I have had handed me for perusal a letter from yourself to Captain Smith enclosing a communication to you from the Governor of Mahon, in relation to a disturbance which took place at the Theatre in that Town on the night of the 3d inst. in which Officers of the American Squadron, Citizens of Mahon, and a Guard of Soldiers were engaged.

The report of Lieut. Pendergrast, a witness, though not a participator on that occasion, which brought this matter officially under your notice, was necessarily of a general nature, and was written under the impression that some or all the Officers who had been forced into this disturbance and cruelly outraged, would have been examined in relation thereto. This not having been done and the Governor having justified the brutal and unheard of attack of the Soldiers, and your own communication showing that the information you have received has induced you to accept of the Governor's explanations, I am compelled by what is due to my own honor, and in justice to the younger Officers engaged on that occasion, to submit in some detail the circumstances of that painful occurrence.

Before doing this however, I beg leave respectfully to remove a very erroneous impression under which you seem to labour and which is embodied in the following paragraph of your letter of the 9th inst. You are pleased to say, "It is a matter of exceeding mortification to me, that a disturbance should have occurred in which American Officers were in any way interested or concerned, particularly as the scene and circumstances, from all I can learn, will not bear examination." There was nothing, Sir, in the "scene or circumstances" which will not challenge the severest scrutiny. It was a licensed public amusement, peculiar to the customs of the Country and resorted to on all occasions by the highest classes of society here and by all foreign Officers, from Commanders of Squadrons down. On the night in question nearly all the first people of Mahon were there assembled, including part of your own family, and that of the American Consul. It has moreover been fully within the knowledge of the Commanders of our Ships that the Officers, old and young, frequented these masquerades and no interdiction was ever laid. The "circumstances" too were highly honorable to the Officers, and however unpleasant, were in no manner to be avoided by them.

I had just descended from the boxes to the floor of the Ballroom, when I perceived a rush of many persons surrounding Pd. Midshipn. J. W. Read and Midshipn. Nicholson, of the *Brandywine*. On advancing, I found these two gentlemen in an altercation with a Citizen of Mahon; neither of them seemed much excited and upon enquiry, the former informed me that he had been severely jostled by a Mahonese, who was otherwise very offensive in his conduct. I earnestly requested him and Mr. Nicholson to give up the point at issue and to avoid in every way being drawn into a "row". Mr. Read replied, though he had been badly treated, if it was my wish, he would say nothing further, and he and Mr. Nicholson turned around and were following me out of the crowd, when the individual above alluded to, construing this into an act of fear, struck down Mr. Nicholson, and followed up his blows against Mr. Read and myself. This, Sir, was the very first onset. I saw the blow given and know the man who aimed it and it was the signal for a simultaneous attack on every Officer in the room, ten or eleven in number only, four or five of them young midshipmen, more than half of the Officers having previously left the Theatre, proving conclusively in my mind, that the affair was premeditated.

We were then assailed in every direction front and rear and were compelled to defend ourselves, unless we preferred being beaten down and killed like dogs. The Guard of some twenty Soldiers with muskets and fixed bayonets then came rushing in, and instead of resorting to the usual methods of quelling such a disturbance, by surrounding or driving the whole mass before them, they joined the original assailants, and while the few Officers were defending themselves in front against some hundred individuals, the Guard fell to work in the rear, and with their muskets clubbed them to the ground, in a manner which beggars all description.

Respectable witnesses who were in the boxes can be brought to prove that the Soldiers directed their whole efforts against the Officers, or if any of the Mahonese were struck at all, it was by accident. Pd. Midshipn. Read was struck several times over the head by the butt of a musket and severely bruised on the thighs by the same weapon. Pd. Midshipn. Chapman was severely beaten in the same manner over the back and hips. Midshipn. Nicholson was struck several times over the head with a butt end, and Midshipn. Dallas, on rising after being knocked down by a Mahonese, received a heavy blow on the back also from the butt end of a musket. Midn. Abbott after receiving a severe blow under the jaw from a Musket, has also a deep gash in the nose inflicted by a bayonet, which required sewing up by the Surgeon. On the other hand, while three men were belaboring at the same time young Midshipn. Fairfax, quite a lad, a soldier stood by and permitted them to proceed with their cowardly work, without the slightest interference. The above Officers belong to the *Brandywine*. From this ship Lieut. Gansevoort, Pd. Midshipmen Renshaw, Parker, LeRoy, and Midshipn. Townsend were repeatedly assailed by the Soldiers, with their muskets, over the head and elsewhere, with all the violence and force which they could give to their blows, most of them requiring surgical aid afterwards, particularly Messrs. Renshaw and Townsend, the latter while stooping to raise up Pd. Midshipn. Read, who had been brought down, was attacked by the Sergeant of the Guard, who drew his sabre, and laid bare his skull, and this was followed by a heavy blow from the butt of a musket, for which severe wounds he is still on the Surgeon's report.

Something has been said of the Officers not being in uniform; most of them, Sir, were in uniform and all were as distinctly known as if they had been. Having succeeded with the Officers who were around me, in dispersing the crowd that had first assailed us, I was passing to another part of the room, not engaged at the moment, when on getting in front of the Guard, one of them dealt me a heavy blow over the back, while a second charged upon me with his bayonet, which I contrived narrowly to evade. I had on my uniform coat, cap and gold band. It may be proper to remark also, that in no single instance was resistance offered to the military by a single Officer engaged. With regard to the attack of the Citizens, however outrageous and unprovoked, and though the leading individuals who incited it could be easily designated and should perhaps have been handed over to the Civil Authority, no complaint was made by the Officers; such events have occurred before and will probably happen again. But that an Alcalde should order in the Military and that he and the Officer commanding them should stand by and see the shamefully partial and brutal manner in which they made common cause with the original assailants, that is siding with hundreds of individuals against ten or eleven men and boys, strangers and Officers, who are required to deposit their arms before they enter — it is such an act as this, which in my humble opinion claims signal reparation. For it seems miraculous that several of the Officers did not lose their lives on that night, and it can only be attributed to the mercy of Providence and to the extraordinary efforts of self defence and mutual protection which were evinced on that occasion.

Under such circumstances, Sir, I trust that you will not think it strange, still less disrespectful, that myself and the Officers who were thus outraged, should be wholly disappointed with the letter of the Governor; and if it were not that you had seen it in so different a light I should not hesitate to say that it adds insult to injury. From what I have heard, I am under the conviction, if the conduct of the Alcalde were properly represented to the Political Chief of Majorca, that he would be stripped of his authority and imprisoned, and it is this individual, the greatest culprit in the whole transaction, to whom the Governor refers for the conduct of the Military — not paying a shadow of respect to the report of the Senior Lieutenant of this Squadron, an eye witness to the whole affair. On the report of this Alcalde, the Governor with perfect self complacency says, "His answer (the Alcalde's) justifies the good conduct of the armed force, and the good opinion I have as well of the Officers, as of the Soldiers of the Garrison of this place, under these circumstances you will perceive there is no motive for further proceedings in a case in which I am officially informed that they have *fulfilled their duty.*" After this warm commendation, on the part of the Governor, of the conduct of the Soldiers on the night of the 3d, it is difficult to understand what he means by saying "if any Gentleman under your command will point out any military individual who has been guilty of insulting him, or giving him offence, he shall be chastised with the utmost rigour of the Law". There was not a Soldier, who on that night did not at one time or other, strike an Officer by a blow specially directed at him, but does the Governor require the very Soldier who struck a particular blow to be designated, or does he allude to offences which may have been committed at other times and places, of which nothing has been said? If the Governor means the former, his sincerity may be tested by stating that the Sergeant of the Guard did on the night in question inflict on Mr. Townsend the most cold blooded violence which occurred in the whole affair.

I find, Sir, my situation a very embarrassing one. I

am earnestly desirous of doing nothing that could bear the semblance of the slightest disrespect to yourself, or of showing anything that might seem an improper spirit in not being satisfied with your decision in this case; still, the extent of the outrage of which I have drawn but a faint picture is so great, attended with circumstances so calculated to rouse my indignation as an Officer and a Citizen of the United States, that I think I owe it to myself, to the Junior Officers who were assaulted with me, and to the defenceless and unoffending youths whose blood was shed on the occasion, to ask for redress through all the appeals which official propriety authorizes me to make. If therefore Sir, you should consider no further steps necessary at this time, I would respectfully request that this report may be forwarded to the Navy Department, and I would at the same time thank you for permission to send a copy of the whole correspondence, to the Senators and Representatives in Congress from my state, as well as to those of the other Officers concerned that they may in conjunction with the Navy and State Department, seek through our Minister at Madrid, or any other channel which may be deemed best, that reparation which I humbly submit the case loudly calls for.

With the Greatest Respect<br>
I have the honor to be, Sir<br>
Yr. Obt. Servt.

Commodore Isaac Hull      S. F. DuPont. Lt.
Com'g U. S. Naval Force
in the Mediterranean.

P.S. Since writing the above, I am credibly informed, that in consequence of the remonstrance of a former Commander of this Station, on the occasion of some similar disturbance at the Theatre of Mahon, the Governor issued an order that under no circumstances should the Military be permitted to enter within the area of the House, even the Sentinel who usually stood within the door of the Pit was removed. The Soldiers were to remain in an adjoining apartment, and receive into custody any individuals, which might be handed over to them by the Civil Police.

Respect'y.<br>S. F. D. P.

U. S. Ship Ohio<br>Port Mahon March 13th, 1840

Sir,

Your communication dated March 10th was enclosed to me by Captain Smith this morning.

It is a matter of regret that a report so much in detail and particularizing the occurrences of the night of the 3d inst. at the Theatre in Mahon was not in the first instance submitted to me, as it contains points and particulars to which no allusion is made by Lieut. Pendergrast in his statement, and which statement was the only report and contained all the facts with which I could be supposed to possess any knowledge.

Whatever may have been the impressions under which that statement was drawn up, it is certain there is no wish or expression in it in relation to an enquiry or an examination to be made by me.

# A RIOT IN THE THEATRE

If the course pursued by the Governor and his reply are unsatisfactory to the Officers of the Squadron, it may in fact be owing to the fact that the grounds on which I was called to act were not so strong as they should have been, at all events your communication presents a much more aggravated case and shows conclusively that stronger grounds were at hand.

I shall immediately forward to the Governor of Mahon your communication to me, or such parts of it as may in my judgment be proper, with a demand that the conduct of the Alcalde and also of the Guard of Soldiers on the night of the 3d inst. at the Theatre in this place, be enquired into and that such steps be taken to punish those who were guilty of the outrages committed upon the Officers of the American Squadron and to prevent like occurrences in future, as are due to those Officers.

Very respectfully<br>
I am Sir,<br>
Yr. Obt. St.

Lieut. S. F. DuPont.      Isaac Hull
U. S. Ship *Ohio,* Port Mahon.    Comr. in Chief of the
                                    U. S. Naval Force in the
                                    Mediterranean.

To His Excellency,
The Governor of
Mahon
Sir,

In acknowledging the receipt of Y. E.'s letter of the 8th inst. in reply to mine of the 6th, I am again impelled to address Y. E. on the subject of the disturbance which occurred at the Theatre in Mahon on the night of the 3d inst., at which several Officers of the American Squadron under my command were severely outraged and most brutally beaten.

Your Excellency's letter of the 8th instant justifies the conduct of the Soldiers on the ground that the presiding Alcalde for that night, whose authority was sustained by the aid of Soldiers facilitated to him by Y. E., had reported favorably of their conduct; but if the Alcalde was obnoxious to the charge of having originated the movements of the Soldiers and implicit obedience to his orders had been promptly yielded, it could hardly be expected that his statement would be unfavourable to their conduct, and in the absence of all proof or admission on the part of the Alcalde as to his orders to the Soldiers, it can only be inferred that he was guilty of authorizing and even justifying the most brutal and uncalled for outrages committed upon the American Officers on that occasion.

I now enclose to Y. E. a more detailed account of what occurred on that night with which I have not been made acquainted until today, and I will add that rumours have reached me that the Alcalde, on the night referred to, did more than once order the Guard to fire upon the American Officers, and that the Officer of the Guard was not present to control its movements, when the blows were dealt exclusively upon the heads and bodies of the American Officers with the butt ends of muskets in the hands of the Soldiers.

The fact that no disturbance occurred until many of

the American Officers had left the Theatre and when their number had been very greatly reduced, that they were attacked by Citizens and Soldiers combined, carries the appearance of premeditated violence and a plan of cooperation to effect the object, and when Y. E. is apprised of the fact that three of the American Officers who were treated in this most brutal manner are youths of not more than fifteen or sixteen years of age who were not only attacked by Mahonese, but received severe blows from muskets in the hands of Soldiers, and that one of those youths was stabbed in the face with a bayonet by a Soldier, Y. E. can hardly doubt the combination nor that violence was premeditated.

These facts are of so glaring a character that I am forced to claim of Y. E. an examination into the conduct of the Alcalde and also that of the Guard on the night of the 3d inst. at the Theatre in Mahon and I trust Y. E. will take such steps to punish those who were guilty of the outrages committed upon the Officers of a friendly Government and to prevent like occurrences in future, as are due to those Officers.

With considerations of high respect I have
the honor to be
Y. E. Most Obt. St.

Isaac Hull
Comdr. in Chief of the U. S.
Naval Force in the Mediterranean.

U. S. Ship *Ohio*
Port Mahon
March 13, 1840

U. S. Ship *Ohio*
Port Mahon March 16, 1840

Sir,

I have received your letter of yesterday's date with statements by Lieut. Marbury and other Officers of the U. S. Frigate *Brandywine* in relation to the outrages committed upon the Officers of the Squadron under my command at the Theatre in Mahon on the night of the 3d inst. by Citizens of Mahon and a Guard of Soldiers combined.

A full, minute and particular account of what took place on that occasion, by two of the Lieutenants of the *Ohio* who were present, with a letter from me claiming an Examination into the conduct of the Alcalde and the Guard on the night of the 3d, are already before His Excellency the Governor of Mahon, in which I express a hope that such measures or steps will be taken to punish those who were guilty of the outrages committed upon the Officers of a friendly Government and to prevent like occurrences in future, as are due to those Officers; His Excellency has since informed me that all the communications and other papers relating to the subject have been committed to the "Assessor of War" for his opinion and that the result will be made known to me.

In this stage of the proceedings I do not think it adviseable for me to institute a formal enquiry, particularly as there exists no complaint against the Officers of the Squadron, but the papers which have been conveyed to me by your letter of the 15th inst. I shall enclose to His Excellency with a request that the same direction may be given to them as the other papers on the subject referred to have received; and should the result of the reference not produce a satisfactory decision it may then be necessary to take the affidavits of our Officers in furtherance of a more full representation to be laid before the Government of the United States.

Very Respectf'y.<br>
I have the honor to be<br>
Your obt. st.<br>
Isaac Hull

| | |
|---|---|
| Capt. Wm. C. Bolton | Commander in Chief of |
| Com'g U. S. Ship | the U. S. Naval Force in |
| *Brandywine,* Port Mahon. | the Medn. |

To His Excellency
The Governor
of Mahon
Sir,

I have the honor to acknowledge the receipt of Your Excellency's attentive note of the 15th inst. and unite with Y. E. in expressing deep regret that the occurrences of the night of the 3d inst. at the Theatre should induce the Officers under my command who have complained of the outrages committed upon them, to insist upon an examination into the affair; but Y. E. cannot doubt that the injuries received by those Officers and the impressions left upon their minds that an unauthorized act was committed, impels them to appeal in strong language for a redress of their grievances; and if in those appeals to their Commanding Officers they have dealt in more heat than the circumstances appear to warrant in the estimation of Y. E., I trust Y. E. will not for one moment suppose it has arisen from any want of respect or high consideration for Y. E.

Y. E. is pleased to apprise me that the whole affair with all the communications and other papers relating to the subject have been committed to the "Assessor of War" for his opinion, and that the result will be made known to me for such purposes as to me may appear proper; thanking Y. E. for this attention, I beg leave to lay before Y. E. some additional papers, in relation to the occurrences complained of by Officers belonging to the U. S. Frigate *Brandywine,* which did not reach me until this morning; and to request that they may receive the same direction.

With considerations of high respect
I have the honor to be

U. S. Ship *Ohio*      Y. E. most Obt. St.
Port Mahon      Isaac Hull
March 16, 1840.      Comr. in Chief of
                                    U. S. Naval Force in
                                    the Mediterranean.

[Translation]

Military Command
of Minorca.

Having passed under date of the 23d inst. to the Assessor of War of this Military Government the verbal process which I ordered to be formed by a decree of the 16th inst. for the purpose of investigating the conduct observed by the Commandant and Troops which formed the piquet at the public masked ball held at the

Theatre of this City in the night of the 3d instant, he tells me among other things under date of yesterday the following: "Proceedings may be stopped in the state in which they are found, as respects the Military Department, with the right however of following it up should there be motives for it, or if any individual produces a formal complaint against any military man, who may have exceeded his duty, remitting the affair to H. E. the Captain General of these Islands, for his superior determination, and passing legal testimony of the whole affair to the Judge of prior Instance of this place, for the purposes that may appear necessary; notwithstanding, your superior illustration will please to direct whatever may appear most to the purpose."

And agreeing in every respect with the foregoing opinion I communicate it to you for the use which you may think proper, the affair being ended on my part by remitting to the Judge of prior Instance legal testimony of what has been done, when I shall send the original to H. E. the Captain General of this Army and Province, for the purposes that may appear necessary, by which I shall have complied with what I offered you in my communication of the 15th of the present month.

God preserve you many years

Mahon 26 March 1840

Sor. Dn. Isaac Hull
Comr. in Chief of the Naval Forces
of the United States
in the Mediterranean
Ship *Ohio,* Port Mahon.

Manl. Lebron

[Report of the Attorney General — Translation]

The accidental Attorney General . . . thought indispensible to request the performance of various diligences in order to ascertain which had been the nature and origin of the occurrence. . . . The performed diligences have produced the desired result, for they have set to light if not the whole of the facts occurred, at least those sufficient to form a right and impartial judgment of the occurrence and of the complaints produced by the American officers.

It appears that the occurrence was the following: a verbal dispute took place between the Midshipmen James W. Read and Sommervil [Somerville] Nicholson and a Countryman; from the words they came to hands, and from particular that at the beginning the quarrel was, it became more general by having taken a part in it other officers that were in the Ball-room and also other Countrymen. Which was the origin of such a dispute? Who was the agressor? It is unknown and it would not be possible to ascertain it. The Americans say that were the Countrymen, and one of them, Mr. Dupont appoints Dr. Benito Mercadal as being him who sent the first blow. This Gent. in his deposition says that before his sending any blow, he had already received two from two different American officers. Dr. Juan Alberty, who is another of those appointed by Mr. Dupont, also says that the Americans disguised were insulting, and that one of them disguised in a devils dress hurt him with its tail, but prudence kept him silent, and finally that when he saw some Americans had taken hold of Dr. Benito Mercadal and were fighting with him, he came near in order to separate them, and received a blow with the shut fist of an American. On the other hand, it appears that the whole was the affair of a moment and that at the very act of its taking place such a confusion was promoted in the Ballroom that prevented those who were mere expectators from seeing, either who had occasioned the disturbance nor those who had taken a part in it; but if it has not been possible to ascertain the origin, it truly results a fact which makes that unnecessary. All the witnesses received, both American and Countrymen of those who took a part in the dispute and of those who were mere expectators, all of them, excepting Miguel Parpal who, says that an American Lieut. drew out a small sword and attacked him with it, a saying which is not credible because before entering the Ballroom, all persons are obliged to leave their arms out, all agree in that none of the disputants did carry any stick or arms of any description; that the fight was carried over with fist blows, without having had considerable transcendency to any of them. Not having intervened any sort of arms nor having been there any effusion of blood, the occurrence does not present any gravity, and is one of those that frequently happen in such festivities, and to which commonly gives rise a misunderstanding, an involuntary action where none can think himself offended because both assailants and assaulted are somewhat guilty. Under which circumstances and that no formal complaint against any determined person has been presented, the Attorney General thinks that all further official investigation is to be suspended.

But, if during the dispute between Americans and Countrymen did not occur any act which had any transcendency of consideration to any one of those who took a part in it, it was not such the case when the soldiers guard obeying the orders of the Alcalde who presided at the Ball cleared away the room. It was from those soldiers that the American officers received the blows, contusions and wounds, and it is against them and against the Alcalde 3d under whose orders they were that the Americans make their bitter complaints; they say that the Alcalde ordered the attack and yet the Commodore in his official letter manifests to have heard some rumors that the Alcalde more than once ordered to fire against the Americans, that the guard directed itself only against them, avoiding the Countrymen, and that without any hostile act from the part of the Americans, the guard gave them repeated blows with the butt-ends of their muskets in the most violent and brutal manner. Having also been committed to writing the investigations on these affairs, here is the result they have produced. As regards the order to fire, it was not heard either by the Lieut. commanding the guard nor by any of the soldiers, to whom it aught to have been addressed; from all the rest who have given their depositions in this proceedings only Mr. Wm. A. Parker manifests to have heard it, but his saying deserves little faith for his being singular, and because he himself acknowledges that he does not speak the Spanish for which reason it would not be surprising that he misunderstood the expression more particularly amidst the confusion and bustle consequent to such disturbance, find-

## A RIOT IN THE THEATRE

ing himself at the centre of the room and at such a distance of the Presidence Box from which it was not easy for him to hear distinctly the words pronounced by such President.

As regards the dispositions taken by the Alcalde to reestablish order, he himself . . . says that they were the following: Observing the disturbance and seeing that his cries were disobeyed, he ordered the commander of the soldiers guard that was there for the purpose of assisting him in case of need, to clear away the room; that this disposition produced a good effect, for the only presence of the soldiers was sufficient to reestablish order, but that scarcely the troops had left the room when the disturbance was renewed; that being then afraid that what in the beginning was but little or nothing, might by degrees produce disagreeable consequences, he repeated again his order to the Commander of the troops, to clear away the room, and that as soon as this was done he ordered the cessation of the Ball. This report of the Alcalde is totally consistent with the deposition of the Sub-Lieut. D. Salvador Nebot, who was the Commander of said guard, and with the result of the proceedings. These dispositions, in the Attorney's General's mind are not censurable. The Alcalde presiding the festivity had the charge of maintaining order in it, finding himself unexpectedly with a fight not between two or three persons, but between a considerable number of them, he had ground to be afraid of the fatal consequences that might result, if he did not put an immediate end to such a large circle: to obtain this with the only two police officers that he had under him, was impossible, as they were not respected; he had no other means but to have recourse to the armed force and have the room cleared away. . . . But if in its execution some excess was committed by the individuals of the guard, if they did make use of more violent means than it was necessary, the Alcalde is not to be answerable for it, because in that very moment the soldiers were no more under his immediate orders, but under those of the officer who commanded them, nor can you, Sir, interfere in the investigations of such excesses because the persons supposed to be the authors of them are not under your jurisdiction. Notwithstanding, the Attorney General can do no less than to manifest regarding the conduct observed by the soldiers of the guard, that one of the principal motives of the American officers complaint is removed: these suppose that the soldiers addressed themselves against them exclusively, carefully avoiding the Countrymen. All the contrary results from the proceedings. Miguel Parpal, D. Juan Alberty y Nidal, and Francisco Calle, all of them Countrymen, declare to have received blows with the butt-ends of the muskets from the soldiers. . . . Witnesses of the fact assure . . . that the soldiers sent their blows indistinctly against all the combatants. . . .

The Attorney General to conclude says: that not having intervened any sort of arms, nor having been any effusion of blood in the quarrel between the Americans and the Countrymen, the occurrence does not present any gravity, and consequently, is not proper that any further investigations on it should be continued whilst no formal complaint against some determined person is not presented; that the dispositions taken by the Alcalde in order to put an end to it were indispensable and right, and finally, that the excesses of which the American Officers complain of, having at all events been committed by the soldiers who cleared away the room, you cannot proceed against said individuals, they being under another jurisdiction, before which the American officers have the right to present their formal complaints as it does correspond.

For which the Attorney General requests the suspension of these proceedings, previously consulting the same with His Excellency the Audiencia terriotorial; notwithstanding, you will resolve what you will think more proper.   Orfila

Mahon 3rd July 1840

Verdict of the Court of 1st Instance of Mahon
[Translation]

Mahon 7th July 1840. Having considered the proceedings made in consequence of the testimony passed to this Court by His Excellency the Governor of this Island relative to the disturbances which took place at the Masquerade ball on the last night of Carnival of the present year, disturbances of which the Commander in Chief and several Officers of the United States Squadron, then anchored in this harbor, complained of, alleging that their Countrymen had been insulted by the Mahonese and that the measures taken by the Alcalde, President of the ball, and the conduct of the Soldiers to re-establish order were all addressed against the former, who suffered a most brutal and violent attack; having also considered what the Attorney General has represented and the reasons produced by him in his decree, Doctor Don Antonio Ballester, Judge of the 1st Instance of this District, pronounces and declares that, There is no ground to proceed criminally against the aforesaid Alcalde, Don Juan Jose Sancho, on account of his behaviour on that night; and that it is not the province of this Court to investigate that of the Soldiers, particularly as the same has been the object of a formal judicial suit before the competent authorities; and lastly, that the proceedings do not produce sufficient ground to proceed officially against any determinate person. A copy of this resolution to be sent to His Excellency the aforesaid Governor requesting him, at the same time, to transmit the same to the Commander in Chief of the United States Naval Forces, but beforehand the same is to be consulted in the Superior Court, to which these original and entire proceedings are to be sent. Thus it is signed by the Judge, of which I testify.

Antonio Ballester

Signed before me Migl. Vicens y Andreu.


[Opinion of the Captain General — Translation]
Military Command
of Minorca.

His Excellency the Captain General of this Province under date of April 24th wrote to me as follows:

## A RIOT IN THE THEATRE

"I have heard the Auditor of War of this Military Government on the result of the verbal process remitted by you on the 9th inst. formed for the purpose of ascertaining whether the Guard at the Theatre of Mahon on the 3d of March last committed an excess, when by invitation of the Presiding Authority they entered the Ballroom to quiet a disorder which had taken place in it and to clear the room; and being of opinion that there is no motive for proceeding against the individuals composing the aforesaid Guard and consequently that proceedings should be stopped as proposed by the Military Assessor of Mahon, approving of this opinion I return you the verbal process to be archived, so long as there appear no proper motives for continuing it, and as the disagreeable motive that occasioned it may produce complaints, perhaps exaggerated from individuals of a friendly Nation, I have communicated to H. M. Government this incident and the result of the verbal process and I doubt not that with your well known zeal you will take care to prevent any disputes between the Troops of the Garrison and the individuals of the American Squadron, without neglecting the preservation of public order, the first obligation of the authorities."

The which I have the honor to communicate to you for your information and use, and in answer to your letter of March 28th in which you so requested me to do.

God preserve you many years

Mahon July 15, 1840

Manl. Lebron.

[Translation]

Military Command
of Minorca.

The Judge of 1st Instance of this District communicated to me on the 28th of September last that which follows:

"I have the honor of transmitting to Y. E. the subjoined testimony of the measures devolved in the suit formed in consequence of the insults and maltreatment which some Officers of the U. S. Squadron stationed in the Mediterranean said they had suffered at the public masquerade ball which took place in this City on the 3d of March last, by which Y. E. will perceive there was not sufficient grounds for proceeding officially against any person in particular.

"Therefore, this affair is considered superseded as long as no particular complaint is produced which may give room for ulterior proceedings. I lay this before Y. E. that you may make it known to the Commodore of that Squadron, trusting Y. E. will acknowledge its receipt."

Which I have the honor of transmitting with a copy of the testimony above mentioned, for your information and purposes which you may think fit.

    God preserve you many years
      Mahon 26th November 1840
          Manl. Lebron.

The Commander in Chief
of the U. S. Squadron
in the Mediterranean.

# A RIOT IN THE THEATRE

To His Excellency,
The Governor of Mahon.

The undersigned Commander in Chief of the United States Naval Force in the Mediterranean, has the honor to acknowledge the receipt of Your Excellency's Official letter of the 26th ultimo, conveying to him the opinion of the "Judge of first Instance of this District" in the case of several Officers of the United States Squadron who complained of outrages and insults inflicted upon them by a Guard of Soldiers and Citizens of Mahon combined, at a Masquerade ball, which took place in this City on the 3d of March last, by which it appears, "there are no sufficient grounds for proceeding against any person in particular".

The undersigned has also the honor to acknowledge the receipt of a Copy of the Verdict of the Court of first Instance of Mahon and the confirmation of that Verdict by the Superior Court at Palma in the same case. For which attentions the undersigned begs leave to present his thanks.

The undersigned takes occasion to say that the Copy of the testimony in the suit intended for his information and use, did not accompany Y. E.'s Official letter of the 26th ultimo.

    With sentiments of high consideration
     and respect
   I have the honor to be
    Your Excellency's

U. S. Ship *Ohio*  Mo. Obt. Servt.
Port Mahon    Isaac Hull
December 2nd, 1840. Commander in Chief of the
        U. S. Naval Force in the
        Mediterranean.

General Order

I have to express my disapprobation of the "Public Masquerades" given at the Theatre in Mahon. I have reason to believe they are resorts for the dissolute and immoral and I have therefore to require that the young Officers of the Ship under your Command be not permitted to remain out of the Ship after eight o'clock P.M., without special permission from the Commanding Officer on board, who will, on granting such permission, require a pledge that they will not attend the Public Masquerades given in Mahon.

               Isaac Hull
                    Commander in Chief of the U. S.

U. S. Ship *Ohio*         Naval Force in the Medn.
Port Mahon
  Feb. 5, 1841
To Officers Commanding Vessels of the
U. S. Squadron in the Mediterranean.

## Chapter XVII
## DISCIPLINE

FLOGGING was the usual punishment inflicted in the navy for offenses committed by enlisted men. Discipline was strict and the cat-o'-nine-tails and colt (rope's end) were freely used. It was done in the presence of the whole ship's company and must have had a brutalizing effect on those who witnessed it, especially the midshipmen and apprentice boys. But reform was on the way. In 1850, after much discussion, flogging was abolished in the navy. Yet the reform was at first unpopular, not only with the officers, but in some degree among the men. Confinement in irons without flogging was another mode of punishment.

In 1838 grog was still regularly served to seamen. After a time commutation of the grog for money was authorized, and later it was forbidden to minors. In 1862 Congress ruled that "the spirit ration in the navy of the United States shall forever cease."

The offenses for which punishment was inflicted were almost innumerable and only a few of the more common may be mentioned: drunkenness, stealing, gambling, disobedience of orders, disrespect to an officer, desertion. Under the date of Sunday, September 29, 1839, the log of the *Ohio* records: "At 10 called all hands, read the Articles of War, performed Divine Service, and mustered the Crew round the Capstan. At 11 called all hands to witness punishment. Punished the following men, viz. James Steerwell, six with the Cats for disobedience of orders; Michael Lanigan [the same] for leaving his boats; Edw. Cutting [the same] for insolence; John Bird [and two others] twelve [lashes] for drunkenness"; and three men got twelve each for "leaving the ship without permission and swimming on shore."

Officers and the more serious offenders among the men were tried by Court Martial. It was provided by law that: "When the trial takes place out of the United States, the Commander of the Fleet or Squadron shall possess full power to pardon any offence committed against these Articles, after conviction, or to mitigate the punishment decreed by a Court Martial." January 29, 1840, Passed Midshipman Carter B. Poindexter was found guilty of disobedience of orders, disrespect to his superior officer, and unofficerlike conduct. He was sentenced "to be suspended from all professional employment on the part of the Government for the space of twelve calendar months" and it was decreed "that this sentence be read at all Naval Stations in the United States and on board such ships or vessels of the United States Navy as may be in commission there or elsewhere." Commodore Hull approved the first part, but not the second part. May 22, 1841, James Reeves, seaman, was found guilty by the Court Martial of "threatening to strike his superior officer whilst in the execution of his office, using abusive, provoking, and reproachful words, gestures, and menaces to and treating with contempt his superior officer, . . . leaving and absenting himself from the U. S. Ship *Ohio* without permission, and attempting to smuggle into said U. S. Ship *Ohio,* a quantity of spirituous liquor." He was sentenced "to receive seventy-five lashes with the cat of nine tails at the gangway of the United States Ship *Ohio* and to be dismissed the naval service of the United States." Commodore Hull "hereby mitigates the punishment decreed in the case of James Reeves, referred to in the foregoing Record, and the said James Reeves is to receive seventy-five lashes with the cat of nine tails at the gangway of the United States Ship *Ohio;* and is *not* to be dismissed the Naval service of the United States."

U. S. S. *Ohio*.<br>At Sea. April 16th. 1839.

Sir.

I have to report that, in obedience to the several Warrants issued by you of date 15th inst., I proceeded at 11 A.M. this day to execute the punishments named therein, and finished with all except [James] Reynolds, who, after receiving twenty five lashes, fainted and was released by the advice of the Surgeon. He has since notified me that he is ready to receive the balance of the punishment before the expiration of the time limited in the Warrant, but I beg leave, as the prosecutor of the charges against Reynolds, to intercede in his behalf, and request that if you shall deem it practicable and proper, the residue of the punishment may be remitted.

Very Respectfully<br>Your Obt. Servt.<br>Jos. Smith<br>Capt. U. S. S. *Ohio*.

Comt. Isaac Hull.
Commr. in Chf of the
U. S. Naval Force in the Medr.
    Present.

U. S. Ship *Ohio*.
At Sea   Oct. 28th, 1839

Honoured Sir,

We the undersigned persons take the liberty of submitting these few lines for your serious, and we trust indulgent consideration.

It is with the greatest regret that we find ourselves charged with crimes of which we never had the least intention.

If we did not express ourselves in a proper style, you may rest assured Sir, it was entirely through ignorance, and in not knowing the *proper manner* of addressing our commander, and not *wilfullness*.

Honoured Sir, rather than be subject to this confinement and have to await the decision of a Court Martial, we are very willing and will be thankfull to you if you will punish us at your own discretion and according to your own judgement; we therefore leave ourselves completely at your mercy.

    Sir, we remain
      Your Humble and Obedent Svts.
        John Hilton
        Peter Miller
        Jas. Brown
To        Saml. Silk
 Commodore Isaac Hull  Thos Carter
 Comdr. in Chief of U. S. Naval Edw'd Kenny.
 Force in the Mediterranean.

U. S. Frigate *Brandywine*
Port Mahon, March 17th, 1840.

Sir;

It is my unpleasant duty to inform you that the First Carpenter's Mate, Thos. Reynolds, has been stabbed in the body, by a dirk, at the hand of the Master at Arms, Saml. J. Reeves, both of this ship.

This circumstance occurred on shore, on the evening of the 15th inst. I would have apprised you of it earlier but I have waited the result of an examination of the wounds by the surgeon, which I now submit to you; as well as all the facts that are known, or can be ascertained, in the case. I am happy to be persuaded that no serious consequences will ensue to Reynolds, though the act of the Master at Arms must be regarded as one of a savage, uncalled for and brutal nature.

It appears that the Carpenter's Mate was on liberty; that his liberty had not expired; that the Master at Arms was not sent for him; that he accidentally met him. Whether any misunderstanding had previously existed is not known. The Master at Arms had been in charge of the liberty apprentices, to see that they conducted themselves properly and went on board in due time. The First Lieutenant's and the Surgeon's reports accompany this, and to them I beg leave to refer you for fuller information.

I am told the crew have evinced great indignation, and the safety of the person of the Master at Arms may be regarded as insecure; therefore I submit to you, after you have examined the 1st Lieutenant and Surgeon, whether it would be well to have the Master at Arms tried by Court Martial, or reduced and discharged from the ship. If he is discharged, will he come on the Consul's hands? or have you the power to get rid of him in a foreign port? or will it be best to have him returned home in the store ship? He has heretofore borne a good character, is an efficient man and has served in several of our ships of war.

The habit of carrying concealed weapons must be discountenanced; if stabbing is countenanced no person will be safe. It appears to me that the Master at Arms should have left Reynolds and repaired on board and reported him. I suppose they were both inebriated. May I suggest to you to have the Master at Arms at your office for examination? I have ordered the First Lieut., Mr. Kelly, to have statements of the occurrence made out by the Master at Arms and Carpenter's Mate, respectively, and will send them to you so soon as I shall receive them. The only person who is conversant with what passed between the above individuals is a boy of about fourteen or fifteen, by the name of France. I will be very happy to receive your orders or advice in this case.

I am, Sir, very respectfully<br>Your obt. sevt.

Como. Hull                    W. C. Bolton, Captain
Commander in Chief, etc. etc.

P.S. The statements above referred to are received and forwarded. They will probably supersede the necessity of your seeing the Master at Arms, or Lieutenant or Surgeon.                    W. C. B.

## Naval General Order.

The President of the United States, believing that greater formality in the infliction of such corporal punishments as are authorized by Law may be adopted in the Navy with beneficial consequences, directs that no such punishment shall be inflicted on any person in the service without sentence of a Court Martial, when that is required by Law, or the written order of the Captain or Commanding Officer of the vessel, or Commandant of the Navy Yard to which he is attached, where the authority to cause it to be inflicted rests in the discretion of the Commanding Officer, specifying the offence or offences and the extent of the punishment to be inflicted, which order shall be read and the punishment inflicted in presence of the Officers and Seamen belonging to the vessel or Navy Yard.

And such orders for punishment shall be entered on the Log Book and a quarterly return made to the Secretary of the Navy, stating the names of the persons punished, their offences and the extent of the punishment inflicted, together with such explanations or remarks as the Commanding Officer may deem necessary to a proper understanding of the case.

The President also directs that the law authorizing the enlistment of Seamen and others for the Naval Service, as it may be in operation at the time of enlistment, shall be printed on the back of the shipping Articles and read to each person desirous to enter previous to his signing them, in order that he may know precisely the engagements and obligations he is about to contract.

J. K. Paulding,
[Secretary of the Navy].

Navy Department
May 29th, 1840

U. S. Ship *Ohio,* Toulon
June 1st, 1840.

Sir

We would respectfully call your attention to a difficulty which occurred today in an attempt to arrest a deserter. We apprehend that lest some further step be taken, an opinion may be entertained by many who were present that we have committed an unauthorised aggression on a Citizen of France. The following are the particulars.

In passing along the Quay between the hours of 1 and 2 P.M. we met Alexander Dubois a deserter from this ship. Conceiving that our duty as officers required us to restore him to the ship, we ordered him down to the landing; on his refusing Passed Midn. Jones took him by the arm to secure his compliance. Immediately a mob closed round us and two of the foremost took Mr. Jones by the arm for the purpose of releasing Dubois. Mr. Jones then let go his hold; the two of the mob mentioned desisted their hold of him but made other demonstrations of an unfriendly nature, thereby securing the escape of Dubois.

The foremost of the mob can be identified by us as well as by a sergeant who afterwards joined us to render assistance in securing the deserter.

Very respectfully
Your Obdt. Servts.
Passed Midn. W. A. Jones
" " Wm. E. LeRoy

To Commr. Isaac Hull
Commander in Chief of the U. S. Naval
Force in the Mediterranean.

[Translation]

Tribunal of Toulon    Toulon  June 1st 1840

Mr. the Commander

A Frenchman, Alexandre Dubois, has come and informed: that having embarked a year since on board of your vessel at Marseilles, in the quality of Ward Room Cook, on condition of quitting this service when he should judge most convenient, he finds difficulties on the part of the officers under your command, in obtaining his discharge, and the payment of wages which are due him, at the rate one hundred and ten francs pr. month, French Money, and that they have refused him. I do not think Mr. Commander, that you would authorize the keeping on board, a Frenchman against his will, and that he should be refused his wages which are due him, nor do I doubt acquainting you with the object of the reclamation of Alexandre Dubois, but that you will find it just and hasten to order your officers to pay this Cook what is due him, and to restore him the effects that he may have on board. Under this persuasion I have the honor to inform you of the complaint that has been brought to me.   I am Sir, etc.

Procureur de Roi


By U. S. Ship *Ohio,* Port Mahon
July 24th, 1840.

Sir,

In obedience to your order dated the 21st inst., in reference to a robbery committed on the person of Bernard Wright a Marine attached to this Ship, directing us to "enter into an examination of this matter, collect as far as possible all the facts in the case and report the result to me in writing, with the names of the parties concerned, and the amount of money, if any, which was stolen," we have the honor to make the following Report:

Bernard Wright states that he went on shore with one Hundred and Twenty french dollars. Before going on shore some of his messmates ask'd him what he was going to do with so much money. He told them it was money which his messmates had given him to exchange for gold. After he went on shore he was in Castle Street near the House kept by a man who goes by the name of Sam Victor, when Edward Williams belonging to the Main Top ask'd him for the loan of a dollar. Wright told Williams he hadn't it to spare at that time, but if he saw him by and by he thought he could lend him a dollar. James Steerwell, also belonging to the Main Top, who was near, ask'd Wright to lend him a dollar also. Wright made the same reply to Steerwell that he made to Williams. Williams then whispered something to Steerwell which Wright could not hear. Williams then returned to Wright and ask'd him if he could not let him have that dollar now. Wright replied that he would sooner not let him have it then. Williams replied "damn your eyes I will have it now" and struck him in the face. Wright said to him "dont be striking me, if you want the money I will give it to you now." Steerwell and Williams then laid hold of Wright and forced him into Sam Victor's house. After they got him in the house, he asked them what they wanted.

"Boys" said he "I will let you have some money if that is all you want." On entering the house Victor closed his front door and said "Boys take him into the back room," at the same time going behind his counter to get the bar to secure the door. They made an effort to get him into the back room. In resisting this effort Wright caught hold of the Counter in the Bar room. Sam Victor forcibly broke his hold of the Counter but not before Wright had got on the side of the room next to the window. Wright then made an attempt to get out of the window. Edward Cutting, also belonging to the Main Top, endeavored to prevent him. At this time, one of them (he does not know which) put his hand into his left hand pocket and turned it inside out, the money which was in it falling on the floor. He does not know how much money was in the pocket, but thinks there were about Eighty five french dollars. As soon as the money dropt, they (Cutting, Steerwell, Williams, and Victor) left him to pick it up and Wright made his escape out of the window.

Calvin Wentworth, a Marine, says Wright and he went on shore togeather. When they first went on shore Wright told Wentworth that he had one Hundred and Twenty dollars with him. Wentworth replied that he thought him unwise to bring so much money with him. Wright said he had brought it ashore to get changed into gold. The first house Wright went into he enquired where he could get it changed into gold and was directed to a place by a woman. After this he went into Castle Street where he encountered five sailors who wanted to borrow money from Wright. Steerwell, Williams, and

Cutting were three of them, the others Wentworth did not know. Wright told them he could not let them have money then, but would let them have it at six o'clock. At first they said it would do, but afterwards said they must have it then.

Williams told Wright he was a shipmate of his and was no man if he did not let him have it and struck Wright at the same time. Four of these men took hold of Wright, and Steerwell took hold of two of the men and said "for God sake let the man alone." They shoved Wright along until they got to Sam Victor's house and shoved him in there. After they had all entered the House Victor said "Take him into the back room." They closed the door and Wentworth saw no more of it until he saw Wright getting out of the window. As he got almost out Wentworth saw the money fly out of Wright's pocket — some of these men had hold of Wright when he was getting out of the window.

John Cogswell, a Seaman, says he was on shore the same day Wright was on shore. He was in Castle Street about eleven o'clock in the morning. There were a number of sailors standing togeather and Steerwell among them. Cogswell heard some sailor ask Steerwell to lend him some money. Steerwell said he had none to spare as he had already lent Ten dollars. Steerwell had some money in a small bag around his neck — does not know the amount, and does not know whether it was silver or copper.

Passed Mid. Jones says he heard Steerwell say that he had been accused of robbing a marine and he be damned if he had robbed him, when he robbed him again he would murder him too. Steerwell was in confinement at the time.

Midshipman Knapp says he heard Steerwell say "yes, I robbed the buggar, and I would rob any other buggar who got his money in the same way he did." That was soon after Steerwell was put in confinement. Mr. Knapp thought at the time that Steerwell referred to the robbery of Wright.

The man called Sam Victor is connected with this transaction in such a manner as to merit particular notice. It appears from the evidence of Wentworth that Victor, after Wright was forced into his house by Steerwell, Williams and Cutting, directed them to take Wright into the back room, and immediately after giving this direction proceeded to bar his front door to prevent Wright's escape. By the evidence of Wright himself it also appears that Victor forcibly broke Wright's hold from his counter while Wright was struggling with Steerwell, Williams, and Cutting. In the interview which we had on board this ship with Victor in the presence of all the parties concerned he presented a bill against Wright for 25 dollars, which he said had been owing to him by Wright for several years and which he could not get Wright to pay. From these circumstances we are induced to believe that Victor was privy to the robbery and a principal actor in it. Wright accounts for his being in possession of the 120$ which he took on shore with him, in the following manner, to wit, he states that 26$ belonged to Kenyon, 31$ to Claystine, 30$ to Kearnes, which statement has been confirmed by them, and that he had about 33$ dollars of his own, of which he lent 2$ to Wentworth and spent about one dollar himself, and that when he returned to the ship and reported the robbery to Mr. Mercer, he had in his possession 35$ dollars from which it appears that he was robbed of 82$.

     Very respectfully
      Yr. Obt. Svts
       Sam. Mercer, Lt.
To       Thomas A. Linton,
 Commodore Isaac Hull  [Captain of Marines].
  Comm'r. in Chief of U. S. Naval
   Force in the Mediterranean
    From U. S. Ship *Ohio*.

      Navy Department
       28 October 1840
Sir,

 The Department has been informed that a Private in the Marine Guard on board the U. S. Sloop of War *Cyane* in the Mediterranean, was punished with unusual severity for being found asleep on his post at a time when the guard was called upon to perform extremely severe duty.

 You will be pleased to furnish the Department with an explanation of the circumstances of this case, and also to report the fact in regard to the duty which has been imposed upon the guard.

    I am respectfully yours
      J. K. Paulding.

Comme. Isaac Hull
Commg. U. S. Naval Forces
in the Mediterranean.

## Chapter XVIII
## IMPRESSMENT

SINCE the early years of the French Revolution all classes of Americans, particularly political, naval, and commercial, had been sensitive on the subject of the impressment of American seamen. In the peace negotiations following the War of 1812 it had not been possible to induce England to renounce this practice. On various occasions after the war England refused to relinquish the right she claimed of impressing seamen.[1]

But as the United States grew stronger and gained confidence in the power to resist aggression and resent injury, the formal acknowledgment of our rights, while desirable, seemed less important. In the United States Senate, in April, 1846, Daniel Webster, defending the Treaty of Washington, in which impressment is not mentioned, said:

"It has been said that the treaty of Washington, and the negotiations accompanying it, leave the great and interesting question of impressment where they found it. With humility and modesty, I must beg to express my dissent from that opinion." He then speaks of the correspondence of the negotiators "as not having left the question of impressment where they found it, but as having placed the true doctrine in opposition to it on a higher and stronger foundation."

Webster quoted from his letter of August 8, 1842, to Lord Ashburton, as follows: "In the early disputes

[1] *Massachusetts Historical Society Proceedings*, XLV (1912), 509.

between the two governments on this so long contested topic, the distinguished person [Jefferson] to whose hands were first intrusted the seals of this department declared, that 'the simplest rule will be that the vessel being American shall be evidence that the seamen on board are such.' Fifty years' experience, the utter failure of many negotiations, and a careful reconsideration, now had, of the whole subject, at a moment when the passions are laid, and no present interest or emergency exists to bias the judgment, have fully convinced this government that this is not only the simplest and best, but the only rule which can be adopted and observed, consistently with the rights and honor of the United States and the security of their citizens. That rule announces, therefore, what will hereafter be the principle maintained by their government. *In every regularly documented American merchant-vessel the crew who navigate it will find their protection in the flag which is over them.*"[1]

Under the circumstances and in view of the somewhat strained relations of the United States and Great Britain at the time, it is hardly strange that the case which is the subject of the following correspondence should have excited the keen interest of the Navy Department and of United States naval officers and consuls in Europe.

Ship *Canton Packet*<br>Off Barcelona Jany. 12th, 1839.

Sir,

I think it my duty to inform you that after getting my ship underweigh this morning bound to the Brazils

---

[1] *Works of Daniel Webster*, V, 145, VI, 325.

I was boarded by a boat from her Majestys Brig *Weasel* Commander Simpson and one of my crew forcable taken from me, the Commanders excuse for taking him being that the man wishd to enter the Brittish Service that his name did not appear on my ships articles and consequently that he had a right to him. I went myself on board the Brig and informd the Commander that the man was enterd on my crew list by our Consul and that by his taking him from my ship would cause me detention, etc. but all to no purpose, it appears that one of the *Weasels* crew had deserted at this port and that my man was taken to fill his place. I hope Sir if this proceeding is unlawful which it appears to me to be you will be pleased to look into it.

The mans name is Wm. Bruce.

    I am Sir very Respectfully
     Yr. obt. servt.
       Robt. F. Chase.

To the Commodore of the
American Squadron
 Port Mahon

[Affidavit]
Barcelona,
13th January 1839.

To Wit:

I William Bruce Seaman do hereby swear that I was born at Whitby in Yorkshire England and left London in the Bark *Ulysses* of Sunderland in Octr, 1838; and that in consequence of ill health I left that vessel and went on board the American ship *Canton Packet,* Captain Chase, at Trieste in Novr. last and have been compelled to leave that ship from the ill treatment I have received from the Captain, and have volunteered to serve on board Her Majesty's Brig *Weazle* at Barcelona this 13th day of January 1839.

Sworn before me at Barcelona this 13th day of January 1839.

James Annesley<br>British Consul.

Memt.

Mr. Bruce had not ever signed articles for the *Canton Packet,* and endeavoured to avoid sailing in her at all, but was imprisoned at Trieste and was obliged; the Commander of the vessel *admitted* that he had not signed; he was entered *subsequent* to this affidavit in Her Majesty's Service.

Jn. Simpson, Lieut.<br>H. M. Brig *Weazle*

Attested Copy
Signed J. M. Bell
Clerk in Charge.

U. S. S. *Cyane*<br>Off Barcelona   Feby. 24, 1839.

Sir,

I have been directed by the Commander in Chief of the United States Naval Forces in the Mediterranean, to call on you for the reasons for your having violated the Sovereignty of the United States, on the 12th ultimo by force of arms in boarding the American Ship *Canton Packet* belonging to the United States, Robert F. Chase, Master, and taking by force therefrom an American Seaman, who had been maintained at the expense of the

United States by the United States Consul on Shore, and put by him, a distressed American Seaman, on board the *Canton Packet,* and entered on the crew list as one of the legal complement of that ship. An act so incompatible with the treaties existing between the United States and Great Britain and the friendly relations and courtesies maintained by the public authorities of each, has excited the greatest surprise, that it could have been committed by a Commander of one of Her Majesty's Ships of War.

Very respectfully, Sir<br>I have the honor to be<br>Your obt. Servt.

Commander Simpson                      [J. Percival]
Commdg. H. M. Brig. *Weasel.*

Consulate of the U. States<br>at Barcelona    Feby. 25th, 1839.

J. Percival Esq.
Commander of the U. S.
Sloop *Cyane.*
Sir,

   I have the honour of receiving your communication dated yesterday by which you request me to put you in possession of all the facts relating to the circumstance of an American Seaman having been forcibly taken out of the American Ship *Canton Packet,* Robert F. Chase, Master, by the Commander of H. B. M. Brig *Weasel* on the 12th ultimo, together with any copies of protest which may have been made relating to the subject.

The information I can give about it is, that at the moment of leaving this port, the mentioned Ship *Canton Packet,* according to the statement made before me by the Master, Robert F. Chase, was boarded by a boat from H. B. M. Brig *Weasel,* Commdr. Simpson, and the American Seaman William Bruce was forcibly taken from her; that the reasons for so acting, alledged by the said British Commander, were that the man wished to be enrolled in the British Service and that his name did not appear in the list of the said ship. Against that, Captain Chase told me that he replied and showed to Commdr. Simpson that the man was entered on his crew list by the Consul of the United States at Marseilles, and that the same man was in duty bound to fulfill his engagement with him, but all this was to no purpose; Captain Chase added that one man of the *Weasel's* crew had just at that time deserted and Bruce was taken to fill the place.

As the foresaid Ship *Canton Packet* was (while all that happened) under sail and exposed to many contingencies, I gave Captain Chase (although in a hurry) a certificate of the case and advised him to make a protest and to act at the first port in which he may arrive according to the directions of the act 28th May, 1796, section 5, upon protection of seamen against seizure by a foreign power.

     I have the honour to be
      Very respectfully
       Your obedient Servant
      Jos. Borras
       U. S. Consul.

Navy Department<br>May 10th, 1839.

Sir,

Your despatches No. 73 and 74, with the accompanying documents, have been received by the Department.

In relation to the impressment of the American Seaman from the American Ship *Canton Packet,* by Her Britannic Majesty's Brig *Weasel,* the Department is of opinion that the proper course for you to have pursued on this occasion would have been to despatch the Sloop of War *Cyane* with a letter to the Commanding Officer of the British naval forces in the Mediterranean, stating the fact and requiring in firm yet temperate language the release of the American Seaman. It is highly probable that such an application would have been immediately successful, but in case of the refusal of that officer to direct his restoration, you would, as you have now done, refer the case to the Department.

If not too late, you will still adopt this course and continue to pursue it in future in all similar circumstances, when it can be done without interfering with the more important operations of the vessels under your command.

I have the honor to be
respectfy. yours<br>J. K. Paulding

P.S. You will promptly apprise the Depmt. of the result of your demand on the British Admiral in order that, if necessary, the affair may be presented to the notice of the British Government.

J. K. P.

Comre. Isaac Hull
Comr. in Chief of the U. S. Naval Force
in the Mediterranean.

Her Majesty's Brig *Weazle*
Malta Sept. 28th, 1839.

Sir,

In obedience to your letter received last night I proceed to make a more detailed statement, relative to the entry of William Bruce, Seaman of her Majesty's Brig under my command.

On or about the 12 January last when lying in Barcelona Mole, the American ship *Canton Packet* arrived, and on the 13th early in the morning there was a great disturbance on board that ship. Men were beaten and loud cries of murder uttered, a seaman belonging to her jumped overboard and swam alongside Her Majesty's vessel for protection; he was a foreigner and I sent him back to his ship, the boat being in charge of Mr. Thomas C. O'D. Whipple, Mate, and while alongside the American on this duty, William Bruce sprang into the boat saying he was an Englishman and kept on board against his will and that his life was in danger from the ill treatment he received from the Mates of the Vessel; he came on board in our boat on her return. I told him that he must make this matter quite clear to the British Consul at Barcelona, James Annersley, Esq. before I could take any steps relative to him, and enquired how he came in the ship. He replied as stated in his affidavit, and that he never had signed articles, which the American Master Chase *admitted to be truth* before me and the officers on board the *Weazle*. William Bruce also stated that when at Marseilles he wrote to the British Consul for protection, but his letter was detained on board the ship, and himself imprisoned while lying there. I then sent him on shore at Barcelona, and afterwards communicated with the British Consul on the subject, who after examining the seaman on oath considered the case to be so clear that he informed me if I did not enter the man he must come upon the Consulate for support as a distressed British subject, and he afterwards came on board in the *Weazle's* boat voluntarily *from the shore and was entered;* during this examination a seaman jumped overboard and swam to us. He was a Swede and I sent him back to the *Canton Packet,* on board of which vessel the most brutal scenes were going forward, and the man was forcibly dragged up in to the ship by ropes, uttering loud cries, of which circumstance I apprised the Swedish Consul at Barcelona and altogether the affair was so disgusting that during my long service of 36 years I never saw the like, and I felt it due to humanity to advise the American Master to a better system of discipline.

The Senior Officer on the SE Coast of Spain being absent I left the report for him at the Consulate as is customary.

I have the honor to remain with every deference and respect

Sir, Your most Obedient and humble Servant<br>
John Simpson<br>
Lieut. and Comr.

To Rear Admiral Sir John Louis, Baronet
    Etc. Etc. Malta.

This letter of Lieutenant Simpson was forwarded to Admiral Sir Robert Stopford who, in a letter to Commodore Hull enclosing it, remarks: "You will see that there was no ground for complaint on the part of the master of the Vessel who claimed the person in question as a subject of the United States."

Commodore Hull was doubtless satisfied, and dissuaded from pursuing the case further. Shipmasters in the American merchant marine, as a class, were of the sort in whom their countrymen could take pride, but Captain Chase and Captain Durkee, the subject of the next chapter, were exceptions.

## Chapter XIX
## A SLAVE SHIP

DURING nearly the first two thirds of the nineteenth century the attempted suppression of the African slave trade occupied much of the attention of the civilized world. England took the lead and endeavored to make treaties with other powers for the accomplishment of this end. Owing to the unwillingness of some of the nations to yield to England the right to search their vessels on the high seas, difficulties arose. The United States joined with England in keeping squadrons cruising for slavers on the west coast of Africa, but refused to agree to the right of search. France also refused, but Spain and other powers made treaties with England agreeing to the suppression of the trade with mutual right of search.

The following correspondence relates to the case of a slave ship virtually under the protection of the Spanish government, and to the unsuccessful attempts of the United States to get possession of her. The attempts to get possession were unsuccessful as far as the matter is disclosed by this correspondence. What the ultimate outcome was remains in doubt.

    Consulate of the United States of America
      Port Orotaro, Tenerife 22 July 1839
Alexander Burton Esqre.
  Consul of the U. States of Amer.
    Cadiz

Sir:

I have the honor to inform you of the arrival at Santa Cruz, of the Brig *Two Friends,* Capt. John A. Durkee, under the American Flag. She is 275 tons, mounts two guns, and a quantity of small arms. The crew consists of 17 American Seamen and Foreigners, with 11 extra hands, Spaniards, shipped as passengers, in all 36 desperate fellows, has no Register, merely a Bill of Sale to cover the property.

She was cleared at New Orleans for Port Praya in the Cape de Verds, but landed her cargo at Gallinas on the Coast of Africa and has come here to keep clear of British Cruisers, until her cargo of slaves may be ready, then run down, take them on board, and be off.

The American Sailors say they shipped for a voyage to the Coast of Africa and back to the Wt. Indies, and only made known to them the objects of the voyage after they had sailed, when the parties concerned offered them $40 Dollars per month for the voyage.

I have passed official notes to the Capt. G[ene]ral and Commandant of Marine, requesting them to prevent her leaving the port until examination into this business. I request you will communicate this intelligence to any of our vessels of war that may be on the Cadiz, Lisbon, or Gibraltar station, as I am convinced, unless some armed vessels of the United States come here to take cognizance of this business, all will go in favor of the Spaniards concerned.

The inclosed paragraph inserted in the Correo. Nacional of June last, copied from the London Sun of the 6th of said month, will convince you of the propriety of giving attention to this business.

I have the honor to be Sir
Your most obt. servt.
Joseph Cullen

[Copy sent by Mr. Burton]
To Commodore Isaac Hull
Commanding the U. States Squadron
in the Mediterranean.

[Affidavit]

Personally appeared at this Consular Office of the United States of America George Anderson, a seaman on board the Brig *Two Friends* of New Orleans commanded by John A. Durkee, and being duly sworn by me to answer truly to such questions as I should put to him concerning the said Brig —

Declareth. That he is a native of Liverpool in England and that he is twenty years of age and has been sailing out of the United States for nine years and that he considers New York as his place of residence.

That he shipped on board the Brig *Two Friends,* Captain John A. Durkee, in New Orleans in April last to go from thence to the Island of Cuba, the Coast of Africa and back to the West Indies.

That when he joined the vessel he found on board a cargo of rice and provisions and ballast; that they went from thence to Cabañas in the Island of Cuba and remained there about three weeks, to the best of his recollection, employed in emptying the Tierces of Rice into bags, taking that and the ballast on shore, filling a number of large water casks that were brought from the shore and afterwards taking on board again the Rice that had been landed and some more that had been brought there in a small schooner.

That when the Brig was laying there the Captain called the crew aft and told them that he would give them the same wages as the Spanish Crew had, namely Forty Dollars to able seamen and Thirty-five to ordinary seamen; that they were going to the Coast of Africa where a cargo was ready waiting for them and that they should not remain there long enough to be affected by the sickness, but should return to the Havannah when they should have plenty of money.

That the Deponent on one occasion asked to be discharged from the Vessel, not wishing to go the voyage, but that the boatswain having asked him how he was to get on shore and one man having run away and been brought on board again, he seeing it was useless to attempt running away, agreed to go and received from the Captain Twenty-five Dollars, to make with the fifteen received at New Orleans Forty for one month's advance.

That on the passage from Cabañas to Gallinas he saw the Boatswain employed fitting iron bars into the Hatchways to make a grating, that the holes made in the coamings were afterwards filled up and painted over and that the boatswain told Deponent those gratings were to keep the negroes from coming on deck.

That when at Gallinas they discharged Rice, the iron gratings and a bag, which as the Deponent handed over the side he felt to contain irons, also some tin pans and a bundle of colors in a bag and also coppers and cooking utensils.

That the only person that landed there was the passenger known as the Spanish Captain. That the Deponent understood from the negroes that came alongside that their cargo of slaves would not be ready for two or three months, for the cargo intended for them had been previously shipped in another vessel belonging to the same owners, and there were only about one hundred slaves collected since. That while laying at anchor Captain Durkee hailed the lookout at the mast head and told him not to look on shore but towards the offing and that the chain cable with which they were moored was unshackled and kept ready for shipping.

That they lay off Gallinas about twenty four hours and put to sea again but that it was not till some days afterwards that he heard they were coming to the Canary Islands, and that after laying there some time they were to return to the same place for their cargo of slaves, upon which the Deponent and his shipmates agreed that they would present themselves to the Consul of the United States to obtain their discharge, not wishing to go into the slave trade.

The Deponent further Declareth, that his real name is John Maguire, but that he was induced to ship by the name of George Anderson to avail himself of the discharge of an American seaman of that name.

All which he Declareth to be the truth. Santa Cruz the thirtieth of July, one thousand eight hundred and thirty nine.

John Maguire

Copy of the original sworn before me.
        Joseph Cullen.

United States Consular Agency
Santa Cruz, Teneriffe
25th October 1839.

Sir,

In complyance with your request I take the liberty to answer the letter you have addressed under this date to Joseph Cullen Esqre., Consul of the United States, enquiring into the state of the proceedings respecting the American Brig *Two Friends* detained here under presumptive evidence of being engaged in the slave trade.

The result of the investigation entered into by the Consul and the Authorities of this place was, that the Spanish Brig *Dos Amigos,* commanded by Juan B. Travala[?], proceeded from the Havanah to New Orleans in March last and was there sold by her Spanish owner Francisco Riera to Michael Moore, Merchant of that place, of which transfer a Bill of Sale was drawn out by David L. McCay, Notary Public of said City, and she was then cleared out by the Custom House of New Orleans as the American Brig *Two Friends,* John A. Durkee Master, with a crew of sixteen protected and eight unprotected men, the Spanish Captain, the Piloto and eight or nine foreigners belonging to the original crew remaining on board as passengers going to Santiago de Praya with a passport given by the Spanish Consul. From New Orleans she proceeded to Cabañas in Cuba and remained there about fifteen days taking in water and provisions. The crew say that while there, having found she was intended for a slaving voyage, they wished to be discharged, to which the Captain would not consent but offered them forty Dollars per month that they might be on the same footing with the Spanish Seamen, to which, finding no means of getting on shore, they consented. From Cabañas they proceeded to Gallinas on the Coast of Africa, but the cargo of slaves not being ready, they landed there the Boilers, Fetters, iron Gratings and a quantity of Rice, and in twenty four hours put to sea again and came here, the Captain reporting the vessel in the Consular Agency as bound on a trading voyage to the Coast for Palm Oil, but soon after the seamen came on shore and denounced the vessel as a slaver, claiming to be paid their wages and discharged, not wishing to go on such a voyage and throwing themselves on the protection of their respective Consuls as British, Sweedish and Portuguese subjects. The Consul of the United States called up the Master and Mate and examined them and the seamen on oath, and ellicited such information as led him to apply to the Authorities to detain the vessel while he took measures to lay these circumstances before the Government.

At same time all the other Consuls passed official notes to the General denouncing the vessel as a slaver and requesting his interference to obtain the discharge of the seamen who had claimed their protection, which the Consul of the United States objected to on the grounds that having embarked as American Citizens he would detain them as such, but he requested the General to order all the passengers to be disembarked and examined and they with the exception of the Spanish Captain and the Piloto declared that they were not such passengers but part of a crew shipped in the Havanah for a voyage to the Coast of Africa in the Brig under Spanish Colors and belonging to Francisco Riera of that place, and that they knew nothing of her being transferred in New Orleans and taking the American Flag, but always considered her Spanish and the Spanish Captain as the Commander, he on the contrary persisting in styling himself a mere passenger.

It having also appeared that during the last voyage of the same vessel to the Coast under the Portuguese Flag she was entrusted with a commission by the Governor of the Island of Principe[1] which she did not perform, the Portuguese Consul called on the General to arrest the Mate Walter Hammond and Boatswain's Mate Manuel Sena, who it appeared were on board of her at the time, the latter as Captain of the Flag.

The Captain General, as Juez Protector de Estrangeros, finding that it appeared that the vessel had been originally dispatched from the Havanah and that it was evident that the parties who really owned her and were concerned in the traffic in slaves, in which she was evidently to be engaged, were Spanish subjects, and that the American Flag had only been assumed in order to cover the property in case of being overhauled by a British Cruizer, and not knowing either how to decide on the reclamations made by the Consuls of other Nations, determined on submitting the case to the Spanish Government that he might be instructed how to proceed. Mr. Cullen at same time has made an application to the Ambassador of the United States at Madrid, and till instructions are received from these quarters the

---

[1] A Portuguese island off the west coast of Africa.

vessel is detained here; the part of the crew that shipped as American Citizens and several of the foreigners having refused to return on board until the matter should be decided and having been very unruly and riotous were put in a castle by the General at the Consul's request, but the expense of maintaining them and the passengers having exhausted the funds created by a sale of some Rice belonging to the vessel, they have this day been put at full liberty by the General with the understanding that they may claim their wages from the vessel as entitled by Law, and that the dayly allowance passed to them is to cease on the last of this month.

This, Sir, is the present state of the matter and nothing further can be done until the Spanish Government communicates instructions to the Captain General respecting the course he is to pursue.

    I have the honor to be,
     Sir,
      Your most obedient humble servant.
       Thomas Mahy, Jr.
Commodore Isaac Hull   U. S. Consular Agent
Commander in Chief of the U. S.
Naval Forces in the Mediterranean.


To the Commander in Chief of the U. S. Ship *Ohio*.
    [Santa Cruz Roads]
Sir

 The brig *Two Friends* of N. Orleans under my command owned by Michael Moore a citizen of the U. States,

Merchant resident of the city of New Orleans, having been unjustiably detained by Joseph Cullen Esqr. Consul for the U. States in conjunction with the Governor of this island, I hereby claim the protection of my flag and call on you as Commander in Chief of the U. States Ship *Ohio* for protection for myself and vessel conformable to the laws of my country, whose interests you have the honour to watch over. As I understand that it is the intention of the government not to surrender my brig to any American Ship of War until it receives advices from its own department at the court of Madrid, and it being your intention to proceed on your voyage, I must request and even ask it as a matter of right that my vessel be removed further from shore and anchored in a place of safety, that she be furnished with the requisite sails to enable me to save the property intrusted to my charge in the event of a gale of wind, (say) two topsails, jib, and trysails as also personal safety for myself from molestation by the authorities of this government after your departure.

I from this hour throw myself on your protection and whilst the flag of my country is seen waving from one of its noblest ships, I hope I call not in vain. Hoping Sir that you will take into due consideration my oppressed state and the tenour of my humble petition

I have Sir the honour to remain yours respectfully

John A. Durkee

Brig *Two Friends*   New Orleans

Santa Cruz, Teneriff   Oct. 26, 1839.

Duplicate via Gibraltar
Consulate of the United States of America,
Tenerife, 4th November 1839.

Sir

I had the honor to receive your communication 27th of last month, in reply to my letter same date covering the Captain General's answer to the letter you addressed him on the subject of the Brig *Two Friends,* Captn. John A. Durkee.

Captain Durkee's letter 26th October of which you were pleased to send me a copy, is at variance from truth. He is a man of no principle, interest his only guide, the honor of the Flag a pass word with him on all occasions, but his proceedings is convincing proof the little respect he has for the honor of the Flag or Laws of his Country, consequently his statements should be received with caution.

I have protected him in the command of his vessel and recommended him to remain quiet on board, knowing that he was in personal danger as well as myself from his licensious crew in conjunction with the Spanish and Portuguese sailors that came in the vessel disguised as passengers, but in fact part of her crew for the slaving voyage, some of them the same men that had the management of a similar concern the previous voyage under another name, when Captn. Durkee commanded her the outward passage to the Coast of Africa, under American colors, and the return voyage to the Island of Cuba under Portuguese colors (as passengers) with a cargo of slaves which arrived in safety.

He has not been so fortunate this trip and I do hope

this lesson will make vessels under similar circumstances keep aloof from these Islands as these proceedings will not be countenanced or connived at by me.

I have communicated the Minister at Madrid your arrival off this Port and what has taken place, and requested him to inform you the result of his application to the Spanish Government for the delivery of the vessel, to be sent to the United States for adjudication, in which case it will be necessary to send an armed vessel here with an officer and a few hands to take charge of her and convey her to the United States.

Captain Durkee and the hands that are on board will continue in her, but he is so connected with persons in this traffic at Cuba and so implicated in this business that it would not be prudent he should have the sole controul, unless accompanied by an officer of your confidence to convey her in safety to the United States. This may be accomplished with little inconvenience as you may have some men to send home that might be sent here and put on board the *Two Friends* and proceed in her to the United States, then return and join the Force under your command, and as she is a first Rate Vessel well found in everything, plenty of water and provisions, a convenient way of sending home any men and dispatches you may have to forward.

It is adviseable the Deposition of the Seaman John Maguire of which a copy inclosed should be confirmed by him in your presence. Also the Deposition of the man that claimed wages due him by Captain Durkee the former voyage, and forward them to the Secretary of State that will convince the Government of my correct proceeding and counteract the charge of injustice on my part as stated by Captain Durkee in his letter addressed to you 26th October.

    I have the honor to be
      with great respect
    Sir
      Your most obedt. and humble servt.
Commodore Isaac Hull   Joseph Cullen.
Commander in Chief of the U. S.
Naval Force in the Mediterranean.

Sir.       Tenerife  25th Jany. 1840.

 I had the honor to address you under date of 12th of December last that I hope may have reached you in safety.

 I have now to inform you the arrival here on the 14th Inst. of the U. States Brig *Dolphin* Commanded by Lieut. Charles H. Bell in 27 days from New York sent here by Govt. to demand the delivery of Brig *Two Friends* Capn. Durkee.

 I have forwarded by this conveyance to the U. States Minister at Madrid a copy of the official correspondence that passed between Lieut. C. Bell and the Capt. General without effecting his object, his Excellency still persisting in detaining the vessel until he receives an order from his Government to deliver her.

 I have also remitted him the publication containing the libellous paragraph on Capt. Percival's conduct, and another circular of the Portuguese Vice Consul, relating to the affair of the *Two Friends* and hope they may be noticed.

I have requested the Minister to communicate you the result of this unpleasant affair to enable you to take such measures as you may deem prudent to get possession of her and send her to the U. S.

The Friends of the Parties interested [in] the slave trade, have used every means to involve the vessel in difficulties and prevent her leaving this place, they appear to meet protection in their proceedings, that I hope will not be countenanced by the Spanish Government and that the Flag of the U. S. will be respected.

The ire of the Capn. Genrl. is directed against me for having opposed his proceedings in the business from the commencement.

Capn. Durkee was forcibly taken from on board the vessel, new hands were put on board by orders of the General, he was confined in a Castle and after some days set at liberty but not allowed to return on board. Yet the General still persists in stating she is not in his possession, but merely under detention same as stated in his reply to your official note 26th Oct. last, thinking by this evasion to exonerate himself from the heavy expenses caused by his detention of the vessel, after you came here to demand her. I hope this will not be the case.

Lt. Bell sails this day for the Coast in search of vessels sailing under the American Flag similarly situated as the *Two Friends*. I have the honor to be

With great respect

Sir, Yr. Mo. Ob. and Hble Svt.

Commodore Isaac Hull      Joseph Cullen
Commander in Chief of the U. S.
Naval Forces in the Mediterranean.
Port Mahon, Island Minorca

Legation of the United States,
Madrid 16th April 1840.

Sir

On the 26th August I had the honor to ask the attention of Her Majesty's Govt. to the consideration of the U. States' Brig *Two Friends,* being at Teneriffe, within the jurisdiction of Spain and suspected, or rather known to be a slave ship. The papers which I submitted to you (asking their return, which you have forgotten) made evident her character; and that she was a vessel of and from the United States. Again the subject was brought to your Excellency's notice on the 14th of November 1839; and to this moment, after a lapse of eight months I am without a decision. Permit me to ask, to solicit, a response, that before my departure, my Govt. may be possessed of the reasons on the part of Her Catholic Majesty's Govt., why a surrender of this vessel is refused, if such be the conclusion that is arrived at.

In the correspondence which has taken place between the Captain General at Tenerife and the Consul of the U. States, her national character has not been questioned at any time. Why then is the vessel detained? The recorded written circumstances show the following facts: that

1st. In August a request was preferred to the Spanish authorities in Tenerife by the U. States Consul, that suspicions were entertained that she was a slaver; and their interference was asked, that she might be prevented from putting to sea, and which request was acceded to.

2d. That Commodore Isaac Hull, Commanding the U. States' Squadron in the Mediterranean, on the 26th October last, appeared off the harbor of Santa Cruz, and asked that the vessel should be delivered. The response was, that the subject was before the Govt. at Madrid, and a hope was expressed by the Capt. General for the matter to abide the decision of this Court. There the affair rested.

3d. A vessel of war, the *Dolphin,* was despatched from the U. States, and on the 20th Jany. a similar application was made, and the reply given that the matter was still before the authorities at Madrid. From the 26th August, the date of my first communication to your Department, have I waited without being informed that any attention has been given to this subject. The U. States most earnestly desire to cultivate a harmonious understanding with all nations, but your Excellency must perceive that forbearance cannot always be esteemed a virtue. They have through their Minister here, respectfully asked that one of their own vessels, which has taken refuge in a Spanish port, should be delivered up, to answer to the laws she has violated; and for eight months no answer has been given. Warned by the present example, the next similar occurrence may cause them to act without appealing to the courtesy of this Govt. and thence the consequence may be a rupture of their friendly relations, which ought by every possible means to be avoided in reference to the interests of both countries.

To the 2d application made on the 20th January by Lieutenant Chs. H. Bell, commanding the U. S. armed Brig *Dolphin,* the same ground was taken by the Captain

General, that the Govt. of H. C. Majesty had as yet given no directions concerning the delivery; and further, that large claims existed against the vessel, on the part of the consignees and others, which would be *required* first to be paid.

I beg to inform your Excellency that the *Two Friends* is the property of the U. S. The circumstance of being a slave ship constitutes her by our laws forfeited, confiscated property, and the crew pirates. Being then the property of the U. S. Govt. as much so as is one of our armed vessels, I cannot conceive by what civilized code the Capt. General of the Canary Islands can claim a right to make the Brig alien for the asserted debts. The moment her illegal character and intentions were ascertained, and this is fully admitted by him in his letter of the 16th August to our Consul, all and everything of private ownership ceased, and thenceforth by the force of forfeiture, she became the property of the U. States; and being such, cannot be detained for any debts which are outstanding against her. Besides, it should be borne in mind that these preferred charges have been occasioned by a tedious detention, of which the U. S. were not the cause.

It is fair to presume that nations will always act towards each other with justice, and thus exclude the idea of any resort to compulsory means, until everything of amicable negotiation has been attempted. And is not this demand of the Capt. General, for the advance of money as a precedent condition to the delivery, a coercive measure? Most assuredly it is. The Govt. of Her C. Majesty would doubtless look with surprise,

## Chapter XX
## WAR CLOUDS

THE half dozen years preceding the ratification of the Ashburton Treaty in 1842 constituted one of the most critical periods of Anglo-American diplomacy. For years the northeastern boundary and the Oregon question had been sources of irritation. An incident of the Canadian Rebellion of 1837-1838 was the destruction of the American steamer *Caroline* at Fort Schlosser on the Niagara River by a party of Canadians, an American citizen being killed. A few years later a Canadian named McLeod, who boasted of his share in this enterprise, was arrested in New York state. His release was demanded by the British minister and refused. Various other instances of friction added fuel. "In 1841, . . . the relations between the United States and Great Britain were so grave that war seemed to be imminent."[1] The Ashburton Treaty settled the points at issue, with the exception of the Oregon boundary, which was adjusted a few years later. The following correspondence began just at the time of the change of administration, from Van Buren to Harrison.

London March 8, 1841

Dear Sir;

Although I am ignorant of your plans and take it for granted you hear regularly from our Government, I yet deem it proper to write and apprise you of the excitement which prevails here, and the fears which

[1] Channing, *History of the United States*, V, 534.

WOODEN BOWL

PRESENTED TO CAPTAIN HULL

many entertain, that we may be *forced into war with Gt. Britain*. Although in my opinion such will not be the immediate result it is by no means improbable that this may be the case. The affair of the *Caroline* Steamer destroyed at Schlosser in 1837, the imprisonment of McLeod, together with the Boundary Question, are the immediate causes of the excitement which now prevails in both Countries. The arrival of the *U. States* Packet a few days ago and the *Westchester* last night brings accounts to the 16 of February. I send you the *Times* of this morning containing the Report of the Committee of Foreign relations, in the House of Representatives, with a short debate on it. I received no communication or [Papers?] from Washington. I hasten to apprise you of the present state of things, to enable you to decide what steps it may be proper to take with our Squadron in the Mediterranean. Would it not be the most judicious course to get nearer home, and within reach of orders from the Department? Unless you have strong reasons for remaining and of which I know nothing, I should think it the safer and more prudent course, to return. I beg however that you will judge for yourself, for really it is a matter of which I know very little. I shall be glad to hear from you as soon as you have decided what you mean to do.

    In haste, believe me dear Sir,
     Yr. obt. svt.
      A. Stevenson
    [American Minister to Great Britain]
Commodore Isaac Hull
Care of Fitch, Brothers & Co.
 Marseilles     Recd per Purser from
        Toulon March 23d 1841

Confidential

London March 11, 1841

[Sir:]

When war is threatened, the Hero of the *Constitution* is present to the mind of every American. I refer you, my dear Sir, to the enclosed extracts from the Ministerial and opposition Journals, the *Chronicle* and the *Times*. My opportunities certainly are not small, as I am in daily converse with Members of both houses of Parliament and I regret to find that in private, as well as in debate, the most decided tone of hostility prevails through all parties. The Tories have declared in the Speeches of Ld. Stanley, of Sir R. Peel, of Sir H[enr]y Hardinge, of Mr. Smith O'Brien, their fixed determination to defend the position taken by the Cabinet in relation to the demands in regard to McLeod. Ld. Palmerston stated in the house of Commons, on the 9th Feby, that the ultimatum had been sent that night to Mr. Fox. Ld. Melbourne said in the house of Lords on the same day, that measures had been taken to uphold the house and dignity of the Nation, and to "SUCCOUR" McLeod. These remarks produced in both houses, from all sides, *loud* and *continued* cheering. Mr. S—— and all men agree as to the meaning of the term "succour", when applied to a man imprisoned in a foreign Country. Notice the preparations for defence — the violent and warlike report of the committee on foreign relations — the reports and resolutions in the Legislature of Maine — the paragraphs of the Ministerial Journal — the *Chronicle,* stating that workmen are employed *in relays* by night and by day to force into readiness the steam Frigates for the American coast; read the "report that 10 sail of the line are ordered to assemble at Gibraltar in consequence of the trial of McLeod". I am aware that the American Minister wrote to you two days since, but in his absence from London for the day I venture, with the approval of Mr. Rush, the Secy of Leg'n, to communicate the news *just arrived*. Mr. Rush's brother,[1] of y[ou]r Squadron, has many of the facts on this important question. I dined yesterday in company with one of my cousins, Cap. Sir James S——, and I assure you that notwithstanding the refined and courteous manners of this gentleman, he betrayed the feeling of readiness for action. His Frigate has just been made ready for sea and it [started?] on the passage for America.

You will pardon an American, whose intrusion proceeds from the desire that Hull shall but be prepared for his Enemy, to add lustre to his name and glory to his country.

I am my dear sir    Most truly
yours
John Hare Powel[2]

Mr. Rush has heard this letter and entirely approves it. The outfit of 2 Frigates is *now* certain
Com. Hull
U. States Squadron in the
Mediterranean.

I have written in the utmost haste to save the mail.

[1] Midshipman Madison Rush, of the *Ohio*.
[2] A prominent American living in London.

Minutes of Proceedings of a Council Composed of the Commanders of Vessels of the Mediterranean Squadron under the Command of Commodore Isaac Hull.

On the twenty fourth day of March, one thousand eight hundred and forty one, Commodore Hull issued his orders, calling a meeting on board the U. S. Ship *Ohio*, in the harbor of Mahon, Island of Minorca, at eleven o'clock A.M. of the same day, of the following Officers viz: Captain Wm. Compton Bolton, Commanding the U. S. Frigate *Brandywine*, Captain Elie A. F. Lavallette, Commanding the U. S. Ship *Ohio* and Commander Ralph Voorhees, Commanding the U. S. Sloop of War *Preble*.

The Officers named assembled in the Poop Deck Cabin of the U. S. Ship *Ohio*, in the presence of Commodore Isaac Hull, on the day and at the time required.

Commodore Hull briefly stated the object of the meeting and, to more fully elucidate it, he directed his Secretary to read the following viz;

Gentlemen,

Commodore Hull desires to say he has called you together for the purpose of placing before you a letter he has received from the Minister of the United States at the Court of Great Britain, enclosing publications taken from the newspapers in relation to the exciting difficulties which exist between the United States and Great Britain; that he is without instructions from the Government, in relation to those difficulties, and, under the circumstances of the case, he deems it necessary that some preparatory movement should take place in the Squadron under his command.

Commodore Hull therefore desires to hear your views in relation to that measure, and states as his own the following, viz; There are three positions which the Squadron can select from: 1st to proceed to Toulon, where the earliest information could be received and where perhaps instructions from the Government of the United States would probably reach him earlier than at any other point; 2d To proceed out of the Mediterranean to some point where he could hear the result of the existing difficulties; and 3d to put the Squadron in motion to return to the United States. The last, however, without more definite information or instructions from the Navy Department, Commodore Hull is not much in favor of. Commodore Hull desires to hear your sentiments on these propositions and will also be glad to have any others that may strike you as better adapted to the present doubtful and uncertain position in which he is left.

After this the said Secretary to Commodore Hull was directed to read the letters hereto appended, from His Excellency A. Stevenson, United States Envoy, dated "London March 8, 1841", and from John Hare Powel Esquire dated "London March 11th, 1841". When the following views and sentiments were expressed by Captain Wm. Compton Bolton: That he had reflected upon this subject and was at first impressed with the belief that the Squadron should at once proceed to Toulon, but that on further consideration he was convinced that the proper and only available course to pursue was to leave the Mediterranean and to proceed outside, where information of events and the actual state of affairs could be learned by or from Vessels traversing between the United States and Great Britain, and if hostilities were to be resorted to, the Squadron would then be so situated as to be enabled to render efficient aid at sea or it might proceed to the United States, where its services would be available on the Coast or in our harbors, the Ships might be converted into moving harbor batteries, to be manned by militia or soldiers, and our Seamen disposed of on the Lakes or to advantage otherwise; another very good consideration is, that by taking this course, the policy or plan of our Government in conducting the threatening war and of which we are now entirely ignorant, would be ascertained, and in case of a favorable termination of the existing difficulties the Squadron could return to the Mediterranean and resume its station there.

The views of Captain Bolton were fully assented to by Captain Elie A. F. Lavallette and by Commander Ralph Voorhees.

And to which Commodore Hull replied, I am prepared to pursue that course.

It was then suggested by Captain Wm. Compton Bolton that definite action on the movements of the Squadron had better be suspended until it should be ascertained if a French Steamer from Toulon, then about entering the harbour of Mahon, brought later news than was already at hand, which suggestion was adopted and the Council broke up.

It having been ascertained that the French Steamer brought no information to change the views already formed, expressed and assented to, the Officers before named again met on the same day in Mahon at half past one o'clock P.M. when a verbal order was given by Commodore Hull to the following effect, viz. that every preparation should be made to proceed to sea tomorrow the twenty fifth day of March, one thousand eight hundred and forty one.

The foregoing minutes contain the views expressed, in corroboration of which we hereunto affix our names.

Done in Mahon, Island of Minorca, the twenty fourth day of March one thousand eight hundred and forty one.

    W. C. Bolton, Captain
    E. A. F. Lavallette, Captain
    Ralph Voorhees, Com'
    Isaac Hull
      Com r' in Chief of the U. S.
      Naval Force in the Med$^r$.

Attest Jn. Etheridge
  Commodore's Secretary.


    U. S. Ship *Ohio*
     Port Mahon March 24, 1841.

Sir,

 Such of the Sick at the Hospital in Mahon under your charge as can be serviceable or useful on board ship will be sent to their respective Ships.

 The Squadron is about to leave this port and you will be left in charge of such Sick as require the comforts and advantages of Hospital treatment. You will be pleased to refer to our Consul for advice in relation to the discharge of the Sick should I not return in time to be referred to.

Very Respectfully
I am Sir
Yr. Obt. St.
Isaac Hull
Commander in Chief of the U. S.
Naval Force in the Mediterranean.

Dr. James Greene
U. S. Navy
Surgeon Hospital    Mahon.
[Endorsed]
Dr. Greene is authorized in conjunction with the U. S. Consul to close the Hospital for the Sick of the U. S. Squadron opened in Mahon. In case of War between the United States and Great Britain Dr. Greene is directed to proceed with all despatch to the United States and to report to the Secretary of the Navy.

U. S. Ship *Ohio*, Port Mahon
March 25, 1841.   Isaac Hull.
Comr. in Chief of the U. S.
Naval Force in the Medr.


U. S. Ship *Ohio*
Port Mahon March 25, 1841

Sir,
Circumstances have rendered it necessary to make rather a hasty movement in the Squadron under my Command.

I have therefore to direct that you proceed to sea and make the best of your way out of the Mediterranean; you will endeavor, either by speaking vessels or by touching at some port, to ascertain the state of affairs between the United States and Great Britain. In case of war you will use every exertion to protect yourself and command and to annoy the enemy, cruising as long as your provisions and other circumstances will admit of, and when a favorable opportunity offers you will run into some port of the United States and report to the Secretary of the Navy; much however must be left to your own judgment.

Should you ascertain that quietness has been restored you will return to the Mediterranean touching at Mahon where you will probably hear from me.

      Very Respectfully
       I am Sir, Yr. Obt. St.
        Isaac Hull
       Commander in Chief of the U. S.
        Naval Force in the Mediterranean

Officers Commanding
Vessels of the U. S. Squadron
in the Mediterranean.

      U. S. Ship, *Ohio*
      Off Cape d'Gat April 1, 1841

Sir,

As it is highly important at this moment that I should get the earliest information possible relative to our affairs with England, and believing that later news than we have yet received may be found at Malaga, or by standing close in with the Spanish Coast for the purpose of speaking vessels which are constantly passing up, I have to direct that you keep close in with the

Coast of Spain until you reach Malaga, speaking such vessels as you may fall in with and making enquiry of their Masters in relation to that subject. At Malaga you will be pleased to communicate with the U. S. Consul there and request of him such information as he possesses in relation thereto, and as soon thereafter as practicable join this Ship off that port; in the event of your not falling in with the *Ohio,* you will proceed to Cadiz and obtain the latest information from the United States and England you can at that place and should the *Ohio* call off that place, you will either join her with the *Preble* or send a boat with such intelligence as you may have obtained with a Pilot for this Ship, should it be found necessary to take her in.

Should you reach Cadiz and ascertain that war has been or will be declared, you will fill the *Preble* up with Provisions and Water and proceed on a cruise where you will be most likely to fall in with the commerce of the Enemy; off Madeira and between that and Teneriff would be good cruising ground. After remaining out as long as you have the means to do so, you will proceed to the United States or to any port in France that will afford you the means of fitting your Ship for a further cruise.

Very Respectfully, I am Sir,<br>
Yr. Obt. Svt.　　Isaac Hull<br>
Comdr. in Chief of the U. S. Naval<br>
Force in the Mediterranean.

Commander Ralph Voorhees
Commanding U. S. S. *Preble*
at Sea

U. S. Ship *Ohio*
At Sea April 1st 1841

Sir.

The Ship under my command having been got in readiness for sea, with provisions and stores for four months (from 1st April), we sailed on the 25th March from Mahon and proceeded down the Mediterranean encountering constant light and head winds which has greatly retarded our passage.

The precarious state of affairs between England and the United States, tending greatly to a rupture between the two Countries, render it necessary for various arrangements to be made in the Ship by the removement of Bulkheads, Mounting of Guns, making tubes and cylinders, fiting spare Topsail and Top Gallant Yards, Stoppers, Shot Plugs, and indeed all things appertaining to the various departments of the Ship in a perfect state of readiness to meet an Enemy. The Crew are daily exercised at the Guns and appear cheerful and contented.

Of the Officers it affords me much pleasure to speak in the most favourable terms. I trust and confidently believe from their ready obedience to orders that the *Ohio* can and will be able to perform all that our Country may expect from her.

Enclosed are the monthly returns of the Purser.

    I am
        Sir
            Very Respectfully
                Yr. Obt. Servt.
            E. A. F. Lavallette

Commodore
    Isaac Hull
Comr. in Chief of the U. S.
Naval Force in the Mediterranean.

U. S. Ship *Ohio*
Off Malaga April 6, 1841

Sir,

The information which you have bro't to me from Malaga in relation to the exciting questions between the United States and Great Britain appearing to be of a character calculated to produce reconciliation, and the tone of the public prints having become so pacific, I do not think it necessary to proceed out of the Mediterranean at this time. You will therefore be pleased to proceed with all practicable despatch to the harbor of Mahon in the Island of Minorca, where you will overhaul and refit your Ship, take on board a full supply of Provisions, Water and Stores and join me at Toulon or at such other port as I may hereafter direct. As it is desirable that the *Preble* should join me at as early a day as possible, I enjoin upon you the necessity of using every exertion to accomplish that object and I request that you will report to me, as soon as you can ascertain the fact, the probable time it will require to refit and overhaul the *Preble*.

Mr. Purser Sinclair will join this Ship with the least possible delay, and if necessary for him to do so by the *Preble,* I request you will afford him the necessary facilities.

I also request you to receive on board the *Preble* three boxes containing private and public papers and for which I ask your best care and attention; they will be sent to you, or application will be made to you for such assistance as may be necessary, by Mr. Purser Sinclair or by Mr. Rich the U. S. Consul at Mahon.

Be pleased to send to me the returns of your Ship for the month of March 1841.

> Very Respectfully, I am Sir, Yr. Obt. St.
> Isaac Hull
> Commander in Chief of the U. S. Naval Force
> in the Mediterranean

Commander Ralph Voorhees
Commanding U. S. Sloop of War *Preble*
Off Malaga, Coast of Spain.

On the same day, April 6, Commodore Hull wrote to Consul Rich: "The news from the United States is so pacific that I have altered my plans. I shall remain in the Mediterranean and probably have the pleasure to meet you and your amiable family in Mahon again, to whom I beg to be remembered with all respect and kindness."

> U. S. Ship *Ohio*
> Harbour of Toulon, France
> April 25, 1841.

Sir,

As the affairs between the United States and Great Britain appear to be at this time pacific and in such a state as to dispel the anxiety which has been felt, I have to direct that, on receipt of this letter, you prepare the *Brandywine* under your Command for immediate service, taking on board a full supply of provisions, stores, etc. When ready for sea, you will proceed with her to the Coast of Italy, touching at the principal ports, communicating with the Consuls, etc. of the United States and rendering all the aid and assistance to our

Citizens and Commerce contemplated by the Government, taking for your guide generally the Instructions from the Navy Department to me, copy of which was sent to you some time since. After passing as much time on the Coast of Italy as may be necessary, you will (should the season not be too far advanced) proceed to the Levant for the same purposes and to give your attention to any acts of piracy there, a knowledge of which may reach you. I however enjoin on you the strictest watchfulness and attention at all times to guard against emergencies which may grow out of the questions pending between the United States and Great Britain. Having completed your summer's cruise you will return to Mahon, where you will report to my successor in command of the U. S. Naval Force in the Mediterranean for further instructions.

Wishing you a pleasant cruise, I am, Sir,
Very Respectfully, Yr. Obt. St.
Isaac Hull
Commander in Chief of the U. S.
Naval Force in the Mediterranean

Capt. Wm. C. Bolton
Commanding U. S. Frigate
*Brandywine* Port Mahon
Island of Minorca.

U. S. Ship *Ohio*
Harbour of Boston
July 22, 1841.

Sir,
Since my return to the United States from the Mediterranean, I have been pained and mortified to find that

your letter to me of the 8th of March last has been made public by an official report made to the Senate by the Secretary of the Navy, and that it has been referred to as the leading cause of the return of the U. S. Frigate *Brandywine* from her station.

It is due to you as well as to myself that a full exposition of the course I pursued on receipt of your letter should be made. The course which has been taken by others you have no doubt seen and I trust you will understand my position.

Your letter and one from J. Hare Powel Esqr. on the same subject were received by me at Mahon on the 23d of March; the information conveyed, together with the tone assumed by the French papers, led me to believe there could be little doubt of the result of the exciting questions pending between G. Britain and the United States. I was without instructions to govern me in case of a rupture and felt myself placed in a very critical situation. The first move might be important and before taking it I deemed it proper to call a Council of the Officers holding commands of vessels in the Squadron. The Council met on the 24th of March at which there were present, besides myself, Capt. Bolton of the *Brandywine,* Captain E. A. F. Lavallette of the *Ohio,* Commander Voorhees of the Sloop of War *Preble* and my Secretary Mr. John Etheridge. The object of the meeting was made known, my views were expressed and your letter and that of Mr. Powel were read, and the officers present were requested to make known their sentiments. Minutes of the proceedings were noted at the time by my direction. This Council was confidential and I do not think the officers of my own ship were acquainted with the views expressed or with the result of the meeting. Captain Bolton requested to be furnished with a copy of the minutes, his request was complied with, not officially however, but intended as a memorandum, as such only was the record taken, only an extract of which was furnished by me to the Navy Department.

On the day after the meeting of the Council I drew up the orders under which the Squadron was to move, in which not one word is said in relation to your letter, neither is reference made to the Council of officers, but they directed the Commanders of Vessels as follows: "That you proceed to sea and make the best of your way out of the Mediterranean. You will endeavour, either by speaking vessels or by touching at some port, to ascertain the state of affairs between the United States and Great Britain. In case of war you will use every exertion to protect yourself and command, and to annoy the enemy, cruising as long as your provisions and other circumstances will admit of, and when a favorable opportunity offers, you will run into some port of the United States and report to the Secretary of the Navy. Much, however, must be left to your own judgment. Should you ascertain that quietness has been restored, you will return to the Mediterranean touching at Mahon, where you will probably hear from me."

The vessels of the Squadron proceeded to sea in company. On the 29th of March Captain Bolton sent his boat to the *Ohio* and on its leaving a verbal order was sent by me, through the officer of the boat, to Captain

Bolton *not to go out of signal distance.* On the night of the 3d of April, however, he separated from my flag and I did not see or hear from him again, until my arrival at this place, although I heard *of* him when at Gibraltar in June last. My astonishment was great to find that he had quitted his station and returned to the United States and I am mortified that he should have resorted to the minutes of the proceedings of the Council, embracing your letter, as the circumstances that influenced his return, copy of which "minutes" he must have sent to the Navy Department. It was not intended by me that your letter should be exposed to the public eye; I considered it one of a friendly character, meant to convey to me the state of your own impressions and to leave me to act as my own judgment should prompt in a case involving the safety of my command.

That Capt. Bolton found it necessary to lean on the "minutes" was a matter of his own choice, arising from the fact that he left his station without orders, but I find it difficult to appreciate the sense of propriety entertained by the Navy Department in furnishing on a call from the Senate, letters which carried with them the character and impress of "confidential", particularly when that propriety was left to its judgment and discretion by the very terms of the call. An investigation into the causes of the return of the *Brandywine* to the United States may and should be instituted that the true causes may appear. Whatever influence the information conveyed to me by your letter may have had on my mind, it should have had none on Captain Bolton, he was under my orders and had no right to go behind them, and in furnishing your letter to the Navy Department as a circumstance which influenced him in quitting the Mediterranean to return to the United States, he has I think deviated from a true military course.

I shall at all times declare that in furnishing Captain Bolton with a copy of the "minutes" referred to, it was not intended that they should be made public and I feel that I have been much injured by their publication.

I have thus given you an exposition of this matter at the earliest moment, and beg leave to add that I deeply regret and deplore the course which has been pursued.

With very great respect, I have the honor to be
Sir, Yr. Obt. St.
Isaac Hull

P.S. If Mr. Powel is still in London will you do me the favour to show him this letter?

His Excellency
A. Stevenson
U. S. Envoy and Minister Plenipotentiary, London

U. S. Ship *Ohio*
Harbour of Boston
July 22, 1841

J. Hare Powel Esqr.
London,
Dear Sir,

I reached this place on the 17th inst. after a passage of thirty one days from Gibraltar. Since my arrival I have been placed in possession of a Report made by the Secretary of the Navy on a call by the Senate of the

Un. States to communicate, "if not incompatible with the public interest, the correspondence of the Minister in England with the Officers of the Mediterranean Squadron, in consequence of which the Squadron left the Station, and the dispatches of Captain Bolton to the Secretary of the Navy connected with that movement", and it has given me exceeding pain to find that your confidential letter to me of the 11th of March last was embraced in the dispatches of Captain Bolton to the Navy Department. It is proper that I should, as I now intend to do, embrace the earliest opportunity to assure you that your letter was not furnished to the Navy Department by me or with my knowledge, nor did I intend it should ever be made public. A copy of it was furnished to Captain Bolton under the following circumstances. On its receipt, with one from His Excellency the Minister in England and in consequence of the tone of the French papers, so important did I consider the information, that I called a Council of the Senior Officers under my command; they met in my Cabin, where views were expressed and opinions interchanged as to the movements of the Squadron. Your letter and that of Mr. Stevenson were read and minutes of the proceedings were taken and written out by my direction. The Council was a confidential one and I do not believe the Officers of my own Ship were acquainted with the proceedings or the result of the meeting. Capt. Bolton requested to be furnished with a Copy of the "Minutes", it was handed to him unofficially and intended only as a memorandum. The Squadron sailed from Mahon the day succeeding that on which the Council was held, under specific instructions from me and having no reference whatever, either to your letter or to the proceedings of the Council. Capt. Bolton parted company as I conceive without cause and certainly without permission and proceeded to the United States and on his arrival saw fit very improperly I think, to send to the Navy Department with his dispatches, copy of the "Minutes" which embraced a copy of your letter to me. He deviated I think from military propriety, he had my orders which bore date subsequently to the "Minutes", and on those orders he should have rested.

I am mortified and truly regret the course which has been pursued by Capt. Bolton and the Navy Department and shall at all times declare that in furnishing Capt. Bolton with a copy of the "Minutes" referred to, it was not with a view that they should be sent to the Navy Department or be made public, and I feel that much injury has been done to me by the course which has been pursued.

I have written to Mr. Stevenson and have perhaps, entered a little more fully into this matter. I have requested him to shew you that letter, and I beg of you to permit Mr. Stevenson to read this.

    With very great respect
      I have the honor to be, Sir, Yr. Obt. St.
        Isaac Hull.

        Boston July 29th, 1841
Sir,
I have the honor to acknowledge the receipt of your letter of the 26th instant informing me that Capt. Bolton

has furnished no explanation of his return to the United States from the Mediterranean deemed satisfactory by you, and that you deem it unnecessary to act further in reference to my letter (sent to the Navy Department under date of the 17th inst.) until you shall hear again from me.

I beg leave to say that the circumstances and facts connected with the matter referred to, so far as they have come to my knowledge, are already before the Navy Department.

I now transmit copy of my reply to Capt. Bolton's communication.

With very great respect<br>
I have the honor to be Sir,<br>
Yr. Obt. St.<br>
Isaac Hull.

Hon. George E. Badger,
Secretary of the Navy
Washington, D. C.

Boston July 29, 1841

Dear Sir,

Previously to the receipt of yours of the 20th inst. I had addressed a communication to the Navy Department, on the subject of your return to the United States from the Mediterranean with the Frigate *Brandywine* under your command, enclosing one to your address to be forwarded to you in case "the Department is not already in possession of satisfactory information from Capt. Bolton upon the points therein embraced", copies of which are herewith enclosed, marked No. 1 and No. 2.

The Secretary of the Navy says "He (Capt. Bolton)

the matter any further. Nor have I entertained any other feelings than such as naturally arose from a sense of obligation due to the Service, to which we both belong.

It was my wish to leave the affair of your return from the Mediterranean wholly to the Navy Department, feeling satisfied that my duty was performed in placing before it the facts, so far as they had come to my knowledge, and if I have not been so understood I trust a copy of this letter, which I shall send to the Department by the same mail which takes this, will have the desired effect.

The Department has been unaccountably reserved towards me in this matter, so much so that I neither know its wishes with regard to your particular case, nor the course intended to be pursued; I shall, therefore, refrain from any further action until more explicitly advised.

I shall leave Boston for a few days, but any further communications you may be pleased to address to me, I shall be put in possession of on my return, when they shall receive my consideration and attention.

      I am, Very Respectfully
       Yr. Obt. St.
Capt. W. C. Bolton   Isaac Hull
U. S. Navy
Claverack, Columbia County
 New York

I have to direct that you proceed with the U. S. Ship *Preble* under your Command to Leghorn, where you will communicate with Mr. Greenough and J. A. Delano (Master of the Ship *Sea*) in relation to this business. You will render any aid and assistance that may be necessary or proper in hoisting the Statue on board the Ship *Sea* and disposing of it in such a manner as to preclude as far as possible any accident in shipping or any injury on the voyage; any alteration that may be required to be made in the Hatches of the Ship *Sea* to receive the Statue, you will be pleased to cause to be made at the expense of the Government of the United States; which being completed you will cause to be prepared for the signature of the Master of the *Sea* five Bills of Lading, to be disposed of as follows, viz: one to be sent to the Secretary of the Navy, one to the Commandant of the Navy Yard at Washington, one to be sent to my address at Boston, one to be kept by the Master of the *Sea,* and the fifth to be retained in your possession; the Statue to be delivered at the Navy Yard at Washington to the order of the Secretary of the Navy.

The copy of the letter from the Secretary of the Navy will give you the views and wishes of the Government, and I particularly urge upon you the greatest care in hoisting and stowing the Statue.

Having executed the foregoing order you will return to Mahon and report to my successor in command of the U. S. Naval Force in the Mediterranean for further orders. You have my permission to touch at Toulon or Marseilles on your return, if you find it necessary.

Should my relief not be found at Mahon, nor any

information of his arrival in the Mediterranean, you will proceed to the Coast of Spain, touching at Barcelona and Malaga and such of the intermediate ports as may be necessary for the protection of the Commerce of the United States. I desire however that you should report to my successor as soon after his arrival as possible.

Very respectfully, I am Sir,<br>Yr. Obt. St.<br>Isaac Hull<br>Comdr. in Chief of U. S.<br>Naval Force in the Mediterranean

Commander Ralph Voorhees
Comdr. U. S. Sloop of War *Preble*
Toulon, France

Navy Department<br>8th December 1840

Sir,

The Secretary of the Navy has, by a Resolution of Congress, been charged with the transportation of the Statue of Washington by Mr. Greenough from a port of Italy to the Navy Yard at this City, when it shall be finished.

No direct or positive information has been received as to this latter point, and you are requested on the receipt of this letter, to address Mr. Greenough, either at Leghorn or Florence or both places, on the subject. You will enquire in the first place as to the precise dimensions of the Statue, its height and other particulars, for the purpose of ascertaining whether it can be safely received and secured between decks in a Sloop of War.

In that case you will despatch the *Cyane,* which vessel will be relieved by the *Preble* now fitting out for that purpose, to the port of Leghorn, where it is presumed the Statue will be brought from Florence, to receive it on board and transport it to the Navy Yard at this place.

Should it however be found impossible to receive and stow it away between decks in the *Cyane,* you will on being apprised of the time when it will be ready for shipment, proceed to charter on the best terms in your power, some safe and competent American merchant ship, of ample dimensions for the purposes above designated, with directions to carry into effect these instructions with as little delay as possible.

You will furnish any aid and assistance Mr. Greenough may deem necessary or proper in hoisting the Statue on board, and disposing of it in such a manner as to preclude as far as possible, any accident in shipping, or any injury on the voyage. Mr. Greenough has been apprised of the contemplated arrangements and requested to communicate with you on the subject.

It is extremely important that great care and circumspection should be used in the selection of a vessel for the transportation of this valuable work, and the Department enjoins on you a scrupulous attention to that object, should the *Cyane* be found not competent to its safe accommodation.

      I am very respectfully
        Yr. Obt. Servt.
          J. K. Paulding.

Com. Isaac Hull
Commanding U. S. Squadron
in the Mediterranean.

## A STATUE OF WASHINGTON

### Charter Party

Toulon, France, April 23, 1841. This Charter party of affreightment, made and concluded upon this twenty third day of April, one thousand eight hundred and forty one, between J. A. Delano, Master of the American Ship *Sea* of Norfolk, of the burthen of eight hundred and seven tons or thereabouts, now laying in the port of Marseilles, through Messrs. Fitch Brothers Co. Navy Agents in the said City, of the one part, and Commodore Isaac Hull, Commanding the United States Naval Forces in the Mediterranean on behalf of the U. S. Government, of the other part, Witnesseth: That the said J. A. Delano as above, for the consideration hereinafter mentioned, has let to freight so much of the said ship *Sea* as necessary for its receiving and proper stowing, so as to preclude as far as possible any accident or injury on the voyage, with the appurtenances to her belonging for a voyage from Leghorn in Italy to the Navy Yard at Washington D. C. in the United States.

And the said Master J. A. Delano aforesaid does by these presents covenant and agree with the said Commodore Isaac Hull as above specified, that the said Ship shall be tight, staunch and strong and sufficiently manned, tackled and apparalled with all things necessary for such a Vessel and voyage and that it shall be lawful to the said Commodore Isaac Hull to put on board the said Ship at Leghorn a Statue of the late General Washington.

In Witness whereof the said Commodore Isaac Hull as above does by these presents agree to put on board the said Statue at Leghorn, by means of assistance to be rendered by the Crew of the U. S. Ship *Preble,* as soon after her arrival at Leghorn as practicable, and will truly pay or cause to be paid to the Master, or Agents or Owners, of the said Ship *Sea* on delivery of the said Statue at the Navy Yard Washington (the dangers of the seas only excepted) the sum of three thousand five hundred dollars in full for freight of same.

And it is also agreed that Capt. Delano shall allow fifteen working days for receiving on board the Statue at Leghorn and its landing at the Navy Yard, these working days to be reversible from the one port to the other.

It is also mutually agreed between the said contracting parties that the shipping and the relanding of the said Statue are to be at the expense and risk of the U. S. Government and that any cutting or alteration necessary to be made to the Ship in order to receive the Statue on board is to be made also at the expense of the U. S. Government. Also that the replacing of the Ship in her present position, or as she may be before receiving the Statue on board is to be done in the Navy Yard at the expense of the said U. S. Government and that within the period of the lay days specified above which may not have been consumed at the port of loading.

The purport of these above stipulations is this: that the Ship *Sea* is to be exonerated from any charges relating to the loading and landing of the said Statue. That she shall receive the net sum of three thousand five hundred dollars, and be restored to her primitive condition if any alteration be necessary, entirely free from any charges connected therewith.

It is also agreed and consented to by Commodore

# A STATUE OF WASHINGTON

Isaac Hull that proceeding from Leghorn, Capt. Delano shall have the privilege of touching at one or more ports in the Mediterranean to take freight or cargo direct to any port in the United States not south of Norfolk, and of landing the same should he require to do so before proceeding with the Statue to Washington. This privilege of taking freight or cargo is understood equally applying to Leghorn as to any other Port in the Mediterranean.

In Witness whereof we have signed the same in triplicate this day and year above written.

                Isaac Hull
                Commander in Chief of the U. S.
                Naval Force in the Mediterranean
                Fitch Brothers and Co.

Witness to all the   John A. Delano
Signatures
John Etheridge.


                U. States Ship *Preble*
                Leghorn, May 15, 1841

Sir

We arrived here early on Sunday morning the 9th inst. the ship *Sea* arrived the evening previous.

I have just returned from Florence to which place I repaired immediately on my arrival here to communicate with Mr. Greenough relative to the shipment of the statue. It will be boxed up ready to leave Florence today. It is to be brought to this place by land, there not being sufficient water in the canal; but the wheels

The commodore spent some time in Boston, attending to public and private business. He then went to New York, and from there to New Haven, where he passed the winter and spring. In the summer of 1842 he moved to Philadelphia, where he bought a house on Spruce Street and settled down for the short remainder of his life.[1] His health had begun to fail and October 26, 1841, he had been granted a leave of absence for one year. At the expiration of this, in October, 1842, Secretary Upshur offered him the "appointment of Commander afloat at Boston," if agreeable to him, but he was not well enough to accept and his leave was extended another year. He continued to fail and died in Philadelphia February 13, 1843, not quite seventy years old. His tomb is in Laurel Hill Cemetery, Philadelphia.

Isaac Hull was one of our great naval commanders. He was of the "old sea-dog" type. Edmund Quincy, in his Life of his father, speaks of having been too young to remember Captain Hull's visit to his father's house in 1812, "but I often saw him in later years and knew him well, as a very young man knows a distinguished elder. His manners certainly were easy, as my sister describes them, and prepossessing in the sense of being eminently suitable to the man and characteristic of him. They were plain, bluff, and hearty, as became 'a rough and boisterous captain of the sea,' and indicated a good heart and a good temper, though not incapable of being ruffled on a sufficient occasion."[2]

[1] Wilson, *Commodore Hull and the Constitution*, in *New York Genealogical and Biographical Record*, XI (1880), 109.

[2] Quincy, *Life of Josiah Quincy*, 263. See above, p. 27.

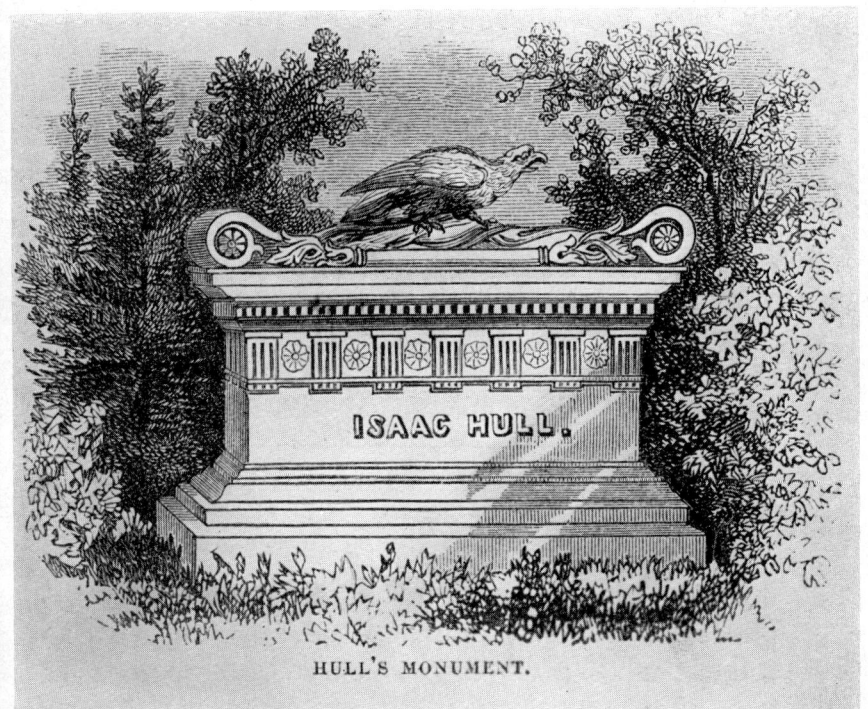

HULL'S MONUMENT.

He was kindly and took an interest in young men. After the Mediterranean cruise he wrote friendly letters to his midshipmen, like this to Daniel Ammen: "I have much pleasure in bearing testimony to your correct conduct during the short period of your service under my late command in the Mediterranean. Accept my best wishes for your health and happiness as well as speedy advancement in the Navy." He was an active, busy man and had no patience with the shiftless and lazy. In 1834 he wrote to his nephew: "You do not tell me what you are about. I hope you find constant employment, for be assured that idleness will soon bring any man to ruin."[1]

Admiral Farragut said to General James Grant Wilson: "Isaac Hull was as able a seaman as ever sailed a ship. If I have done the country any service afloat, it is in no small degree owing to the ambition and enthusiasm he created in me when I was a youngster by his fair fight with and capture of an English frigate. I always envied Hull that piece of good luck."[2]

---

[1] *New York Genealogical and Biographical Record,* XI, 109. See Hibben, *History of Washington Navy Yard,* 70.

[2] *New York Genealogical and Biographical Record,* XI, 101.

## THE END

# INDEX

Abbot, Joel, lieutenant, 62, 63, 64.
Abbott, J. Francis, midshipman, 229.
Adams, George, lieutenant, 205.
Adams, John, president, 55, 60.
*Adams,* U. S. frigate, 4.
Adelaide, Queen, 107.
Alberty y Nidal, Juan, 242, 246.
Allen, Edward, midshipman, 169.
Allen, Herman, 81, 82.
Allen, Samuel, captain, 201, 202.
Ambler, John, 79, 80, 81, 87, 89.
*America,* U. S. ship of the line, 84.
Ammen, Daniel, midshipman, 331.
Amstead, Joseph F., 171.
Amsterdam, 14, 16, 18, 20.
Anderson, George, seaman, 279, 281.
Anderson, John, 186.
Annersley, James, British consul at Barcelona, 270, 274.
Apprentices, 166, 179.
*Argus,* U. S. brig, 4, 5, 6, 7, 8, 10, 12.
Ashburton treaty, 267, 268, 296.
Athens, 100, 106, 119, 120, 121, 123, 124, 125.

Badger, George E., secretary of the navy, 83, 317.
Bainbridge, William, captain, 5, 30, 41.
Balch, George B., midshipman, 168.
Ballester, Antonio, 248.
Barlow, Joel, U. S. minister to France, 12, 13, 15, 21.
Barron, James, commodore, 9.
Barron, Samuel, commodore, 6.
Barry, Richard, 75.
Bartlett, Edwin, 52, 54.
Bates, John A., purser, 65, 67.
Baury, Frederick, midshipman, 12, 13.
Beadle, Mr. and Mrs. 128.
Beale, George, purser, 65, 66.
Beirut, 106, 127, 128.
Bejar, Don Jose, acting governor of Mahon, 207.
Bell, Charles H., lieutenant, 289, 290, 292, 295.
Bell, J. M., clerk, 270.

Belt, William J., lieutenant, 73.
Benjamin, ——, Rev., 125.
Bennett, Sarah, 1.
Binney, Amos, 65.
Bird, John, seaman, 254.
Blair, Henry, seaman, 193, 194.
Blanco, ——, admiral, 51.
Blockade, 5, 13, 14, 19, 31, 32, 35, 42, 44, 46.
Bolivar, Simon, general, 44, 45, 46, 52, 55.
Bolton, William Compton, captain, in command of the *Brandywine,* 106, 114, 238, 295; his musicians, 185; his crew on liberty, 211, 213; reports a case of stabbing, 258; at council of war, 300, 301, 302, 303, 311, 314, 315, 318; orders for, 310, 312, 313; returns home, 313, 316, 317, 319.
Borras, Joseph, U. S. consul at Barcelona, 272.
*Boston,* U. S. sloop of war, 61.
Bourne, Sylvanus, U. S. consul at Amsterdam, 20.
*Boxer,* H. M. S., 31, 32.
*Brandywine,* U. S. frigate, takes Lafayette to France, 55; on the Pacific station, 58, 60; on the Mediterranean station, 106, 111, 113, 114, 206, 257, 295, 300; orders for, 131, 132, 309; officers of, 151, 228, 230, 238, 240; crew of, 194, 210, 211, 212; returns home, 311, 313, 317.
Breese, Samuel L., commander, 88.
Bridge, Horatio, purser, 152.
Briggs, Samuel S., 70, 73.
Brown, Charles, seaman, 193, 194.
Brown, James, 256.
Browning, Robert L., lieutenant, 155.
Bruce, William, seaman, 269, 270, 272, 274.
Buell, Jeremiah, gunner's mate, 196.
Burrows, William, lieutenant, 32.
Burton, Alexander, U. S. consul at Cadiz, 277, 279.

## 334 INDEX

Caldwell, Charles H. B., midshipman, 169.
Callao, 43, 44, 45, 46, 47, 51, 52, 54, 58, 60, 66, 67.
Calle, Francisco, 246.
*Cambridge,* H. M. S., 44, 50.
Campbell, Hugh G., captain, 4.
*Canton Packet,* American ship, 268, 269, 270, 271, 272, 273, 274, 275.
Cape Horn, 43, 61.
*Caroline,* steamer, 296, 297.
Carr, Thomas N., U. S. consul at Tangier, 150.
*Carrier,* American brig, 194.
Carrington, Abijah, 192.
Carrington, Charles, 191, 192.
Carter, Thomas, 256.
Cass, Lewis, secretary of war, 74.
Cassoni, Philip, pilot, 320, 321.
Chapman, George W., passed midshipman, 229.
Charter parties, 201, 325.
Chase, Robert F., American, shipmaster, 269, 270, 271, 272, 274, 276.
Chasseaud, Jasper, U. S. consul at Beirut, 129.
Chauncey, Isaac, commodore, 9, 40, 63, 114, 196.
Cherbourg, 13, 17, 18, 21, 22.
*Chesapeake,* U. S. frigate, 9, 10, 11.
Claystine, ——, 265.
Cobb, ——, U. S. vice-consul at Arica, 57.
Cogswell, John, seaman, 264.
Colby, Frederick W., midshipman, 169.
Collins, John, seaman, 194.
*Columbus,* U. S. receiving ship, 92, 196, 197, 198, 329.
*Congress,* U. S. frigate, 32, 35.
Congressional inquiry, 64, 65, 66, 67.
*Constitution,* U. S. frigate, in the war with France, 2, 3; in the Tripolitan war, 4, 5; cruising, 12; at Cherbourg, 13, 21, 22, 23; at the Texel, 14, 15, 16, 17, 18, 19, 20; fired on, 21; at Portsmouth, 21, 22; returns home, 23; refitting, 24; chased by British squadron, 25; her battle with the *Guerrière,* 26, 27, 28, 29; at Boston, 29; captures the *Java,* 30; in dry dock, 74; ordered to the Pacific, 111; hero of, 298.

Cooper, G. C., purser, 206.
Cooper, James Fenimore, 3, 24.
Council of war, 300, 301, 302, 303.
Court martial, 9, 32, 63, 151, 162, 164, 172, 173, 174, 175, 176, 254, 258, 259.
Court of inquiry, 9, 63, 64, 79, 151, 318.
Cox, John W., lieutenant, 155.
Crowninshield, Benjamin William, secretary of the navy, 78.
Croxall, D. C., U. S. consul at Marseilles, 193, 194.
Cullen, Joseph, U. S. consul at Tenerife, 279, 281, 282, 284, 286, 289, 290.
Cushing, T. H., general, 34.
Cutting, Edward, seaman, 254, 263, 264, 265.
*Cyane,* U. S. sloop of war, on Mediterranean station, 87, 95, 151; at Mahon, 95, 98, 105, 132, 134, 159, 161, 190; cruising, 100, 103, 104, 105, 137, 161; commander of, 104, 105, 113, 158; crew of, 104, 105, 115, 116; at Messina, 104, 107, 170, 186; returns home, 106, 324; at Naples, 107; beats the *Ohio,* 112; at Piræus, 120, 121, 123, 124, 125; at Smyrna, 130; at Spezia, 152; officers of, 159, 162, 163, 164; midshipmen on, 160, 167, 168, 169, 170, 171, 176, 177, 178, 181, 182; teacher on, 167, 168, 169, 170, 171; punishment on, 266; off Barcelona, 270, 271, 273.

Daggett, David, U. S. senator, 37, 39, 78.
Dallas, Alexander J., Jr., midshipman, 229.
Davis, E., seaman, 193, 194.
Debts, 99, 110, 111, 144, 149, 265.
Decatur, Stephen, lieutenant, 4; captain, 5, 10, 28, 29.
Delano, John A., captain, 322, 325, 326, 327.
Derne, 6, 7.
Deserters, 9, 21, 22, 148, 149, 185, 186, 260, 261.
DeWinter, ——, admiral, 19.
Dickerson, Mahlon, secretary of the navy, 70, 71, 75, 80.
Discipline, 43, 67, 96, 99, 136, 139, 146, 172, 179, 253.

# INDEX    335

*Dolphin,* U. S. brig, 289, 292, 295.
*Dolphin,* U. S. schooner, 43, 45, 52, 60, 65.
*Dos Amigos,* brig. See *Two Friends.*
Dove, Benjamin M., lieutenant, 124.
Downes, John, commodore, 76, 87, 171, 172, 178.
Downes, John, Jr., midshipman, 87, 160, 169, 171, 177, 178, 181.
Dubois, Alexandre, wardroom cook, 260, 261.
Duelling, 151, 182.
Dunn, Henry, landsman, 213, 214.
Du Pont, Samuel F., lieutenant, 140, 155, 157, 159, 233, 234, 235, 242.
Durkee, John A., American shipmaster, 276, 278, 279, 281, 282, 286, 287, 288, 289, 290.

Eakin, James, master, 10.
Eaton, John Henry, U. S. minister to Spain, 294, 295.
Eaton, William, general, 6, 7.
Eckford, Henry, naval constructor, 84.
*Eclair,* H. M. S., 60.
*Elizabeth,* American bark, 192.
Elliott, Jesse D., commodore, 77.
Ellison, Francis B., lieutenant, 133, 163, 164, 165.
Emerson, American ship-master, 186.
*Enterprise,* U. S. schooner, 4, 5; brig, 31, 32.
*Erie,* U. S. sloop of war, 197.
*Essex,* U. S. frigate, 196.
Etheridge, John, commodore's secretary, 65, 66, 76, 83, 303, 311, 327.
Evans, Samuel, lieutenant, 7.

Fairfax, Reginald, midshipman, 230.
Farragut, David Glasgow, midshipman, 166; admiral, 331.
Fitch Brothers & Company, 98, 143, 297, 325, 327.
Flogging, 146, 253.
Foltz, Jonathan M., surgeon, 199.
Fosdick, Benjamin H., clerk, 63, 64.
Fountain, George, seaman, 103.
Fox, Gustavus Vasa, midshipman, 167, 168, 176, 177.
Fox, Henry S., British minister at Washington, 298.
*Franklin,* U. S. ship of the line, 43, 58, 59.

*Frederic,* brig, 45.
*Fulton,* U. S. steamer, 94, 95.

Gallatin, Albert, secretary of the treasury, 14, 15.
Gansevoort, Guert, lieutenant, 155, 230.
Garretson, Isaac, purser, 14, 16, 19, 20.
*General Greene,* U. S. receiving ship, 23.
German, Juan, alcalde, 209.
Gero, John, seaman, 194.
Gerry, Thomas R., 89.
Gibraltar, 4, 8, 80, 95, 100, 102, 104, 145, 150, 179, 206, 299.
Gilman, John Taylor, governor of New Hampshire, 33.
*Globe,* American ship, 53.
Godon, Sylvanus W., lieutenant, 155.
Goldsborough, Charles W., chief clerk of navy department, 10.
Gomila, James, hospital steward, 194.
*Good Hope,* American brig, 65.
Gosselman, ——, captain in Swedish navy, 99.
Greene, James M., surgeon, 148, 195, 304.
Greenough, Horatio, sculptor, 320, 321, 322, 323, 324, 327.
Grier, John W., chaplain, 155.
Grog, 139, 146, 200, 253.
*Guerrière,* British frigate, 26, 27, 28, 29.
*Guerrière,* U. S. frigate, 196.
Guise, ——, admiral, 44, 46.
Gunboats, 4, 5, 8, 33.

Hamet Pasha, 6.
Hamilton, Paul, secretary of the navy, 11.
Hammond, Walter, mate, 284.
Hardinge, Sir Henry, 298.
Harris, ——, captain, 29.
Harrison, William Henry, president, 104, 296.
Hart, Anna McCurdy, 30. See Hull, Mrs. Isaac.
Hart, Elisha, captain, 30, 79.
Hart, Jeannette, 43, 59, 74, 88.
Harvard College, 86.
*Hastings,* H. B. M. ship of the line, 104, 107.
*Havana,* H. M. S., 22.

## INDEX

Hawaii, 52, 53.
Hawthorne, Nathaniel, 152.
Hazleton, David, seaman, 194.
Health, 199, 200.
Hill, ——, 121, 126.
Hilton, John, 256.
Hitchcock, Robert B., lieutenant, 206.
Hogan, Michael, U. S. consul at Valparaiso, 65, 67.
Hogan, William, member of congress, 64, 65.
Holland, Thomas, seaman, 22.
*Hornet,* U. S. sloop, 7.
*Hornet,* U. S. sloop of war, 23.
Hospital, 194, 199, 303, 304.
*Hotspur,* H. M. S., 23.
Houstin, ——, Rev., 125.
Howard, William L., lieutenant, 155.
Hudson, William, musician, 189.
Hull, Eliza, 81, 82.
Hull, Isaac, birth and boyhood, 1, 2; lieutenant in the navy, 2, 4; in war with France, 2; sails the *Constitution* in a race, 2, 3; commands a cutting-out expedition, 3, 4; in the Tripolitan war, 4, 5, 6, 7; commands the *Enterprise,* 4; commander, 5; commands the *Argus,* 5, 6, 7, 8; at Derne, 7; letters, orders, etc., of, 7, 8, 9, 16, 17, 18, 19, 20, 31, 32, 37, 38, 40, 69, 78, 80, 81, 82, 83, 100, 132, 134, 135, 138, 144, 148, 165, 196, 198, 205, 215, 219, 222, 235, 237, 239, 240, 251, 252, 304, 305, 306, 309, 310, 314, 316, 317, 318, 319, 321, 323, 327; captain, 8; builds gunboats, 8; on Barron court of inquiry, 9; commands *Chesapeake,* 10; in Boston, 11; commands *President* and *Constitution,* 12; at the Texel, 14, 16, 17, 18, 19, 20; in the English Channel, 21, 22; refuses to surrender deserter, 22; returns home, 23; chased by British squadron, 25; his battle with the *Guerrière,* 26, 27, 28, 29; at Quincy, 28; at Boston, 29; honors bestowed, 29, 30; married, 30; in command of Boston and Portsmouth navy yards, 30, 31, 32, 33; views on defense of Portsmouth, 33, 34, 35; on rank and command, 37, 38, 40; navy commissioner and commandant of Boston navy yard, 39; commodore, 41; ordered to the Pacific station, 42; sails in flagship *United States,* 43; at Callao, 44, 45, 47, 50, 51, 52, 53, 56, 57, 59, 60; cruising, 52, 54; relieved and returns home, 60, 61; charges against, 62, 63, 64, 65, 66, 67; vindicated, 64, 67; commandant of Washington navy yard, 68, 69, 70, 71, 72, 73; has trouble with workmen, 69, 70, 71, 73; at opening of Boston dry dock, 74; on leave, 74, 75; on board of revision, 76, 77; ordered to the Mediterranean station, 77, 87; private affairs, 78, 79, 80, 81, 82, 83; frees his slave, 79, 80; reports to, 91, 93, 97, 101, 108, 112, 113, 116, 119, 122, 126, 136, 137, 140, 141, 142, 145, 147, 150, 158, 179, 191, 192, 195, 199, 211, 214, 217, 233, 250, 260, 266, 276, 279, 285, 289, 290, 295, 297, 299, 307, 328; joins the flagship *Ohio,* 94; in command of the Mediterranean station, 97, 98, 113; at Lisbon, 102; saluted, 102, 104; notified of conditions in the Levant, 106, 128; Captain Smith's letter to, 117; Captain Percival's letters to, 154, 161; charges preferred to, 173, 176; midshipmen solicit orders, 176, 177, 178, 182; affairs of enlisted men referred to, 185, 189, 191, 192, 195, 197; medical and sanitary reports to, 199, 203; survey ordered by, 205; local affairs at Mahon reported to, 208, 209, 213, 214, 215, 217, 218, 219, 220; views on theatre riot, 222, 226, 235, 237, 239, 240, 251, 252; reviews courts martial, 254, 255; orders report on case of robbery, 261, 262; on supposed case of impressment, 270, 273, 276; on case of a slaver, 285, 288, 290, 292, 295; calls council of war, 300, 301, 302, 303; prepares to leave the station, 303, 304, 305, 306, 307; decides to stay, 308, 309, 310; on Captain Bolton's return, 311 to 319; arranges for transportation of statue, 321, 323, 325, 326, 327; returns home and hauls

# INDEX

down his flag, 329; death of, 330; character of, 330, 331.
Hull, Mrs. Isaac, 31, 39, 43, 59, 74, 80, 87, 88, 89, 153.
Hull, John, 1.
Hull, Joseph, lieutenant, 1, 78.
Hull, Joseph, Jr., 81, 82.
Hull, Richard, 1.
Hull, William, general, 1.
Hunt, ——, 10.
Hurst, William D., master, 206.

Impressment, 267, 268.
*Independence,* U. S. ship of the line, 196.
*Intrepid,* U. S. ketch, 5, 6.

Jackson, Andrew, president, 74.
Jackson, E., 191.
*Jasper,* U. S. storeship, 65, 66.
*Java,* H. M. S., 30.
Jefferson, Thomas, president, 55, 60; secretary of state, 268.
*Jersey,* British prison-ship, 1.
*John Adams,* U. S. frigate, 4.
Jones, Jacob, commodore, 60.
Jones, William, secretary of the navy, 32, 34, 36.
Jones, William A., passed midshipman, 260, 264.

Kavanagh, Edward, U. S. *chargé d'affaires* at Lisbon, 145.
Kean, Marcus, seaman, 194.
Kearnes, ——, 265.
Kelley, Anthony, captain, 65.
Kelly, John, lieutenant, 212, 258.
Kenny, Edward, 256.
Kenyon, ——, 265.
Keyes, Mr. and Mrs., 128.
King, ——, Rev., 121, 125, 126.
Knapp, Robert A., midshipman, 169, 265.

Lafayette, Marquis de, general, 55.
Lanigan, Michael, seaman, 254.
*La Reine,* Sardinian frigate, 114.
Latimer, William K., commander, in command of the *Cyane,* 105, 112, 134, 138, 158; reports of, 105, 113, 116, 126, 160, 182; at Beirut, 106; at Athens, 119, 120, 121, 122, 126; at Smyrna, 130; charges preferred by, 161, 163, 164.

Lavallette, Elie A. F., captain, in command of the *Ohio,* 99, 134, 135, 148, 205, 206; reports of, 136, 137, 140, 141, 142, 147, 150, 185, 213, 307; recommends tea in place of grog, 139, 147, 200; at council of war, 300, 302, 303, 311.
Lawrence, James, lieutenant, 12; commander, 23.
Lebron, Manuel, governor of Minorca, 204, 210, 214, 225, 241, 249, 250.
Lee, ——, U. S. consul at Bordeaux, 12.
*Leopard,* H. M. S., 9.
LeRoy, William E., passed midshipman, 230, 260.
*Levant,* U. S. sloop of war, 89.
Liberty, 43, 111, 141, 170, 177, 178, 207, 208, 210, 211, 212, 215, 216, 220.
Lima, 44, 45, 47, 48, 49, 50, 54, 55, 56, 57, 60, 66.
Linton, Thomas A., captain of marines, 266.
Log-book, of the *Constitution,* 12, 13, 14, 20, 21, 22, 23, 24; of the *United States,* 43, 51, 52, 54, 60, 67; of the *Ohio,* 92, 94, 95, 99, 102, 103, 104, 200, 201, 253, 254, 329.
Long, John C., lieutenant, 65.
Louis, Sir John, rear admiral, 275.
Lyndall, George, 70, 73.

McCall, Edward, 66, 67.
McCauley, Daniel Smith, U. S. consul at Tripoli, 109, 119.
McCauley, Edward, 118, 119.
McCay, David L., notary public, 282.
McDonough, Charles S., midshipman, 160.
Macdonough, Thomas, commodore, 62.
McLeod, Alexander, 296, 297, 298, 299.
McRae, Archibald, midshipman, 168.
McWilliams, Alex, 73.
Maguire, John, seaman, 281, 288.
Mahon. See Port Mahon.
Mahy, Thomas, Jr., U. S. consular agent, 285.
Major, James, professor of mathematics, 168, 169.

## 338  INDEX

Maling, ——, captain, 48, 51.
Marbury, A. H., lieutenant, 238.
Marines, 3, 10, 84, 85, 96, 97, 261, 263, 266.
*Mars,* H. M. S., 23.
Marseilles, 98, 99, 100, 105, 112, 131, 132, 138, 143, 158, 192, 274, 297.
Matzen, John, captain of hold, 195, 196.
Maurant, John, 219, 220.
Mediterranean station, 77, 87, 95, 98, 111, 134, 151, 199, 207.
Melbourne, Lord, 298.
Mercadal, Benito, 242.
Mercer, Samuel, lieutenant, 103, 155, 166, 205, 266.
Merchant marine, 42, 52, 53, 67, 98, 130, 131, 187, 268, 276.
Metzer, John. See Matzen.
Midshipmen, 149, 160, 166, 167, 168, 169, 170, 180, 181.
Miller, Peter, 256.
Mills, Elijah H., member of congress, 39.
Minorca, island of, 95, 204, 207, 220, 222, 248, 250, 300, 303, 308.
Miskell, John A., 70, 73.
Missroon, John S., lieutenant, 140, 155.
Mitchel, John, seaman, 194.
Moore, Michael, merchant, 282, 285.
Morris, Charles, lieutenant, 12, 22, 25, 27; captain, 63.
Morris, Charles M., midshipman, 89.
Morris, John, boatswain, 197, 198.
Morris, Lewis, colonel, 89.
Morris, Richard V., commodore, 4.
Morse, James, seaman, 95.
Murray, Alexander, captain, 9.
Mutiny, 53, 56, 58, 59.
Myrick, ——, captain, 56.

*Nautilus,* U. S. schooner, 7.
Naval Committee, 65, 67.
Navy Commissioners, 37, 38, 39, 63, 68, 76, 92.
Navy Department, letters and orders of, 11, 30, 34, 35, 53, 66, 69, 70, 75, 109, 113, 114, 130, 133, 134, 144, 186, 200, 259, 273, 297, 301, 310, 311, 321, 323, 330; reports to, 26, 32, 80, 83, 107, 131, 132, 179, 304, 305, 312, 315, 316; and navy commissioners, 37, 38, 76; views of, 40, 62, 79, 268, 313, 319; agents of, 145, 201, 325.
Navy Yard, Washington, 23, 24, 68, 69, 70, 71, 73, 74, 320 to 326; Boston, 30, 37, 39, 41, 62, 63, 64, 78, 87, 90, 171, 196, 197, 198, 329; Portsmouth, 30, 31, 32, 33; New York, 92, 93; Mahon, 98, 147, 200, 204.
Nebot, Salvador, 245.
Newcomb, Henry S., midshipman, 173, 174.
Nicholls, Andrew, seaman, 194.
Nicholson, Samuel, captain, 2.
Nicholson, Somerville, midshipman, 228, 229, 242.
Nixon, Z. W., lieutenant, 48, 50.
*North Carolina,* U. S. ship of the line, 111.

Obregon, Don Manuel, governor of Mahon, 208.
O'Brien, Smith, 298.
Officers, 92, 97, 98, 151, 152, 154, 155, 159, 221, 222, 247, 250, 252, 307.
*O'Higgins,* Chilean frigate, 51.
*Ohio,* U. S. ship of the line, building of, 84; dimensions of, 84; battery of, 84, 100, 101, 102; officers and crew of, 85, 96, 99, 100, 102, 103, 136, 137, 139, 140, 141, 142, 146, 149, 151, 155, 157, 160, 210, 211, 212, 216, 253; cost of, 86; Captain Smith in command of, 86, 99; fitting out for service as flagship, 87, 90, 91, 93; going into commission, 87, 91, 92; at New York, 92, 94; log of, 92, 94, 95, 99, 102, 103, 104, 200, 201, 253, 254, 329; sailing qualities of, 93, 95, 96, 100, 101, 103, 112, 137, 139; health of, 93, 94, 199, 200, 202, 203; at sea, 95, 100, 112, 134, 136, 138, 148, 154, 202, 255, 256, 305, 307, 329; at Port Mahon, 95, 98, 103, 116, 131, 132, 140, 142, 144, 147, 159, 161, 172, 190, 204, 206, 213, 219, 225, 251, 252, 261, 290, 300; Captain Lavallette in command, 99, 134; condition of, 101, 109, 135, 140, 148; at Trieste, 135; at Smyrna, 137, 139; at Toulon, 146, 260, 309, 320; at Gibraltar, 150, 179, 329; at Bos-

# INDEX 339

ton, 165, 310, 314, 329; at Spezia, 166; in quarantine, 203, 204; liberty on, 210, 211, 212; at Tenerife, 100, 285, 292; council of war on, 300, 311, 318; preparing for war, 307; returns home, 329; out of commission, 329.
Olivies, Bartolome, alcalde, 209.
*Ontario*, U. S. sloop of war, 88.
Orfila, ——, attorney general, 247.
Orlop, 92, 93, 97, 102, 109, 151, 154, 155, 156.
Otho, king of Greece, 121.

Pacific station, 42, 43, 60.
Palmerston, Lord, 298.
Pando, ——, 60.
Parker, William A., passed midshipman, 230, 244.
Patterson, Daniel T., commodore, 76, 87.
Paulding, Hiram, lieutenant, 47.
Paulding, James K., secretary of the navy, 107, 111, 115, 130, 170, 186, 188, 259, 266, 273, 324.
*Peacock*, U. S. sloop of war, 52.
Pearson, John, seaman, 218.
Peel, Sir Robert, 298.
Pendergrast, Garrett J., lieutenant, 99, 140, 212, 221, 222, 225, 226, 227, 234.
*Pennsylvania*, U. S. ship of the line, 84.
Percival, John, lieutenant, in command of the *Dolphin*, 52; commander, in command of the *Cyane*, 104; his crew, 104, 185; relieved, 105, 113, 158; salutes queen, 107; letters to Commodore Hull, 154, 161; his midshipmen, 168, 170, 171, 177, 178, 181; on destitute seamen, 188; on case of supposed impressment, 271, 289.
Percey, J., captain, 23.
Perdicaris, Gregory A., U. S. consul at Athens, 122, 123, 125, 126.
Perry, Matthew Calbraith, midshipman, 29.
Perry, Oliver Hazard, lieutenant, 12.
Perry, William, seaman, 194.
*Philadelphia*, U. S. frigate, 5.
Pinckney, Richard S., lieutenant, 148.
Piracy, 98, 106, 108, 118, 129, 310.

Place, Charles W., midshipman, 169.
Poindexter, Carter B., passed midshipman, 254.
Porter, David, commodore, 39, 63, 105, 196; U. S. minister to Turkey, 105, 106, 129, 130.
Porter, David Dixon, admiral, 31.
Port Mahon, headquarters of U. S. Mediterranean station, 95, 98, 145, 207, 300, 308; navy yard at, 98, 147, 200, 204; governor of, 99, 203, 204, 207, 208, 214, 216, 219, 220, 221, 225, 235, 238, 239, 247, 251; hospital at, 194, 199, 303; laws and regulations of, 207, 208, 214, 215, 216, 217, 219, 220; theatre at, 221; robbery at, 261.
Porto Plata, 3.
Portsmouth, defense of, 31, 33, 34, 35, 36.
*Potomac*, U. S. frigate, 196.
Powel, John Hare, 299, 301, 311, 314, 318.
Pratique, 200.
Preble, Edward, commodore, 4, 5, 6, 8, 9.
*Preble*, U. S. sloop of war, on the Mediterranean station, 98, 106; ordered to Toulon, 142, 143; at sea, 145; at Malaga, 146; at Mahon, 300; ordered to cruise, 306, 308; at Leghorn, 320, 321, 322, 324, 325, 327.
*President*, U. S. frigate, 12, 29.
Provisions and stores, 142, 149, 200, 201, 202, 203, 204, 205, 206.
Punishment, 99, 142, 146, 149, 253, 254, 255, 256, 259, 266.

Quarantine, 108, 200, 203, 204.
Quimby, James, seaman, 189, 190.
Quincy, Edmund, 27, 330.
Quincy, Josiah, 27.

Raguet, Condy, U. S. *chargé d'affaires* at Rio de Janeiro, 59.
Rank and grade, 37, 38, 40, 41.
Read, James Withers, passed midshipman, 228, 229, 230, 242.
Recruiting service, 9, 10, 24, 35, 36.
*Redpole*, H. M. S., 21.
Reeves, James, seaman, 254, 255.

340

INDEX

Reeves, Samuel J., master at arms, 257.
Renshaw, William B., passed midshipman, 230.
*Revenge,* U. S. schooner, 12.
Revision, Board of, 76, 77.
Reynolds, James, seaman, 255.
Reynolds, Thomas, carpenter's mate, 257, 258.
Rhind, Alexander C., midshipman, 172, 173, 174, 175, 176.
Rich, J. H., acting consul at Mahon, 217, 218.
Rich, Obadiah, U. S. consul at Mahon, 98, 149, 201, 202, 203, 204, 208, 308, 309.
Ridgely, Charles G., commodore, 93.
Riera, Francisco, ship-owner, 282, 284.
*Rimac,* brig, 44.
Robbery, case of, 261 to 266.
Rodgers, John, commodore, 9, 12, 25, 28, 38, 39, 63.
Rodil, ——, general, 43, 47, 48, 51.
Rush, Benjamin, secretary of legation at London, 299.
Rush, Madison, midshipman, 299.
Russell, Jonathan, U. S. *chargé d'affaires* at London, 21.

*Sally,* sloop, 3.
Salutes, 8, 13, 43, 51, 52, 54, 55, 60, 94, 95, 99, 102, 104, 107, 329.
Sancho, Juan Jose, alcalde, 209, 248.
Sanitation, 199.
*Sarah and Esther,* American brig, 201.
Sardinia, king of, 114.
Schlosser, Fort, 296, 297.
School, 166, 167, 168, 169, 170, 171, 179, 180.
*Sea,* American ship, 321, 322, 325, 326, 327.
Seamen, American, welfare of, 98, 184, 185, 187, 188, 192, 193.
Selden, Carey, 80, 81.
Sena, Manuel, boatswain's mate, 284.
Sequi, Francis, acting president, board of health, 204.
Shields, Wilmer, midshipman, 182, 183.
Shurtleff, George G., seaman, 190.
Silk, Samuel, 256.

Silsbee, Nathaniel, member of Congress, 40.
Simpson, John, lieutenant, 269, 270, 271, 272, 275, 276.
Sinclair, William, purser, 143, 206, 308.
Slave-ship, 100, 277, 278.
Slave-trade, 277, 295.
Smith, Joseph, captain, on board of revision, 77; in command of the *Ohio,* 86, 99, 172; letters and reports of, 91, 93, 94, 97, 101, 102, 109, 112, 117, 155, 158, 172, 174, 175, 176, 180, 185, 189, 191, 196, 203, 255; ordered to submit report, 100; private letter to Commodore Hull, 117; letter to officers on orlop, 155; prefers charges, 172; report on apprentices, 179, 180; mentioned, 178, 226, 234.
Smyrna, 106, 130, 132.
Somers, Richard, commander, 6.
Somers, William, apprentice, 102.
Southard, Samuel Lewis, secretary of the navy, 53.
Spencer, John C., surgeon, 198.
Spencer, S., 195.
Sprague, Horatio, U. S. consul at Gibraltar, 105, 206.
Stanley, Lord, 298.
Steerwell, James, seaman, 253, 262, 263, 264, 265.
Stepto, James, seaman, 193.
Stevenson, Andrew, U. S. minister to Great Britain, 297, 299, 300, 301, 314, 315, 316, 318.
Stewart, Charles, lieutenant, 4; commodore, 42, 58.
Stockton, Robert F., commander, 87, 97, 99.
Stopford, Sir Robert, admiral, 276.
Sumner, Charles, 86.
Surveys, 200, 201, 204, 205.
Sussey, Comte de, 15.
Swan, ——, captain, 192.
Swift, Samuel, captain, 65, 66.
Swift, ——, lieutenant, 20.

Talbot, Silas, commodore, 2, 3.
Tattnall, Edward F., midshipman, 160, 169.
Taylor, Alfred, lieutenant, 155.
Teneriffe, 106, 277, 282, 286, 287, 289, 291, 295.
Texel, the, 14, 16, 17, 18, 19.

# INDEX

Thomson, Mr. and Mrs., 128.
Throop, Enos Thompson, U. S. chargé d'affaires at Naples, 107.
*Thunderer,* H. M. S., 104.
Ticknor, Benaiah, surgeon, 109, 199.
Toulon, 103, 105, 138, 143, 145, 146, 148, 149, 297, 302, 308, 309, 320, 321, 325.
Townsend, Robert, midshipman, 230, 232.
Travala, Juan B., captain, 282.
Treasury Department, 15, 20, 66, 79.
Trefethen, Henry, captain, 32.
Tripoli, war with, 4, 5, 6, 7; U. S. consul at, 108, 109, 118, 119.
Tudor, William, U. S. consul at Lima, 44, 45, 50, 51, 56, 57, 60.
*Two Friends,* American brig, 278, 279, 282, 285, 286, 287, 288, 289, 290, 291, 293, 295.

Ufford, J. L., 82.
*Ulysses,* British bark, 269.
*United States,* American packet, 297.
*United States,* U. S. frigate, flagship of Pacific squadron, log of, 43, 51, 52, 54, 55, 60; at Callao, 43, 44, 45, 51, 52, 67; cruising, 47, 54; orders for, 53; returns home, 60, 61; officers of, 65, 66; crew of, 94, 171.
Upham, ——, colonel, 33.
Upshur, Abel P., secretary of the navy, 83, 330.

Vail, Edward M., lieutenant, 143.
Valparaiso, 43, 52, 54, 65, 67.
Van Buren, Martin, vice-president, 74; president, 107, 296.
Van Staphorst, Messrs., 15, 18.
Van Wyck, Edward H., assistant surgeon, 200.
*Vermont,* U. S. ship of the line, 197.
Vicens y Andreu, Miguel, 218, 248.
Victor, Sam, 262, 263, 264, 265.
*Victorieuse,* French corvette, 104, 149.
*Vincennes,* U. S. sloop of war, 60.

Voorhees, Ralph, commander, in command of the *Preble,* 106, 144; letters of, 145, 328; brings dispatches, 146; at council of war, 300, 302, 303, 311; orders for, 306, 309, 321, 323.

Walbach, John Baptiste de Barth, colonel, 34.
Wallace, William, seaman, 22.
War of 1812, 1, 24, 25.
War Department, 34, 35, 36, 74.
Warden, David Bailie, U. S. consul general at Paris, 12, 13, 14, 15.
Warrington, Lewis, captain, 192.
War scare, 296.
Warsdale, William, U. S. consul at the Helder, 17.
Washington, George, birthday of, 52, 99; statue of, 320 to 327.
*Washington,* U. S. ship of the line, 32, 196.
Watson, Henry B., lieutenant of marines, 165.
*Weasel,* H. B. M. brig, 269 to 275.
Webster, Daniel, 267.
Wells, ——, 80.
Wentworth, Calvin, marine, 263, 264, 265, 266.
Werden, Reed, midshipman, 168.
*Westchester,* 297.
Whipple, Thomas C. O'D., mate, 274.
Williams, Edward, seaman, 262, 263, 264, 265.
Williamson, David, midshipman, 160, 168.
Willink, Jan, 15, 18.
Willink, Wilhem, 15, 18.
Wilmer, J. B. B., chaplain, 143.
Wilson, James Grant, general, 331.
Winship, ——, captain, 194.
Wise, Henry A., midshipman, 169.
Woodbury, Levi, secretary of the navy, 74.
Worden, John L., midshipman, 169.
Wright, Bernard, marine, 261 to 265.
Wright, Mathew, 73.

*Yankee,* smack, 32.